Emerging Markets Megatrends

Rajiv Biswas

Emerging Markets Megatrends

palgrave
macmillan

ISBN 978-3-319-78122-8   ISBN 978-3-319-78123-5   (eBook)
https://doi.org/10.1007/978-3-319-78123-5

Library of Congress Control Number: 2018940748

Cover credit: Pierre BRUMDER/Alamy Stock Photo

Printed on acid-free paper

This Palgrave Macmillan imprint is published by the registered company Springer International Publishing AG part of Springer Nature
The registered company address is: Gewerbestrasse 11, 6330 Cham, Switzerland

Contents

List of Figures

Preface

Adventures in Emerging Markets

The city was on fire. I could see the night sky glowing a lurid smoky orange above the central district as it burned, with artillery fire continuing to pound the city throughout the night. At dawn, the fighter jets returned, rocketing and strafing the artillery positions located in the nearby woods. At midday, despite the ongoing fighting, I walked through some side-roads to a hotel that had been designated a UN safe zone, and watched from an upper floor window as fighter jets flew overhead, glinting silver in the burning sun. I leant with my back against a pillar, watching as the fighters circled above the city and then dived to bomb various key targets.

In the early afternoon, I went downstairs to the hotel lobby for a short while, and when I returned to my upper floor lookout, there was a bullet embedded in the pillar that I had been leaning against, just about at head height. In war, the difference between life and death was just a game of random chance. I learnt that lesson again a couple of days later, when a bullet zinged past my head and slammed into a nearby metal door with a tremendous clang. Taking cover near the door, I saw the spent bullet lying in the rubble and picked up the burning hot metal, putting it into my jacket pocket as a reminder of my close call.

Later I personally witnessed the incredible bravery of two UN military personnel who were guarding the entrance to the designated UN safe zone at another major hotel. The hotel was marked with Red Cross and UN flags on the roof, so that fighter jets circling above the city would not attack the building. However, the UN soldiers protecting the main gate were confronted by a platoon of heavily armed soldiers who tried to force their way into the safe zone, to set up a machine gun post on the hotel roof to shoot at the fighter jets that were strafing and bombing the city. However, had they done so, the fighter jets would have been entitled to attack the hotel in retaliation, potentially killing many civilians who were taking refuge in the safe zone.

The UN officer in charge was Canadian, evident from his red Maple Leaf shoulder flashes. He was armed with only a pistol and supported by just one Norwegian UN soldier with a sub-machine gun. When the leader of the Greek Cypriot platoon, swathed with belts of machine gun ammunition, cocked his .30 calibre heavy machine gun, his platoon also cocked their other weapons and tried to push their way in through the gate. The UN soldiers responded by cocking their weapons and stood their ground, staring down the platoon. Had firing commenced it was obvious that both the UN soldiers would have been killed since they were heavily outnumbered and outgunned. I would probably have joined them in the spray of gunfire, since I was sitting in a car right next to them. I still marvel at the bravery of those two UN soldiers, doing a very tough job and risking their lives in the middle of someone else's war.

While luck was on the side of those two UN soldiers that day, the total number of fatalities of UN peacekeeping forces during active operations since the end of World War Two has reached 3718 by March 2018, highlighting the tremendous sacrifice made by soldiers from many nations taking part in UN peacekeeping operations in scores of developing countries worldwide.

Often the UN peacekeepers have to operate with very limited support and light weapons as a counterbalance to highly aggressive and heavily armed military units. The UN peacekeeping forces also have very strict rules of engagement limiting their ability to use force except in extreme circumstances. The blue beret of the UN peacekeeper is a true badge of courage in many conflict zones worldwide, with a total of 48 UN peacekeeping operations having been conducted since the end of World War Two.

The United Nations was created in the aftermath of World War Two, coming into existence on 24 October 1945. A key objective for the United Nations was to foster international peace and security, following the devastation and tens of millions of lives lost during World War Two.

Yet seven decades later, the world continues to witness conflicts occurring in many developing countries, including present-day conflicts in Syria, Libya, Yemen, Myanmar and Iraq. After the Nazi genocide during World War Two, the international community aspired to prevent such a horrific event from occurring again, but genocides have happened in a number of countries such World War Two, including in Cambodia, Rwanda and Bangladesh.

Images in recent years on TV channels of tens of thousands of Rohingya refugees fleeing from Myanmar, and of Syrian and Libyan refugees desperately trying escape to Europe, reinforce the fear that the world is still deeply divided along tribal lines, along religious schisms, along racial divides. In a moving opening line in a recent Hollywood movie called Wonder Woman (Warner Bros, 2017), Gal Gadot, the actress (and former military combat instructor) playing the role of Diana, says of this planet that "the closer you get, the more you see the great darkness simmering within". There is great truth in that statement—this planet is still ravaged by conflict, genocide, slavery, organized crime and despotic rulers.

The conflicts that have occurred in many developing countries since the end of World War Two have been a major factor preventing their economic development. When I lived in Ethiopia many years ago, it was a very poor country but still relatively peaceful, although there had been a recent history of conflict when the Ethiopian army had fought with Eritrean rebel forces.

It was a time of relative political stability and Addis Ababa was a peaceful, bustling city. We often spent weekends visiting the Awash National Park, sometimes camping by the banks of the Awash River, where one could often spot crocodiles floating by. Finding crocodile clawprints outside my tent one morning was a troubling memory. When we made the long journey driving from Addis Ababa to Asmara in a Land Rover, burnt out vehicles were often visible on the roadside near Asmara, grim reminders of the fighting. The drive through over 1000 kilometres of mainly dusty, dirt roads was dangerous and challenging, but had its rewards. There were hardly any cars travelling along that road in those days, and when we did a short detour to visit the Blue Nile Falls, we had the spectacular rugged scenery just for ourselves.

However, Ethiopia's period of relative peace and stability was later shattered by decades of violent repression and renewed border conflicts, with the nation struggling through a number of major famines. It is only relatively recently that Ethiopia has again emerged as a hub of economic development in East Africa.

Life in Somalia was a fantastic bush adventure. Somalia was also a very poor country at the time, but still peaceful. On most weekends we would go hunting in the bush country with rifles and shotguns, shooting guinea fowl, partridges, warthogs and various local deer such as gazelle and smaller dik dik. Guinea fowl were plentiful, and were a staple on the dinner table, although one had to be careful to avoid swallowing or biting the shotgun pellets embedded in the meat.

We would also swim in the Indian Ocean, which was teeming with fish, and Bruno Carini, our big game hunter Italian friend, would either snorkel or scuba-dive in the ocean and inevitably return with several big grouper fish that we could slice up and take back home in the chiller box. If we were lucky, we would also come across the occasional duck while driving through the bush, which was always a choice selection amongst the bountiful game.

Visiting Carini's house in Mogadishu was also an adventure, as he had several cheetahs and would bring one out to sit with us as we had evening drinks, which was never a comfortable experience. Carini was a character who could have come straight out of a Hollywood movie script, a larger than life Italian version of a Stewart Granger-style big game hunter, but he was a wonderful person with a very friendly personality and a generous heart.

Somalia later descended into decades of bitter civil war and conflict, and despite its extreme poverty at the time we lived there, the situation was far better than what was to come in the years ahead.

From the wilds of Africa, my own career eventually took me to an office in a royal palace in London, quite a remarkable contrast. Working for the Commonwealth Secretariat, an international government organization made up mainly of former British colonies, was a fascinating experience. One of the privileges of working for the Commonwealth Secretariat was that it was headquartered in Marlborough House, a royal palace just adjacent to St James's Palace, which was then the official residence of Prince Charles. It was always a very pleasant start to the day walking past the two sentries from the Foot Guards regiment standing outside St James's Palace, dressed in their impressive bearskin hats and red tunics, on the way to my office just next door. Marlborough House was originally designed by Sir Christopher Wren, the famed architect of St. Paul's Cathedral, as the town house for Sarah Churchill, the Duchess of Marlborough. It was later the residence for several of the Princes of Wales, and the birthplace of King George V.

Marlborough House is a very beautiful royal palace, with spacious, mani-cured gardens and a lovely interior with elegant staircases and walls lined with grand paintings from the Royal collection. Many of the paintings in the main entrance commemorate the victory of General John Churchill, the first Duke of Marlborough, at the decisive Battle of Blenheim—a 'glorious victory'—as he himself described it in a note to his wife Sarah written from the battlefield. Marlborough House made a spectacular venue for the official receptions and formal dinners that were often held during international government con-ferences. The highlight was the annual Commonwealth reception at which Queen Elizabeth II, the Head of the Commonwealth, would meet all the Commonwealth staff. It was very exciting for me on one such occasion when

Prince Charles took a moment to shake hands with me and made time to ask me a few questions about my own work and my background.

Soon after I joined the Commonwealth Secretariat, Don McKinnon, a former New Zealand foreign minister, was elected by the Commonwealth nations to be the incoming Secretary General. He brought a refreshing, friendly mood to the organization in typical New Zealand style. His opening address to greet the staff of the Secretariat was marked by a group of Maoris performing the traditional Haka war dance on the lawns of Marlborough House, making a memorable start to his term of office.

Working in the Commonwealth Secretariat was very exciting for an international economist, giving me the opportunity to take part in meetings of Commonwealth finance ministers and central bank governors. I also regularly visited the IMF and World Bank in Washington, DC, having very intense discussions about key international macroeconomic issues with highly capable international experts in global finance and development.

The main focus of the work in the Commonwealth Secretariat was on building co-operation among the Commonwealth governments for economic development and better governance, with the British government playing a key role in helping to finance international development initiatives. With many Sub-Saharan African countries being members of the Commonwealth, an important part of the Commonwealth's work was on initiatives to catalyze economic development in Africa. Following the UK's Brexit referendum in 2016, with the United Kingdom negotiating with Brussels on conditions for leaving the European Union, the Commonwealth may take on even greater importance for the UK as it refocuses on building new trade and investment partnerships outside of the EU. Some of the world's largest emerging markets, including India, South Africa, Nigeria, Pakistan and Bangladesh, are part of the Commonwealth family of nations and important potential future growth markets for British exports.

Working in Marlborough House was a unique experience. Every morning, our work would be interrupted by the various regiments of the Foot Guards playing stirring military marches just outside our windows, always a very pleasant morning interlude for me. Having been a British military cadet myself previously, I had a great affection for the various military ceremonies and parades that were a regular routine on the streets adjacent to Marlborough House and along the Mall to Buckingham Palace throughout the year. A highlight was always the Trooping the Colour parade on the Queen's Birthday, which takes place in the very pleasant summer weather in June.

Many years earlier, during my years as a British military cadet and later when I had been attached as a military cadet to the British Army of the

Rhine (BAOR), I had done my own share of 'square bashing' and endless drills and marching to the dulcet tones with which various British Army sergeants conveyed their instructions. In the BAOR, this discipline was mixed in with military exercises that were conducted in the vast Luneburg Heide.

When I was visiting the BAOR, the tank regiment I was attached to, the 1st the Queen's Dragoon Guards, which for historical reasons happens to have the Austrian Imperial eagle as its regimental emblem, arranged a visit to the nearby former Nazi concentration camp site of Bergen-Belsen. Belsen is located in northern Germany, close to the British Army Bergen-Hohne base I was assigned to. Visiting the site of the mass graves of thousands of victims and seeing the photographic archives and old newsreels of the initial discovery of the concentration camp by advancing British troops was an awakening to the horrors of the Holocaust.

Adding to the grim experience, the regimental barracks I was living in on the British military base had been a former Nazi SS barracks, with some of their military emblems still embedded in various structures of building, such as carvings into the wooden gun racks in the barracks. Many years later, when I visited Amsterdam, I found myself struggling to hold back the tears when I visited the house of Anne Frank in Prinsengracht and saw in the last section of the display in her house that she had died in Belsen just before the end of the war. It is still horrific for me to contemplate that this wonderful inspirational and talented girl died in such horrific conditions and is lying in one of those mass graves I had seen in Belsen. She was one of an estimated 11 million souls, including millions of the Jewish faith, Russian nationals, Polish citizens, as well as victims of many other nationalities, who were murdered in the Nazi concentration camps and in other Nazi atrocities against unarmed prisoners in Europe during World War Two.

Although the United Nations was created at the end of World War Two in order to prevent conflict and create a peaceful new world order, there have been many conflicts in developing countries since 1945.

Since the end of World War Two, conflicts have been a regular hallmark of developing countries globally, with scores of civil wars in Africa, Asia, the Middle East and Latin America. An estimated one million people were killed during the partition of India and Pakistan in 1947, in a hellish cacophony of communal riots and murders. Mass graves are still being uncovered in Indonesia from the civil war after the failed Communist coup attempt in 1965, when an estimated one million people were killed in the fighting and subsequent aftermath of reprisals.

Wars between nations have added to the endless mounting human toll of conflict since 1945, from the Korean peninsula to the Indian subcontinent and many Middle Eastern wars. More than 2 million people died during the Korean War from 1950 to 1953, which ravaged the entire Korean peninsula.

Famine and malnutrition have also caused millions of deaths in developing countries. While living in Ethiopia, I recall handing out bread and salt from the back of a Land Rover to desperate skeletal figures dressed in grey rags. The Ethiopian famine of 1973–1974 is estimated to have claimed 300,000 lives, and a subsequent famine in 1983–1985 took another 400,000 lives in the same country.

While global measures of human development do show significant progress in poverty alleviation since the end of World War Two, an estimated 766 million globally still live in extreme poverty. The number of people who are chronically undernourished is around 815 million people, according to the Food and Agricultural Organisation of the United Nations in its 2016 estimate. One of the greatest challenges facing the international community over the next two decades will be to eradicate global poverty and help the least developed nations of the world to join the ranks of the world's middle income nations.

Failure to achieve these objectives risks creating escalating contagion to the world's advanced economies through an increasing global refugee crisis as those in the poorest nations try to flee conditions of extreme poverty out of desperation. Those countries mired in poverty may also become fertile breeding grounds for social unrest and extremist ideology that could generate terrorism and encourage organized crime.

Therefore, the advanced economies cannot easily isolate themselves from the megatrends impacting on developing countries, and the international community will need to strengthen global partnerships and joint initiatives to tackle the major challenges confronting developing countries. While national governments and international government organisations will have a key role to play in addressing these challenges, the private sector has much to contribute, as demonstrated, for example, by the work of the Bill and Melinda Gates Foundation. Conflict prevention and resolution will remain one of the most important global priorities, with regional and international mechanisms for dialogue being critical for creating a more peaceful international economic order.

I would like to acknowledge the help and advice of friends and colleagues who have been positive influences during my many years of work on emerging markets.

I would firstly like to express my appreciation to Danika Biswas for the research help on this book, which is much appreciated.

I would like to particularly thank Zbyszko Tabernacki, Elisabeth Waelbroeck-Rocha, Ambassador Pradap Pibulsonggram, Tan Sri Dato' Michael Yeoh, Indrajit Coomaraswamy, Professor Joergen Oerstroem Moeller, Ambassador Tormod Endresen, Vivek Tulpule and Paul Morris for their great helpfulness over the years. I would like to especially thank Shane Akeroyd for being a very positive motivating force for my economic research on the Asia-Pacific region. Special thanks are also due to Heng Qian in Beijing and Yong Ngee Ng in Singapore. I am also most appreciative of the advice and guidance from the editorial team at Palgrave Macmillan.

The views and opinions expressed in this book are entirely my own, based on a lifetime of research on, and living in, many developing countries, and should not be attributed in any way to any organization I have worked for or been associated with, whether public or private, or to any other person.

Rajiv Biswas

Introduction: The Rise of Emerging Markets

The End of the Colonial Age

The tectonic shifts in the global economic landscape due to the rising economic weight of emerging markets in the world economy began after World War Two. After that protracted conflict, which resulted in tens of millions of deaths and brought devastation to many parts of Europe and Asia, the age of colonialism by European nations that had prevailed for many centuries came to a rapid end.

At the outset of the Second World War, the European colonial powers had sprawling empires that straddled the globe, including British colonial rule in much of South Asia, as well as Hong Kong, the Malayan peninsula, various colonies in the Middle East, Sub-Saharan Africa and the Caribbean. France also had colonies in North Africa, Sub-Saharan Africa, Indochina and the Caribbean. The Dutch still ruled in Indonesia, while Portugal had colonies in Mozambique, Goa and Macau.

However, World War Two transformed the colonial landscape. The European colonial powers, including Great Britain, France and the Netherlands, had been ravaged by the tremendous human and economic costs of World War Two. In some Asian colonies, colonial subjects seized the opportunity for self-governance, as revolutionary forces filled the political vacuum left by the retreating Japanese occupation forces from French Indochina and the Dutch East Indies. This resulted in bloody independence struggles in some countries, including Indonesia and Vietnam, as the revolutionary forces fought the returning military forces of their colonial rulers.

In Britain, the colossal economic costs of the World War Two accelerated plans for giving independence to some of the British colonies, including India. British plans for a peaceful transfer of power in the Indian subcontinent ended in the partition of India in 1947, with British India divided into India and Pakistan. The creation of separate nations resulted in large-scale movements of refugees amidst communal riots and civil conflict that resulted in an estimated one million lives being extinguished in a savage bloodbath.

Step by step, during the 1950s and 1960s, the European colonial powers retreated from their colonies, sometimes due to the mounting costs of insurgencies and sometimes by political decisions to peacefully hand over power to their colonial subjects.

At the beginning of the Second World War, there were 60 sovereign states, a number that rose to 90 sovereign states by 1950 as the global political map was redrawn after the end of the Second World War and its aftermath. The process of transition away from colonial rule continued during the 1950s and 1960s. By 2017, the total number of sovereign states had more than doubled compared with 1950, rising to 195.

Many of the new nations that have become sovereign states since 1945 have been afflicted by conflict, either due to civil wars or wars with neighboring countries. The Cold War between global superpowers since the end of World War Two has also resulted in proxy wars being fought in developing countries, although another world war has been averted so far.

The Proliferation of Global Conflicts

Despite the resolution of nations at the end of World War Two to avoid future global conflicts and to prevent another genocide after what the world had experienced during World War Two, the geopolitical events of the next seven decades has left a trail of recurrent genocides worldwide. These include the horrors of the Rwandan civil war, the killing fields of Cambodia, massacres of civilians as Bangladesh fought for independence, and another modern-day European genocide in Bosnia.

Since the end of World War Two, conflicts have been a regular hallmark of developing countries globally, with scores of civil wars in Africa, Asia, the Middle East and Latin America. The partition of India and Pakistan created a tragic end to British colonial rule in India, with an estimated one million people murdered. Mass graves are still being uncovered in Indonesia from the civil war after the failed Communist coup attempt in 1965, when an estimated one million people were killed in the fighting and subsequent aftermath of reprisals.

The sheer magnitude of the civilian casualties of genocide and war are so large in some countries that many smaller conflicts with thousands of causalities are often overlooked by the international community and forgotten over time.

Tragically the global resolve to try to prevent future conflicts when World War Two ended ebbed away rapidly in the face of geopolitical confrontations between superpowers such as the Korean War and the Cold War. During the 1971 war of independence in Bangladesh, the total number of victims of the genocide committed by the Pakistani army in a military operation that began in March 1971 which was ordered by then Pakistani President Yahya Khan is estimated to range between 300,000 and 3 million, according to different historical estimates. Then US President Richard Nixon wrote in a handwritten letter on White House letterhead to Yahya Khan dated 7th August 1971 the words:

> those who want a more peaceful world in the generations to come will forever be in your debt.
> (Source: RG 59 PPC S/P, Directors Files (Winston Lord), Box 330, National Security Archive Electronic Briefing Book No. 79, George Washington University)

Development Challenges Confronting Developing Countries

The concept of "emerging markets" was originally created in 1981 by Antoine van Agtmael, an economist with the International Finance Corporation, part of the World Bank Group. The name was intended to create a more positive image for developing countries among private sector investors, rather than the term "Third World countries", the phrase that was then being used to refer to developing countries (International Finance Corporation, "Establishing Emerging Markets"). It was intended to identify a group of developing countries that had achieved rapid economic development and industrialization, and were progressing rapidly towards becoming "developed" or "advanced" economies. Using this new terminology for "Third World countries", the IFC was able to pioneer the development of emerging markets funds to attract private capital for investment into emerging equity markets.

However, the definition of what is an "emerging market" rather than a "developing country" has been very vague since the phrase was originally coined. While some nations have progressed rapidly from being low-income developing countries towards becoming developed nations, defined as "advanced economies" by the IMF, others have languished, remaining trapped at low per capita GDP levels, with slow progress towards improving their standard of living and reducing poverty. Indeed, some developing countries have moved in the opposite direction, falling backwards in their economic development, often due to the impact of conflict on their economies.

Yet the remarkable economic achievements of East Asian economies such as South Korea, Taiwan, Hong Kong and Singapore highlight the tremendous progress that some low-income developing countries have made despite tremendous obstacles. After the end of the Korean War, South Korea was devastated, a nation left in ruins with its people in abject poverty. General McArthur was moved to comment that in his view, barring a miracle, it would take one hundred years for the South Korean economy to be restored. Yet an economic miracle did happen, the 'Han River miracle', as South Korea's per capita GDP rose from USD 67 per year in 1953, among the poorest nations in the world, to USD 27,500 in 2016, having joined the ranks of the advanced nations when it entered the OECD in 1996.

China's achievements since its economic liberalization commenced under senior leader Deng Xiaoping have also amounted to a miracle of economic development, lifting an estimated 800 million people out of poverty. China's poverty rate fell from 81% in 1981 to below 2% by 2014. This has made a major contribution to the overall reduction of global poverty over the past four decades.

Hong Kong has become one the world's leading free market economies since the Second World War, with its per capita GDP having risen to USD 46,000 by 2017. Its continuing success has been based on its role as a leading international financial services centre as well as a major regional aviation and shipping hub.

Singapore has followed a more strategic development model, with its government having played an important role in building competitive advantage and helping to establish new growth industries to replace industries that have faced a loss of competitiveness due to factors such as rising labour costs. As a result, Singapore has been transformed from a poor, low income nation at the time of its independence in 1965 into one of the world's richest nations, with a per capita GDP of USD 53,000 by 2017. Singapore's first prime minister, Lee Kuan Yew, wrote a marvellous book called "From Third World to First: the Singapore Story 1965–2000" (HarperCollins, 2000) describing the economic transformation of the nation from a poor developing country into an advanced economy within just one generation.

The reasons why some developing countries such as China, South Korea and Singapore have 'emerged' while others 'submerge' are complex and vary considerably. I am not aware of any book about Argentina called from "First World to Third: the Argentina Story" yet, but Argentina's descent from being the world's richest nation in terms of per capita GDP in 1895 to 55th in the world according to the World Bank's 2016 ranking based on nominal GDP per capita, and back to developing country status, is a sorry tale of economic mismanagement over many decades. A vast range of factors can impact upon the pace of economic development of developing countries, including the type of political governance, the impact of conflicts, vulnerability to natural disasters, the economic model being utilized by a government, as well as many other aspects of economic governance, such as the business climate for investors and level of corruption.

Among the factors that have impeded the economic development of developing countries, conflict has been a protracted and devastating cause that has prevented the economic progress of many nations. The large number of conflicts that have taken place in developing countries since their independence has been a major factor that has prevented many countries from achieving sustainable economic development. Even today, a large number of developing countries are being ravaged by conflict, including Syria, Afghanistan, Iraq, Somalia, South Sudan and Yemen. Even when an entire nation is not engulfed by conflict, insurgencies have been significant destabilizing factors for some regions, such as the Boko Haram insurgency in Nigeria, the Naxalite rebellion in some Indian states and the Islamist insurgency in Mindanao in the Philippines.

In addition to the devastating impact of conflict, developing countries also face tremendous economic and social challenges in their economic development ambitions from a wide range of trends.

Demographic change and rising urban populations are major policy challenges for many developing countries, creating tremendous pressures on governments to generate employment for new cohorts of young adults joining the population of working age, while rapid growth in urban populations in many countries also requires large new investment in urban infrastructure such as public transport and housing. The rapid projected growth in Sub-Saharan Africa's population over the next three decades will create massive economic and social challenges for this region, with large potential transmission effects to other countries if these escalating population pressures result in intensifying social unrest, emigration and new conflicts.

While many of the global development measures produced by international development agencies and national governments highlight the reductions in the share of population living in extreme poverty, there is less policy focus on the large share of the population living in developing countries who are close to the poverty line and are considered vulnerable to rapidly falling back into poverty due to loss of employment, ill health or disability. For farmers, crop damage due to adverse weather events can also have a devastating impact on their lives due to loss of income and damage to their subsistence or cash crops. Lack of social welfare safety nets and insurance protection for a large share of the vulnerable population of developing countries is also a key global policy concern.

Climate change is another major challenge, with many low-lying developing countries facing risks from rising sea levels, while the impact of changing weather patterns is expected to have a significant effect on agricultural production worldwide as well as increasing the frequency of extreme weather events such as cyclones in some regions.

The impact of disruptive technological change is also creating new uncertainties about the future industrial landscape, as the repercussions of the Fourth Industrial Revolution and robotics could alter the competitiveness of nations for low-cost manufactured products.

Weak governance and conflict in some developing countries have also triggered global spillover effects to the advanced economies. Large waves of emigrants and refugees are fleeing nations with low living standards and poor governance in search of better lives. This in turn is creating social and economic shockwaves in higher income countries as refugees and migrants enter their borders. The political and social turmoil in the Middle East since the Arab Spring has increasingly created a refugee crisis in the European Union, as hundreds of thousands of refugees have fled North Africa and the Middle East to seek a more stable life in Europe.

Terrorism and organized crime have also escalated, thriving on the weak governance in many developing countries and taking advantage of the liberalization of global borders for commerce and trade as a result of globalization.

Europe's refugee crisis combined with the escalation in major terrorism attacks has contributed to the rise of European nationalism as a backlash, as some voters seek various types of barriers to protect their borders from the threats of migration, terrorism and crime. This voter backlash has been evident during the Brexit referendum vote in the UK as well as the US Presidential elections during 2016.

In Germany, the large influx of an estimated 1 million refugees in 2015–2016 has triggered considerable tensions, as a number of violent attacks instigated by refugees from the Middle East have provoked a political reaction from some segments of German society. One town that has been badly impacted by these tensions is Cottbus, in an East German mining region, where confrontations between local residents and refugees have escalated considerably during 2017–2018.

Meanwhile, in the French port of Calais, there have been ongoing clashes between African and Middle Eastern migrants and local police for several years, with the violence having also escalated into ethnic violence between different migrant groups.

The economic gulf between developed countries and developing countries still remains very large, with 47 developing countries still being classified as least developed countries with per capita GDP levels that are only a fraction of the levels in developed nations. Moreover, the list of developing countries that have crossed the divide to become developed nations remains low. For many developing countries, any aspiration of reaching the ranks of the rich nations still seems like a forlorn dream.

Ongoing political, economic and social turmoil in many developing countries will continue to result in large flows of refugees and create breeding grounds for terrorism and organized crime unless advanced countries are able to take more decisive and coordinated policy measures to help tackle these problems. While the advanced countries cannot resolve all the myriad political and economic problems that afflict the developing world, there is still considerable scope for more decisive action that can at least help a substantial number of these developing countries. With many developing countries confronting a crisis in governance and economic management, tackling these challenges will require coordinated global policy action to prevent further deterioration in the global security landscape.

The famous poem by English poet John Donne written in 1624 is still as relevant today.

No man is an island entire of itself; every man is a piece of the continent, a part of the main; if a clod be washed away by the sea, Europe is the less, as well as if a promontory were, as well as any manner of thy friends or of thine own were; any man's death diminishes me, because I am involved in mankind. And therefore never send to know for whom the bell tolls; it tolls for thee.

John Donne, Meditation XVII, Devotions upon Emergent Occasions

1

Demographic Trends in Emerging Markets

The Changing Demographic Landscape

The hard facts of demography will have a profoundly wrenching impact on the balance of world economic power.
(Alan Greenspan, "The Age of Turbulence—Adventures in a New World", page 411, Penguin, 2007.)

Over the next three decades to 2050, global demographic trends will substantially alter the distribution of the world's population. Among the advanced economies, many nations are facing demographic ageing and low fertility rates, with some nations such as Japan projected to experience declines in the total size of their populations.

This will create a witches' brew of economic and social problems, including rising fiscal burdens of health care, pension and social security costs for the elderly. This will be accompanied by a rising elderly dependency ratio as a share of the total population and declining new cohorts of young workers joining the labor force.

However, among the developing countries, there are considerable contrasts in the demographic outlook over the period to 2050. Based on United Nations population projections (United Nations World Population Prospects, the 2017 Revision) using the medium variant of their projections, the total population of different developing regions of the world will show considerable variation in structural trends.

The most dramatic change in the total size and relative distribution of the global population will come from the projected growth in the total

© The Author(s) 2018
R. Biswas, *Emerging Markets Megatrends*,
https://doi.org/10.1007/978-3-319-78123-5_1

population of the African continent, which is expected to grow from 1194 million in 2015 to 2527 million by 2050. This indicates that the total population of Africa is expected to double by 2050, creating significant challenges for African governments to manage the social and economic impact of such rapid growth in the total size of the region's population.

The UN's very long term population projection to 2100 indicates that Africa's population will increase to 4468 million by 2100. In 2017, Africa's population was equivalent to around 28% that of Asia's population and around 17% of the world's population. By 2100, these relative shares change drastically according to the UN medium variant projections, with Africa's population rising to almost become equal to Asia's total population, equivalent to around 93% of Asia's population and accounting for 40% of the world's population.

The Middle East region, defined as "Western Asia" under the UN classification, will also see a large rise in population, from 258 million in 2015 to 397 million by 2050. A large increase in the population of Southern Asia is also projected, rising from 1823 million in 2015 to 2382 million by 2050.

However, other parts of Asia are projected to experience quite different demographic trends, with the population of China projected to decline slightly, from 1397 million in 2015 to 1364 million by 2050. In Southeast Asia, the total population is expected to show a more moderate increase compared with Africa and Southern Asia, rising from 634 million in 2015 to 798 million by 2050.

In Latin America and the Caribbean, the total population is projected to increase from 632 million in 2015 to 780 million by 2050, an increase of 148 million. This is remarkably similar to the population trends in Southeast Asia, where the total population will reach 798 million by 2050 and will increase by 164 million over the 2015–2050 period (Fig. 1.1).

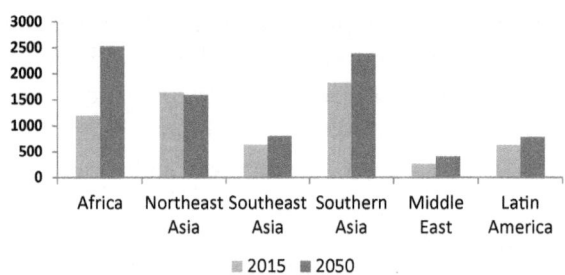

Fig. 1.1 Population by region, 2015–2050 (population in millions) (*Source* UN)

If the UN population projections are analyzed on the basis of per capita GDP levels, then one of the most challenging and troubling projections is that the global grouping of low income developing countries will experience a tremendous rise in total population from 642 million persons in 2015 to 1413 million persons by 2050. This represents a similar proportionate rise in population to the African continent as a whole, with the population more than doubling over the next three decades. To a significant extent this does reflect the overlap in composition of the grouping of low-income countries with African low-income countries. This serves to highlight the importance of global policy initiatives to boost the economic development of the African continent, particularly Sub-Saharan Africa.

Africa's Demographic Time Bomb

In the coming three decades to 2050, more than half of the total increase in the world's population is projected to be in Africa, according to the medium variant of the UN 2017 population projections. The total increase in Africa's population between 2017 and 2050 is projected to be 1270 million persons. The rapid projected growth of the total population in the African continent is particularly attributable to the population growth in Sub-Saharan Africa, which is projected to increase from 969 million in 2015 to 2168 million in 2050. The longer range population projections by the UN for Sub-Saharan Africa give considerable cause for even greater alarm, as they project that Sub-Saharan Africa's total population will increase to 4000 million by 2100. If these population projections are realized, the total population of Sub-Saharan Africa will be four times larger in around eight decades time.

The economic and social consequences of such rapid population growth are very troubling, particularly since the per capita income levels of many of the Sub-Saharan African countries are still classified as low income, with a significant share of the population of many of these countries still living in poverty or close to poverty thresholds.

Furthermore, the demographic profile of Africa's population is extremely young, with youth aged 24 years or less accounting for 60% of the total population in 2017. An estimated 41% of Africa's population is currently aged 15 years or less. With these UN demographic projections indicating that large cohorts of youth will join the working age population each year for many decades ahead, this will create considerable pressure on African governments to generate sufficient new employment opportunities each year in order to prevent the number of people who are either unemployed or underemployed from rising rapidly.

The implications of this long-term demographic outlook is that unless the Sub-Saharan African region can sustain rapid economic growth over many decades, the region could face significant social unrest and economic malaise due to high levels of unemployment and low or no improvement in the standard of living.

With the rapidly growing population putting increasing pressure on the rural sector to generate sufficient employment, there is likely to be a significant flow of rural population towards urban areas, resulting in rapidly growing urban populations with rising pressure on urban infrastructure such as health care, housing, public transport and sanitation.

A scenario of stagnant or slow improvement in living standards in Sub-Saharan Africa would also have considerable adverse consequences for advanced economies, particularly in the European Union, as it will imply a continuous exodus of migrants leaving Africa in search of a better standard of living elsewhere. The most obvious path of migration for African migrants will be towards Europe, since the route to most other developed economies faces much more difficult routes across large distances of ocean.

Clearly from the European Union's perspective there is no realistic capability for the EU to provide a solution to Africa's demographic problem by absorbing large numbers of refugees. However, there is likely to be a strong attraction for millions of economic refugees from Africa to try to find a new home in the EU over the next eight decades if Sub-Saharan Africa remains mired in a poverty trap with very low-income levels, combined with ongoing risks of conflict in some countries.

Politically the issue of such large-scale migrant inflows has already become one of the key concerns dominating the political debate in many EU countries. The issue of migration has generated considerable momentum for far right political parties in the EU who have galvanized support for their parties based on the migration issue.

However, even if the political, cultural and ethnic issues involved with such potentially large flows of immigrants are set aside, large-scale immigration of potentially millions of African refugees or migrants to the EU does not offer any kind of economic solution to the fundamental economic problems confronting Africa, and is also unlikely to be economically sustainable for the EU. If Africa's population is indeed going to increase by an additional 1270 million people by 2050, the emigration of even tens of millions of Africans to other regions will not significantly alter the economic challenges confronting the African continent.

Therefore, if international policymakers wish to prevent such a scenario of substantial outflows of African migrants attempting to reach the EU and other countries each year for many decades ahead, large-scale international initiatives will be needed to try to accelerate the economic development of low income African countries and create sufficient economic growth momentum so that the push factors forcing emigration are significantly reduced.

Such a large-scale initiative would require co-ordinated economic policy measures by the world's largest economic powers, including the EU and other European nations, as well as China and Japan, taking a joint approach over a number of years to try to help Africa's low income nations to breakout of their poverty trap.

A key focus for such a global action plan would need to be on an economic and social development program for Nigeria, which is Africa's most populous country although it is not classified by the UN as one of Africa's least developed countries. However, with Nigeria's total population forecast to rise from 181 million in 2015 to 410 million by 2050, addressing Nigeria's economic challenges will be an important part of any overall co-ordinated international policy response to catalyze Africa's economic development.

Nigeria is already struggling with a long-running insurgency by the Islamist Boko Haram rebels in the northeastern region of Nigeria. The insurgency has been quite protracted, having commenced in 2009 and so far having resulted in 20,000 persons being killed.

Nigeria has also been suffering from another militant uprising in the Niger Delta region, where rebel groups having also been attacking oil infrastructure as a response to the extreme poverty of communities in the region.

Nigeria is therefore already being impacted by several insurgencies, some of which are linked to extreme poverty in some areas. The risks of further political unrest if the numbers of unemployed rise significantly in future decades is a major potential future challenge.

Another major focal point for long-term international development support will be East Africa, notably Ethiopia, which is Africa's second most populous nation. Ethiopia's population is projected by the UN to rise from 100 million in 2015 to 191 million by 2050, representing an increase of 91 million persons.

Three other populous East African countries are also projected to experience significant increases in population. Tanzania's population is projected by the UN to rise from 54 million in 2015 to 138 million by 2050, rising by 84 million over this timeframe. Kenya's population is projected to rise from 47 million in 2015 to 95 million by 2050, while Uganda's population is projected to increase from 40 million in 2015 to 106 million by 2050.

Therefore, for these four East African nations, total population is projected to increase from 240 million in 2015 to 530 million by 2050, an increase of 290 million persons. Three of these four nations, Ethiopia, Tanzania and Uganda, are currently classified by the UN as least developed countries, highlighting the importance of international development assistance for these countries in order to accelerate economic development.

Another populous Sub-Saharan African country that will experience rapid population growth is the Democratic Republic of Congo (DRC), whose population is projected to increase from 76 million in 2015 to 197 million by 2050, which amounts to a population increase of 121 million persons.

In Southern Africa, South Africa is the most populous nation and also the second-largest economy in Sub-Saharan Africa, with a much higher level of per capita GDP than many other Sub-Saharan African nations. Due to its economic size and large population, the accelerated economic development of South Africa would also contribute significantly to the region's economic stability, although South Africa's demographic outlook is not as severe a policy challenge as for some of the other populous Sub-Saharan nations. South Africa's population is projected to rise from 55 million in 2015 to 73 million by 2050, an increase of 18 million persons.

Due to the demographic importance of these seven nations for Sub-Saharan Africa's overall demographic trends to 2100, international initiatives to boost economic growth in these African countries would, if successful, have potentially significant implications for absorbing a large proportion of the new cohorts of young people of working age entering the Sub-Saharan working age population each year. Sustained rapid growth in these countries could therefore be an important mitigating factor that could help to contain risks of rising regional unemployment and potential social unrest.

Another important implication of creating rapid growth in these countries which have significant population sizes is that a sustained period of strong economic growth will drive consumer expenditure growth rates, creating new growth markets for exports from other African countries.

Therefore, focused economic development initiatives by the international community to accelerate the economic development of some of the most populous Sub-Saharan African countries could play an important role in stabilizing the region's economic and social outlook and lifting much of the region's population of poverty.

How international policymakers in the global economic powers address Sub-Saharan Africa's demographic change will therefore have far-reaching implications for Sub-Saharan Africa's future and the human development of the 4 billion people projected to live in Sub-Saharan Africa by 2100.

South Asia's Demographic Challenges

Southern Asia is defined by the UN classification to include the nations of the Indian subcontinent but also includes the major emerging market economy of Iran in the grouping. The UN demographic projection indicates that Southern Asia will experience considerable further growth in the size of its total population, which is projected to rise from 1823 million in 2015 to 2382 million by 2050. This implies that the region's population will increase by an additional 559 million persons over the next three decades.

India is set to become the world's most populous nation, with its total population rising from 1309 million persons in 2015 to 1659 million persons by 2050, an increase of 350 million persons, or around 63% of the total population growth in Southern Asia by 2050.

The proportionate rate of growth of India's population is not as severe as in Sub-Saharan Africa since the number of births per 1000 persons will be significantly lower than in Sub-Saharan Africa throughout the 2020–2050 period. India's crude birth rate is projected by the UN in its medium variant scenario to decline from 18.7 births per 1000 persons annually in 2020 to 12.5 births by 2050, significantly below the Sub-Saharan African crude birth rate over the same period, which is estimated to be 35.7 in 2020 and decline to 25.4 by 2050.

Nevertheless, the total increase in India's population is so large that it will put a significant burden on the Indian government in terms of additional infrastructure requirements for health care, education, transport, urban infrastructure and sanitation.

One of the demographic advantages that India will continue to have over the next three decades is its relatively youthful demographic structure. The old age dependency ratio in India was 9% in 2015, and is projected to rise to 20% by 2050. This is far below the old age dependency ratios in Northeast Asian industrial economies. In Japan, the old age dependency ratio by 2050 is projected to be 71%, while in South Korea the comparable ratio is projected to reach 66% by 2050. Although China's pace of demographic ageing is not as severe as either Japan or South Korea, nevertheless by 2050 the old age dependency ratio in China is projected to reach 44%.

Therefore, India will have a relative comparative advantage compared to the Northeast Asian economies due to its youthful demographic profile, which limits the burden of health care and social services costs for the elderly. Meanwhile, India's child dependency ratio is also projected to decline over the 2020–2050 period due to falling birth rates.

However, India will face another major challenge due to the very large projected rise in the population of working age, which is estimated to increase from 860 million in 2015 to 1123 million by 2050 (Fig. 1.2). This implies that the working age population will increase by 263 million between 2015 and 2050, according to the UN medium variant demographic projections. Consequently, on average around 7.5 million persons will join the Indian working age population each year over the next three decades. This will require sustained rapid jobs growth for decades ahead in order to prevent rising unemployment and social unrest.

For the Southern Asian region as a whole, the old age dependency ratio will also remain relatively low over the next three decades, similar to the Indian old age dependency ratio. After India, Pakistan and Bangladesh are the two most populous nations in Southern Asia.

Like India, Bangladesh will also face a significant total increase in the size of its population, which is projected to increase from 161 million in 2015 to 202 million by 2050, which implies a 51 million increase in total population size. Bangladesh's old age dependency ratio is projected to rise from 8% in 2015 to 24% by 2050, keeping the fiscal burden of demographic ageing relatively moderate.

However, as in India's case, a key policy challenge for Bangladesh will be generating sufficient employment for the rapidly growing population of working age, which is expected to increase from 106 million in 2015 to 135 million by 2050, a net rise of 29 million persons between 2015 and 2050.

In Pakistan, the total population is projected to rise from 189 million in 2015 to 307 million by 2050, which will result in a 118 million increase

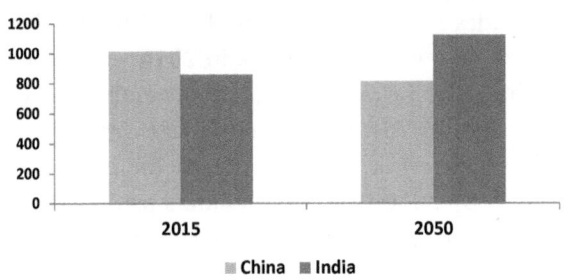

Fig. 1.2 Working age population China versus India (millions, 2015–2050) (*Source* UN)

in the total size of the population. This is similar to the rate of India's population growth over the same period, with Pakistan's population rising by around 62% between 2015 and 2050, compared with a 63% rise for India. The total population of working age is projected to rise from 115 million in 2015 to 205 million by 2050, implying a total increase of 90 million persons. As with India, this highlights the significant challenges Pakistan's policymakers will face in generating sufficient employment to absorb such a large increase in the size of the working age population.

Although the total population of Nepal is much smaller than that of some of its South Asian neighbors, notably India, Pakistan and Bangladesh, nevertheless its population dynamics are also important due to the political instability that has affected the nation since the Maoist insurgency that commenced in 1996. Nepal's population of working age is forecast to increase from 17.8 million in 2015 to 25.2 million by 2050, an increase of 7.4 million persons. The projection indicates that Nepal's working age population would increase by 42% between 2015 and 2050. This would require very substantial new employment growth over the next three decades for a country that is still ranked as a least developed country and has a relatively weak capacity to generate rapid employment growth based on the current economic structure of the economy.

Iran's population is projected to rise from 79 million in 2015 to around 94 million by 2050, a net increase of 15 million. However, the population of working age remains relatively stable, rising from 56.6 million in 2015 to 58.2 million by 2050, a very small increase of only 1.6 million persons over a period of three decades. Therefore, Iran does not face a significant policy challenge in terms of generating new employment growth for its youth joining the labour force over the next thirty years.

Overall one of the key implications for Southern Asia's long-term economic outlook from the youthful demographic profile of Southern Asia is that such significant increases in total population will also generate large cohorts of young people of working age joining the workforce each year. Therefore, for most Southern Asian governments, large-scale employment creation will be a top economic priority for decades ahead.

Another key challenge for Southern Asian governments will be to finance sufficient infrastructure spending for their rapidly growing populations for key requirements such as schools, hospitals, transport, power and other critical infrastructure. If the pace of economic growth is insufficient to maintain improving per capita GDP levels and achieving significant progress in human development indicators, this could result in growing frustration and social tensions. The Arab Spring serves as an important warning of the potential risks of high levels of unemployment and lack of social and economic progress.

Demographic Ageing in Northeast Asia

Unlike the demographic challenges of rapid population growth confronting Africa and Southern Asia, the Northeast Asian region faces a very different demographic outlook due to the impact of population ageing. The advanced economies of Japan and South Korea face the most severe challenges from demographic ageing.

Japan

Although Japan is an advanced economy, it is instructive to consider the implications of ageing demographics that are currently underway in Japan, as this gives important insights into the implications of demographic ageing for developing countries that will experience significant demographic ageing in the near future, including China and Thailand.

Japan's total population is projected to decline from 128 million in 2015 to 109 million by 2050, a decline of 19 million persons. This will have very significant repercussions for the Japanese economy and its potential economic growth rate, since the total size of the Japanese consumer market will be declining every year, acting as drag on long-term consumption growth rates. Japan's crude birth rate per 1000 persons has fallen dramatically, dropping from 24 in 1950 to an estimated 8.5 by 2015.

The total number of births in Japan in the 2016 calendar year fell below the 1 million level for the first time since birth records began to be kept in 1899, dropping to just 977,000 births for the year compared with a peak of 2.7 million births in 1949.

As a result, the number of young Japanese persons aged below 15 has fallen dramatically, from 29.2 million in 1950 to just 16.6 million in 2015, and is projected to fall further to 13.7 million by 2050. The number of young people entering the workforce each year has also fallen dramatically, creating structural problems for the overall composition of the workforce.

The drastic decline in the total number of schoolchildren in Japan has also had a significant impact on school infrastructure, with a net decline in the total number of elementary schools of around 7000 since 1960.

Japanese cities and towns are also projected to face severe implications from the impact of the combination of demographic ageing as well as declining population levels. The overall impact of Japan's declining population is expected to erode Japan's long-term potential GDP growth rate, pulling it gradually lower in future decades.

Meanwhile, the impact of demographic ageing will significantly increase the share of persons aged over 65 as a share of the total population, resulting in rising costs of health care and social welfare in total fiscal expenditure. Japan's old age dependency ratio defined as the ratio of the population aged 65 years or over to the population aged 15–64 is projected to rise alarmingly over the next three decades, according to the UN World Population Prospects 2017 Variant. The old age dependency ratio is projected to increase from 43% in 2015 to 53% by 2030, rising to an alarming ratio of 71% by 2050.

The consequences of such extreme demographic ageing are very severe. One example of the repercussions on Japanese society is that around 4.6 million Japanese are estimated to already have various levels of dementia. By 2025, it is projected by the Japanese Ministry of Health that 7.3 million Japanese will have dementia, or roughly one-fifth of the population aged over 65 years. With government fiscal resources unable to cope with the sharp rise in health care and social welfare costs, the burden of care is increasingly falling upon families to provide care for the elderly. Waiting lists for nursing homes have also been growing.

For the Japanese corporate sector, the impact of such severe population decline also has substantial negative consequences for many companies, since it implies that the domestic market size for many goods and services will be experiencing ongoing annual declines every year for many decades ahead. This will increasingly force Japanese firms to refocus on growth markets abroad, with fast-growing consumer markets in emerging market economies becoming increasingly important for the long-term growth of corporate revenues. Japanese firms are also likely to ramp up their foreign direct investment into fast-growing emerging markets to manufacture close to their end consumer markets, tapping lower wage and more abundant labour supply in these markets.

Japan's population of working age has already declined significantly, from 88 million in 1995 to 78 million by 2015, a drop of 10 million persons in just twenty years. However, this decline is projected to continue, with the working age population projected to fall to 56 million by 2050, a fall of 22 million over the next three decades. This will continue to put pressure on Japanese manufacturing companies to increase the scale of their overseas operations. Meanwhile, firms which need to expand their domestic Japanese workforces, such as hotel chains catering for the fast-growing numbers of international tourists or institutions providing health care and social services for the elderly are likely to face increasing challenges to recruit local workers.

As the Japanese government has so far maintained a strict immigration policy that does not permit large-scale inflows of immigrant workers, it still seems unlikely that Japan will be able to rely on large-scale immigration to address any shortages of workers, unlike some other advanced economies such as Singapore, Australia and Germany which have used immigration to address challenges from ageing demographics and labor shortages.

Over the very long term to 2100, Japan's population is projected to fall to around 85 million persons, representing a total decline of 43 million persons when compared with 2015. Compared with 2015, this implies that Japan's total population would be one-third lower by 2100, with far-reaching implications for the size of Japan's economy, its long term GDP growth rate, and the urban landscape.

South Korea

South Korea does not face such severe population decline as Japan over the next three decades, with its overall population estimated to be 50 million in 2015 and then projected to rise to 52.7 million by 2030 before declining to 50 million again by 2050. However, the structure of the population will experience severe demographic ageing during this period.

The old age dependency ratio is projected to increase from 18% in 2015 to 66% by 2050, very similar to the 71% old age dependency ratio in Japan projected for 2050. This will imply significantly higher future fiscal costs related to health care and social spending for the elderly. Furthermore, the impact of ageing demographics will also result in a lower long-term potential GDP growth rate.

The IMF's Article IV Report on South Korea in 2016 states that:

> With one of the lowest birth rates in the world, Korea is also one of the world's most rapidly aging societies, and fiscal outlays are expected to rise sharply. The fraction of the population that is of working age is projected to peak in 2017 and decline rapidly thereafter, depressing potential employment and growth. The overall population is expected to start declining after 2025, with negative implications for domestic demand.

The IMF also stated in its 2016 Article IV report that South Korea's potential GDP growth has been trending lower.

> In South Korea, potential GDP growth dropped quite dramatically as well - from the record high of 8 per cent in 1991 to below 3 per cent in 2015 – reflecting a decline in the contributions from labor, capital inputs, and productivity.
>
> IMF, "Staff Report for the Republic of Korea Article IV Consultation", Annex V., Page 38, Washington D.C., 2016.

Due to the dramatic demographic changes projected for South Korea, significant economic policy reforms will be needed to try to boost productivity growth and undertake other economic reforms to mitigate the impact of ageing demographics. Like Japan, South Korea has historically had a very homogenous society, so significant reforms to immigration policy still seem unlikely to be used as a policy lever to address demographic ageing. This will put more pressure on policymakers to make other substantial economic reforms in order to try to address the economic impact of demographic ageing.

China

Like Japan, China's population will also experience some decline over the next three decades, albeit on a much more modest scale compared to Japan when measured as a share of their respective populations. China's total population is projected to fall from 1397 million in 2015 to 1364 million by 2050, an overall decline of 33 million persons. However, China also will confront severe demographic ageing over the following five decades. By 2100 the decline in China's population is expected to be much more rapid than in the 2015–2050 period, with the total population projected to contract to 1021 million persons by 2050. This would amount to a total decline of 376 million persons compared to 2015, based on the UN 2017 Population Projection Medium Variant.

A combination of factors have contributed to the ageing demographics of China, including China's one child policy that was introduced in 1980, as well as other contributory factors such as the impact of improving education levels as well as the effect of the rising share of China's urban population. As a result of these factors, China's crude birth rate per 1000 persons has declined steadily from around 42 in 1950 to 12.6 by 2015. By 2050, the crude birth rate is projected to decline to just 9 per 1000 persons, based on the UN 2017 World Population Prospects Medium Variant projections. Meanwhile, the old age dependency ratio is projected to rise from 13% in 2015 to 44% by 2050.

Although China's total population is not projected to fall sharply by 2050, as China's population ages, the population of working age is projected to decline significantly, as the number of young workers entering the workforce each year becomes smaller. China's population of working age is projected to decline from 1015 million persons in 2015 to 815 million by 2050, which would be a net contraction of 200 million persons over a 35 year period. Such a large decline in the working age population will have significant implications for the overall Chinese employment system, as the number of young workers entering the workforce each year continues to decline.

China has already been facing rising manufacturing wage costs in its coastal provinces over the past decade, as the rapid growth of inland Chinese provinces has resulted in the diminishing supply of surplus labor willing to move to the coastal provinces. With the Chinese government having invested heavily in infrastructure development of Chinese inland provinces and encouraging industrial development in inland regions, there have been greater employment opportunities for workers to find employment in their own home provinces, reducing the incentive for internal migrant labor flows to the coastal provinces. Furthermore, migrant labor have faced much more difficult working conditions than local workers, due to government restrictions on their ability to become local residents and benefit from the various entitlements for those originally from these regions. These factors have contributed to the slowdown in internal migrant worker flows to the coastal provinces, helping to drive up manufacturing wages and increasing labor supply pressures on the manufacturing sector.

Increasing demographic pressures due to the ageing population and projected declines in the total size of the working age population in future decades have resulted in considerable review of China's population policies, which have been centered around the "one child" policy that has been in place since 1980. As a result of reviews of the economic implications of China's demographic ageing, the Standing Committee of the National People's Congress passed new laws in 2013 that liberalized the "one child" policy for couples where one of the partners was an only child. These new rules came into effect in 2014, resulting in some increase in the annual birth rate. However, the Chinese government took further measures to liberalize its regulations, allowing a new "two child" policy that took effect in January 2016. Total births in China rose to 17.9 million in 2016, the highest level since 2000 and an increase of 7.9% compared with 2015. Based on this increase in births, the National Health and Family Planning Commission of China has estimated that the working age population will be 30 million higher by 2050 than previously projected prior to the change in the "one child" policy. Although this would significantly mitigate the projected decline in working age population based on the UN 2017 World Population Projections, it would still imply a net decline of 150 million persons in the population of working age between 2015 and 2050.

While the liberalization of the "one child" policy has helped to boost the birth rate in China, other structural trends are continuing to constrain the birth rate, including higher levels of education and the shift towards more urbanization in China. Therefore, Chinese policymakers may have to recognize that while the birth rate can be lowered by tight regulatory controls, the opposite effect of raising the birth rate cannot be achieved by shifting to a higher regulatory limit on family sizes. This is often due to the impact of other factors such as higher education, urbanization and rising child care costs on the decision about optimal family size. Indeed, in 2017, the total number of births in China fell by 3.5% to 17.23 million births, compared to 17.9 million births in 2016.

Consequently, the Chinese economy may eventually confront similar demographic challenges to other Northeast Asian economies, notably Japan and South Korea, due to demographic ageing and the declining size of their working age population. This is expected to gradually reduce the long-term potential GDP growth rate of China, resulting in the further slowdown of Chinese GDP growth rates over the next three decades (Fig. 1.3).

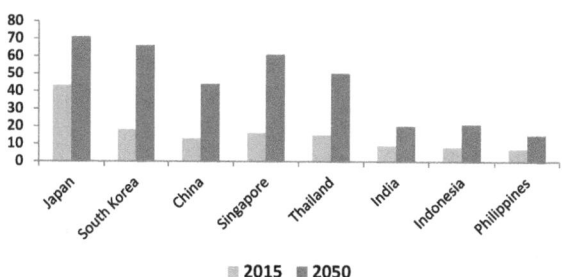

Fig. 1.3 Asian old age dependency ratios 2015–2050 (as share of working age population) (*Source* UN)

Southeast Asia

Although the total population of Southeast Asia is projected to rise significantly over the 2015–2050 period, increasing by 164 million persons, the individual nations of the region will experience varying demographic trends.

For Singapore and Thailand, the next three decades will result in significant demographic ageing. Singapore's working age population is projected to decline from 4 million in 2015 to 3.6 million by 2050, while Thailand's working age population will fall very substantially, from 49 million in 2015 to 38 million by 2050, a decline of 11 million. The old age dependency ratio in Singapore is projected to rise from 16% in 2015 to 36% by 2030 and 61% by 2050. In Thailand, the old age dependency ratio is expected to also rise sharply, from 15% in 2015 to 50% by 2050.

In Singapore, the public policy debate about immigration inflows has become more intense in recent years, putting some constraints on the extent to which inflows of foreign workers can be used to resolve the impact of demographic ageing. Therefore, efforts to boost the participation rate, improve the productivity of labour and encourage later retirement are some of the strategies that will contribute to the mitigating the impact of demographic ageing.

Vietnam's working age population is projected to increase from 65.7 million in 2015 to 70.6 million by 2050, a relatively moderate increase of 4.9 million over a period of over three decades. Vietnam's working age population is projected to begin to decline after 2040, falling by 2.2 million between 2040 and 2050, then continuing to contract over the period to 2100.

In contrast, some of Southeast Asia's other populous countries are expected to experience significant further population growth as well as large increases in their working age population (Fig. 1.4).

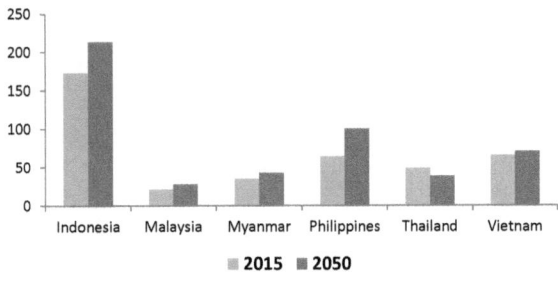

Fig. 1.4   ASEAN working age population 2015–2050 (millions) (*Source* UN)

Indonesia, which is Southeast Asia's most populous nation, is projected to have its working age population increase from 173 million in 2015 to 213 million by 2050, a total increase of 40 million persons. However, the pace of increase of the working age population slows rapidly over the next thirty years, and between 2050 and 2060, the net change in working age population is projected to be a contraction of 100,000 persons. Therefore, the next fifteen years will create substantial pressures on Indonesian government policymakers to generate rapid employment growth, in order to maintain social stability and economic progress. However, due to Indonesia's youthful demographic profile, the old age dependency ratio will remain low over the next thirty years, rising from 8% in 2015 to 21% by 2050.

The Philippines is also projected to undergo a very large increase in its working age population, which is expected to rise from 64.3 million persons in 2015 to 100.3 million persons by 2050, a net increase of 36 million persons. This will put considerable policy pressure on the Philippines government to transform its economy in order to generate such substantial employment growth over the next three decades. With the Philippines already having significant labour migration overseas due to the lack of sufficient employment opportunities at home, such rapid growth in the labour force will be a critical economic policy priority for the government.

Although the total size of Malaysia's population is relatively moderate compared to populous Southeast Asian nations such as Indonesia, Vietnam and the Philippines, Malaysia also faces a large economic policy challenge over coming decades due to the rapid growth in its population of working age. Malaysia's working age population is projected to increase from 21.3 million in 2015 to 27.9 million by 2050, a net increase of 6.6 million persons. As Malaysia is expected to reach advanced economy status by around 2025 due to rising per capita GDP levels, it will be in a much better position fiscally than many other developing countries to put in place economic and industrial policies and new investment programs to try to address the rapid rise in the working age population.

Nevertheless, this is a significant demographic challenge for Malaysia, particularly over the period from 2015 to 2030, when the population of working age will increase by 3.9 million persons. Over the period from 2030 to 2050, the increase in the working age population will not be as large, but will nevertheless be significant, amounting to a net increase of 2.7 million persons.

Middle East

The Middle East region, defined as Western Asia in the UN geographic classification of regions, is projected to have a large increase in size of its population, which is expected to rise from 258 million in 2015 to 397 million by 2050. A key driver for the rapid population growth of the Middle East region is attributable to Iraq, whose population is projected to increase from 36 million in 2015 to 82 million by 2050, a net increase of 46 million persons. Saudi Arabia's population is also projected to show a significant increase, rising from 32 million in 2015 to 45 million by 2050, a net increase of 13 million. While Saudi Arabia's population growth is much more moderate than the very rapid growth in Iraq's population, it nevertheless is a significant increase relative to the total population size, growing by around 40% over the 2015 to 2050 period. Turkey's population is also expected to record a significant increase, rising from 78 million in 2015 to 96 million by 2050, an increase of 18 million persons.

In terms of the implications for the labor force, the very large increase in Iraq's population is also expected to be accompanied by a large rise in the working age population. Iraq's population of working age is projected to rise from 20 million in 2015 to 50 million by 2050, a net rise of 30 million. This will create tremendous economic and social policy challenges for Iraq in order to generate sufficient jobs growth to prevent escalating rates of unemployment. Given the protracted conflict in Iraq over the past 15 years, this large rise in the size of the working age population over the next three decades could be a further destabilizing factor as Iraq tries to rebuild its economy and restore peace.

Saudi Arabia's population of working age is projected to increase from 22 million in 2015 to 30 million by 2050, indicating a net increase of 8 million persons to the size of its working age population. While this is relatively moderate compared with Iraq, it implies significant economic policy challenges for the Saudi government over the next three decades. One of the greatest economic challenges for Saudi Arabia will be to transform their economy away from its dependence on oil and downstream petroleum products, towards a more diversified economy that has greater capacity to generate employment growth across a wide range of industry sectors. As Saudi Arabia has achieved a very high standard of living and high per capita GDP due to its oil wealth, it will also be challenging to create large numbers of well-paying jobs in order to meet expectations of Saudi citizens regarding their standard of living and salary levels.

In Turkey, the working age population is projected to increase from 52 million in 2015 to 60 million by 2050, a relatively moderate overall increase in the working age population of only 8 million, similar to the net increase in Saudi Arabia's working age population over the same time period. However, the net increase in the working age population as a share of the 2015 level is relatively low compared with Saudi Arabia.

An important advantage for Turkey is that the structure of its economy is more diversified than many other Middle Eastern nations, with a relatively industrialized economy as well as a large tourism sector. The well-diversified economy should facilitate the generation of sufficient jobs. As a result, the rise in the working age population is less of a public policy concern for Turkey compared with other large Middle Eastern emerging markets such as Saudi Arabia or Iraq.

Latin America and the Caribbean

The Latin America and Caribbean region is projected to have an overall increase of 148 million people in its population over the next three decades to 2050. In South America, the total population is projected to rise from 416 million in 2015 to 500 million by 2050, an increase of 84 million persons. Much of this increase will be due to population growth in the two most populous countries in the region, Brazil and Mexico, which are both classified as upper middle income countries. The combined population increase of Brazil and Mexico from 2015 to 2050 is projected at 49 million persons, or around 58% of the total population increase of South America over this time period.

The population of Brazil is projected to rise from 206 million in 2015 to 233 million by 2050, an increase of 27 million persons. Over this period, the population of working age is projected to rise from 143 million in 2015 to 145 million by 2050, implying a total increase of around 2 million in the number of persons of working age. Therefore, Brazil is not facing a significant economic challenge in terms of generating employment growth for future cohorts of young workers. This reflects the ageing demographic structure of Brazil's population over the next three decades, with the elderly dependency ratio projected to rise from 11% of the working age population in 2015 to 37% by 2050.

In Mexico, the population is projected to increase from 126 million in 2015 to 164 million in 2050, a net increase of 38 million. The population of working age is projected to rise from 83 million in 2015 to 105 million in 2050, a net increase of 22 million persons. Therefore, Mexico will face a more significant challenge than Brazil in terms of generating sufficient new jobs growth for its working age population. The elderly dependency ratio is projected to rise from 10% in 2015 to 37% by 2050. This does signal that the ageing population will also become a gradually increasing fiscal burden for the Mexican economy, albeit not as severe as in some of the Northeast Asian economies.

Policy Implications for Emerging Markets

The demographic outlook for the different emerging market regions varies considerably over the next three decades, creating widely differing economic policy challenges for policymakers in developing countries.

In Northeast Asia, the focus for policymakers will be on the impact of demographic ageing and the impact of declining populations on the long-term potential economic growth rate. The implications of demographic change for the fiscal outlook will also be a key policy concern, as the rising share of the elderly population as a share of the total population will increase the fiscal burden of health care, social welfare and pension costs.

In contrast, the demographic outlook for Africa is for rapid growth in total population size, creating considerable pressure for governments to address the social and physical infrastructure costs of rapid population growth. A major political and economic challenge will be to generate sufficient employment growth for the rapidly growing working age population. Given the structure of many African economies continues to be heavily dependent on production of agricultural and minerals commodities, a key policy issue for most African governments is whether their existing economic structure will be able to generate sufficient employment growth to meet the large numbers of youth joining the labor force each year. Helping African nations to address the impact of demographic change will be a key policy challenge for donor governments as well as for the international financial institutions. This will require a global development initiative for Africa similar in nature to the Marshall Plan for rebuilding Europe after World War Two.

In the Middle East region, a number of the more populous nations will also face the impact of rapid growth of the population and number of persons of working age, notably Iraq, which is projected to experience very rapid population growth. Saudi Arabia also faces demographic challenges, as it tries to transform its economy to generate more employment to meet the projected expansion of its working age population over the next three decades.

Similarly, Southern Asia also faces significant increases in the total size of its working population during the next three decades to 2050, although the moderating birth rate in many of the nations means that the pace of growth of the working age population does slow down over this period. Nevertheless, governments across the Indian subcontinent will face a very difficult task to generate sufficient employment growth for the fast-growing labor force.

Therefore, although the demographic outlook for different developing countries does vary considerably, the challenges created by demographic change will be among the most important megatrends impacting on the political, economic and social outlook for most developing countries over the next three decades.

2

The Emerging Markets Consumer Boom

The Shift from West to East

Since the 1950s, a dramatic transformation has taken place in the structure of the global economy due to the rising economic importance of developing countries. Much of this shift represents a return to the historical economic order that existed prior to the age of rapid industrialization of Europe and the US.

Estimates by the eminent economic historian Angus Maddison done for the Organization for Economic Co-operation and Development (OECD) indicate that in 1820, China and India were dominant economies in the global economic order, which was then still largely based on agrarian, subsistence economies. At that time, China and India together accounted for around 44% of the global economy, with the Asian region as a whole accounting for around 57% of world GDP and 69% of the global population. Africa and Latin America together accounted for around a further 7% of global GDP in 1820.

However, following the industrial development of Europe and the US as well as the economic impact of the era of colonialism, by 1992 the combined share of China and India in world GDP had declined to just 17% (Angus Maddison, OECD, 1995).

However, the economic significance of developing countries has again begun to rise over the past four decades. According to modern national accounts measures of world GDP based on IMF data, in 1980, developing countries worldwide accounted for 24% of world GDP, based on GDP measured in USD terms in current prices (IMF data). While only producing one-quarter of the world's GDP, developing countries were estimated to have

© The Author(s) 2018
R. Biswas, *Emerging Markets Megatrends*,
https://doi.org/10.1007/978-3-319-78123-5_2

75.7% of the world's population in 1980. By 2016, the developing country grouping's share of world GDP had risen to 39%, while its share of world population had risen to 83% (Fig. 2.1). Based on IMF world GDP forecasts, the developing countries' share of world GDP will increase further to around 44% of world GDP by 2022.

The very significant rise in developing countries' share of world GDP since 1980, amounting to an additional 15% of world GDP, reflects their relatively higher average GDP growth rate compared with developed countries over the 1980–2016 period. As a result of this increase in the developing countries' share of world GDP over the past three decades, their consumption expenditure has also shown strong growth. With developing countries' GDP growing at a more rapid pace than in developed countries, this has underpinned strong growth in consumer spending for developing countries as a group, although the individual performance of nations varies considerably depending on a wide range of political and economic factors (Fig. 2.2).

With the developed nations having accounted for the dominant share of world GDP during the 1950–1980 period, the growth in consumption in North America, Western Europe and Japan had been the main drivers of global consumption expenditure growth. The affluent consumer societies in the developed nations were the growth engines of world consumption demand during these decades. However, real GDP growth rates in the advanced economies have subsequently moderated due to factors such as the impact of demographic ageing and declining productivity growth rates. The impact of the global financial crisis in 2008–2009 also had a protracted adverse impact on European consumer spending, as consumer sentiment plunged while unemployment rates rose above 12% for the Eurozone as an average for the region.

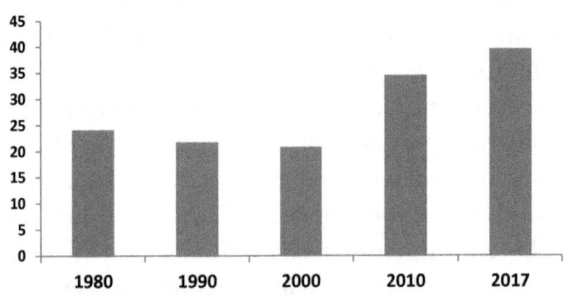

Fig. 2.1 Developing countries share of world GDP (*Source* IMF data)

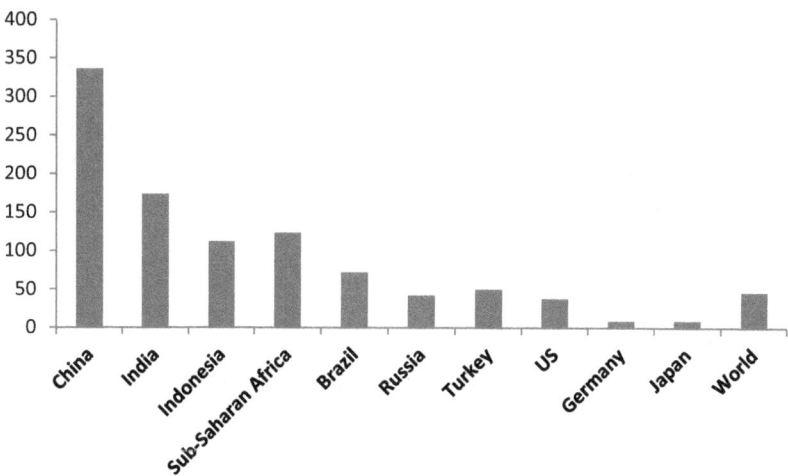

Fig. 2.2 Household consumption growth (percentage change from 2006 to 2016) (*Source* World Bank data)

In contrast, many large developing countries have maintained higher average long-term GDP growth rates since 1980, compared to the global GDP growth average, resulting in much more rapid per capita GDP growth, which has helped to drive consumer spending. The average per capita GDP levels of developing countries in 2017 was 5.7 times higher than in 1980, rising from USD 863 in 1980 to USD 4960 by 2017. In contrast, developed countries' per capita GDP levels have risen by a multiple of 4.4 times over the same period.

Large emerging markets such as India, Indonesia, Brazil and Turkey have experienced rapidly rising consumption expenditure as the size of their affluent middle classes have grown fast. In the decade from 2006 to 2016, the size of the consumer markets of India, Indonesia and Sub-Saharan Africa more than doubled, compared to the relatively slow growth of mature consumer markets of major developed countries such as the United States, Germany and Japan. However, the single most important megatrend in emerging markets that has driven the rise in developing countries' share of world GDP and household consumption is China's economic ascendance since 1980.

The rapid growth of household incomes in Asian developing countries led by China, India and Indonesia is resulting in the growing importance of Asian consumer spending in world consumption. Forecasts by the OECD indicate that Asian consumers will dominate the global growth in the number of middle-class consumers over the 2010–2030 period.

According to the OECD forecasts, the global middle-class population with spending power of between USD 10 and USD 100 per day when measured in equivalent purchasing power terms will rise from 1.8 billion in

2009 to 3.2 billion by 2020 and 4.9 billion by 2030. An estimated 85% of this growth in middle-class consumer population is expected to be in Asia, notably in the fast-growing populous Asian consumer markets of China, India and ASEAN. The OECD study projected that the total number of Asian middle-class consumers would rise from 500 million in 2010 to over 3 billion by 2030. This will push up Asia's share of middle-class consumers globally from 28% in 2012 to 66% by 2030, which will make Asia the world's most important consumer market.

China's Ascendance in Global Consumer Markets

When China's economic reforms under visionary Senior Leader Deng Xiaoping began in 1978, China was still a very poor nation. The per capita GDP of China in 1980 was just USD 309 per year measured in current prices, according to IMF data, with total annual household consumption expenditure estimated at USD 98 billion for the nation as a whole. In comparison, the per capita GDP of the United States was USD 12,575 and the total size of US household consumption expenditure was USD 1.76 trillion, about 18 times larger than China's consumer market.

However, as China embraced far-reaching economic reforms and attracted large foreign direct investment inflows into building low-cost manufacturing production in the coastal provinces of China, the Chinese economy grew at a rapid pace, with average annual real GDP growth of 10% per year for a period of 30 years from 1980 to 2010.

As a result of this sustained rapid economic growth, the total GDP of China rose from an estimated USD 305 billion in 1980 to USD 11.2 trillion by 2016, measured in GDP at current prices in USD terms. In 1980, the size of China's GDP was equivalent to 10.7% of US GDP, but due to China's rapid economic growth relative to the developed countries average, its share of US GDP has risen to 60% by 2016. According to IMF GDP forecasts, China's GDP measured as a share of US GDP will rise further in the medium term, to around 78% by 2022.

When measured as a share of world GDP, China has also achieved a remarkable ascendancy from around 2.7% of world GDP in 1980 to an estimated 14.9% of world GDP by 2016. Within the decade from 2006 to 2016, China's share of world GDP has risen from 5.4 to 14.9%, a very significant increase in just a decade.

As a result of this very rapid relative increase in the size of the Chinese economy compared to the global economy since 1980, the importance of

China's consumer market has also risen significantly. In 1980, the total size of Chinese household consumption expenditure was estimated at USD 98 billion according to World Bank data on world consumption expenditure. By 2016, this had expanded by many multiples, to reach an estimated size of USD 4.37 trillion. In 1980, Chinese household consumption spending was only around 5.5% of total US household consumption spending and 1.5% of world household consumption. However, by 2016, China's household consumption was equivalent to around 34% of US consumption expenditure and 10.7% of world household consumption expenditure.

Although Japan had been Asia's largest economy for decades and a global leader in manufacturing, Chinese GDP surpassed Japanese GDP in 2009. By 2014, the size of Chinese GDP rose to a level that was more than double Japan's annual GDP. This has also been reflected in the relative size of their respective consumer markets. In 1980, Japan's household consumption expenditure was USD 582 billion, compared with China's consumer market size of USD 98 billion. However, by 2016 Chinese annual household consumption spending reached USD 4.37 trillion, significantly exceeding Japan's household consumption of USD 2.76 trillion in the same year.

The rapid growth of the Chinese economy and household consumption since 1980 has been an important factor contributing to the overall rising share of the household consumption of developing countries compared with global consumption. In the decade from 2006 to 2016, world household consumption rose by USD 13.9 trillion, of which China contributed USD 3.4 trillion, or 24% of the total increase in world household consumption expenditure.

Overall, developing countries ranked as low-income and middle-income nations by the World Bank accounted for 59% of the total increase in world household consumption between 2006 and 2016. Therefore, China alone accounted for about 40% of the total growth in household consumption among the low- and middle-income developing countries in the past decade.

The rapid growth of China's consumer market has not only been an important domestic growth engine for the Chinese economy, but has also created a fast-growing export market for the rest of the world's exports. In the Asia-Pacific region, this is one of the key megatrends transforming the region's economies, as China has risen in importance as a key export market, with the impact particularly notable over the last decade. By 2016, one-third of Australia's merchandise exports were destined for mainland China. China is also becoming increasingly important for Australia's services sector exports, with an estimated 40% of international students studying in Australia being from mainland China. China is also the largest export market for South Korea, with around 26% of total South Korean exports sent to China in 2016. Similarly, Taiwan exported around 27% of its total exports in 2016 to China. For Japan, China is also a key export market, accounting for around 18% of total exports in 2016.

As China's rapid economic expansion has propelled it to the rank of the world's second-largest economy since 2009, it has also been a fast-growing market for agricultural and mineral commodities. This has also made China an increasingly important export market for many developing countries in Africa, the Middle East and Latin America, due to the importance of primary commodities in their overall structure of exports.

China's Fast-Growing Consumer Market

The impact of China's fast-growing consumer market on the world economy is increasingly evident in many different sectors of world manufacturing and services. The rapid growth of consumption expenditure in China over the past decade reflects strong growth in household per capita incomes, with Chinese per capita GDP having risen from USD 2110 in 2006 to USD 8582 in 2017. This has propelled China into the ranks of the world's upper middle income countries according to World Bank classifications, with the prospect of becoming a high-income country within the next decade.

Although such rapid growth in per capita GDP is a remarkable achievement in just over a decade, some of China's largest cities have reached much higher average per capita income levels. The per capita GDP of Beijing reached USD 16,920 in 2016, according to Chinese government statistics, which would classify the population of Beijing as high income under the World Bank definition. Shanghai and Tianjin would also be considered high-income cities, with a number of other major Chinese cities close to reaching high income per capita levels.

Such rapid growth in Chinese per capita GDP levels has driven buoyant consumer spending for a wide range of goods and services, ranging from manufactured products such as cars, white goods, computers and mobile phones to services such as financial services, tourism and health care. The strong growth in the size of the consumer middle class in Chinese cities has also underpinned demand for privately owned housing, which has driven demand for manufactures required for new homes, including building products and home furnishings.

An important bellwether of the growing global significance of the Chinese consumer has been the rapid rise of Chinese domestic auto sales, which overtook US auto sales for the first time in 2009. In 2009, Chinese light vehicle sales in the domestic market reached 13.6 million, and have doubled since then. By 2016, total Chinese light vehicle sales reached an estimated 28 million vehicles, according to the China Association of Auto Manufacturers. By comparison, US light vehicle sales in 2016 reached 17.6 million, compared with 10.4 million sales in 2009.

China has also become the world's largest retail e-commerce market, over-taking the United States in terms of total value of e-commerce sales in 2013. By 2016, total online retail sales of goods and services in China reached USD 743 billion, increasing by 26.2% compared to 2015. This is more than double the growth rate for the value of all retail sales in China, which rose by 10.4% year-on-year in 2016. Online retail sales of physical goods rose by 25.6% year-on-year in 2016, creating very fast growth in demand for logistics services in China to deliver these goods bought online.

The impact of China's growing consumer market size has not only been felt in domestic retail sales but is also becoming increasingly evident in other countries as Chinese international tourism visits have risen rapidly during the past two decades.

In 2000, Chinese international tourism visits were estimated at 10 million visitor trips annually, according to UN World Tourism Organization (UNWTO) statistics. By 2016, the total number of Chinese outbound international tourism trips had increased by a multiple of 12, reaching a total of 135 million visitor trips, according to UNWTO estimates, with total spending by Chinese tourist visitors abroad in 2016 reached USD 260 billion. The rapid growth of Chinese tourism spending abroad has made China the world's largest source market for international tourism since 2012. In 2016, Chinese tourism spending abroad was estimated to be more than double US international tourism spending, which was around USD 122 billion according to UNWTO data.

For other Asian countries, the impact of the rapid growth of Chinese tourism has been particularly strong, with China now having become the largest source of tourism visitors to Japan, South Korea and Thailand.

For Thailand, the impact of Chinese tourism has been a very significant growth driver for the tourism economy, which accounts for around 8% of GDP directly, and after taking into account indirect multiplier effects, around 15% of total GDP. Chinese tourism visits to Thailand have risen from 1.7 million visits in 2011 to 8.76 million visits by 2016, increasing by a multiple of over four in a period of just 5 years. This rapid growth in Chinese tourism visits to Thailand has made China the single most important source of tourism visitors to Thailand, accounting for around 25% of total international tourists in 2016. The boom in Chinese tourism has been an important positive factor supporting the Thai tourism economy and contributing to overall GDP growth momentum during a period when the Thai economy had experienced soft domestic demand due to the impact of ongoing political turmoil on consumer and investor confidence.

Chinese tourism has also had a similarly powerful impact on the South Korean tourism industry. As Chinese outbound tourism has boomed, South Korea has become a very popular destination due to its proximity and good flight connections to major Chinese cities. China accounted for almost half of total international tourist visits to South Korea in 2016. A total of 8.067 million Chinese tourists visited South Korea in 2016, up 34.8% on the previous year. In 2016, Chinese tourism accounted for 46.8% of total international tourism visits to South Korea.

However, the importance of Chinese tourism for the South Korean economy became a double-edged sword for South Korea in March 2017. At that time, South Korea faced escalating economic measures from China in response to South Korea's decision to install US THAAD missiles to counter the North Korean missile threat. As part of its economic measures, Chinese authorities advised Chinese travel agencies to desist from arranging Chinese group tourist visits to South Korea. This had a severe impact on the South Korean tourism industry, as Chinese tourism visits fell sharply. During 2017, Chinese tourism visits dropped by around 48% compared to 2016.

Consequently, the rise of Chinese international tourism does have the potential to be used as a form of economic leverage in China's international political relations with other nations. With only 10% of Chinese nationals currently estimated to have passports and be travelling abroad, the future rapid growth of Chinese tourism could result in an even greater share of Chinese tourism in the overall tourism economies of many Asian nations. Therefore, other Asian nations may become more vulnerable in future if China uses tourism as a form of economic leverage to strengthen its negotiating position on bilateral matters with other Asian nations.

Japan is also experiencing a significant surge in Chinese tourism visits, with Chinese tourists accounting for an estimated 26% of total international tourist visitors and 39% of total spending by international tourists in Japan in 2016. The pace of growth of Chinese tourist visits to Japan has also been very rapid over the past 5 years, with Chinese tourism arrivals in Japan growing by 27.6% in 2016 compared to 2015.

As Japan has also been subject to political and economic tensions with China in the relatively recent past, there may also be concerns in Japan about the growing importance of Chinese tourists for its overall tourism industry. In 2012, when geopolitical tensions between China and Japan flared up over a territorial dispute over the sovereignty of some islets in the East China Sea, this triggered anti-Japanese riots in China, with some Chinese consumers boycotting purchases of Japanese retail brands such as Japanese cars and Japanese beer.

I recall staying in a hotel in Beijing belonging to a famous European hotel chain during 2012, when the territorial dispute between China and Japan was still at its height. One evening at a restaurant in the hotel, I rather innocently chose a Japanese beer from the hotel's drinks menu, and the waiter went away and soon came back to politely tell me that brand was not available. I thought that another Japanese brand beer from the menu would make a perfectly acceptable substitute, and when I informed the waiter of my new selection, he again went away and promptly came back to tell me that this too, was not available. I was rather taken aback that such a large international hotel chain was turning out to be the proverbial "pub with no beer" made famous in a song by Australian country singer Slim Dusty. It was only later with hindsight that it dawned on me that I had also been impacted by the anti-Japanese economic retaliation measures that were taking place in China at that time.

Therefore, the consumer spending bonanza that has been unleashed by China's rapidly growing consumer market has brought large export growth opportunities for many nations worldwide, but the experience of South Korea and Japan in the recent past also points to some geopolitical risks as China becomes increasingly important as an export market for some countries.

The Indian Consumer Market

Although the size of the Chinese economy and its consumer market currently is considerably larger than the Indian consumer market, the medium to long-term outlook is for India to also account for a large share of the global consumer market. India's total household consumption in 2016 was estimated at USD 1.35 trillion, compared with China's consumer market which was USD 4.37 trillion in the same year. Therefore, the Indian consumer market is still only around 31% of the size of the Chinese consumer market.

However, with the Indian population projected to become larger than China's over the next decade while the Indian economy has the potential to grow at a pace of 6–7% per year over the period to 2030, the size of the

Indian consumer market is also expected to expand rapidly, albeit still relatively smaller than the Chinese consumer market.

The Indian auto industry is one example of the rapid growth of Indian consumption spending, with total passenger vehicle sales rising above 3 million passenger vehicles for the first time in 2016–2017, reaching a total of 3.046 million domestic passenger vehicle sales for the fiscal year, according to data from the Society of Indian Automobile Manufacturers. Total Indian production of passenger vehicles reached 3.79 million in the fiscal year, with exports of 759,000 passenger vehicles. Domestic passenger vehicle sales have risen by more than double the level of 2007–2008, when sales were at 1.20 million.

The rapid growth of consumer spending on passenger vehicles combined with the liberalization of India's auto sector since the 1990's has resulted in a remarkable transformation of the Indian auto industry. Prior to 1982, due to Indian government import protection for the domestic auto sector, only three Indian car manufacturers were producing antiquated models of cars. Hindustan Motors was producing the Ambassador car from 1958 based on the British Morris Oxford Series III car designed in the 1950s, and production of this vehicle continued until 2014. Premier Automobiles was manufactured a car based on the Fiat 1200 Grand Luce Berlina designed in the 1960s, which was produced in India from 1970 until 1998. The third Indian auto design produced in India was manufactured by Standard Motor Products. This was the Standard Herald, based on the British Standard-Triumph design, and commenced production in 1961.

However, after the Indian government began to liberalize the domestic auto industry and allow international competition, the Indian auto industry was transformed over the next 30 years into a globally competitive industry that has become a major international exporter of autos as well as auto parts. Major international auto manufacturers with significant production in India include Hyundai Motor Company, Toyota, Honda and Ford Motors. Maruti Suzuki India Limited, which was originally a joint venture between the Indian government and Japan's Suzuki Motor Company, is now majority-owned by Suzuki. It has become the leading Indian auto manufacturer, with 1.44 million passenger vehicle sales in 2016–2017. Hyundai Motor Company established operations in India in 1996, and has become India's second-largest auto manufacturer, with state-of-art manufacturing plants that produce nine models, with significant export sales. In 2016, Hyundai Motor India Limited exported 162,000 autos from its Indian production.

The process of liberalization and international competition in the Indian auto sector has also strengthened the capabilities of Indian domestic auto manufacturers, with Tata Motors a major Indian multinational that produces cars, trucks and a wide range of other vehicles including buses. Tata Motors has also become a large global player following its acquisition of the Jaguar and Land Rover brands in 2008 from Ford Motor Company. In 2017, Jaguar Land Rover opened a new engine plant in Changshu in China as part of a joint venture with China's Chery Automobile Limited.

With Indian per capita GDP expected to show strong growth if the economy can achieve sustained average long-term growth in the 6–7% range, this will drive buoyant growth in Indian consumer spending. India is still a lower middle-income country, and therefore rising per capita GDP levels are expected to trigger strong consumer spending on a wide range of manufactures and services, ranging from cars and motorbikes to health care and tourism.

The growing importance of the Indian consumer market for world consumption growth is already evident when compared to the size of Japan's consumer market. The size of the Indian consumer market was still only half the size of Japan's consumer market in 2016 when measured in USD terms. However, India's consumer market size has converged considerably towards Japan's when compared with 1980, when India's consumer market was only around one-quarter the size of Japan (Fig. 2.3).

Therefore, the Indian consumer market has already become increasingly significant at a size that has reached half that of Japan's consumer market. With Japan's economy expected to grow very slowly indeed over the next three decades due to the impact of demographic ageing and the burden of very high fiscal debt, India is already an important locomotive for future growth in Asian consumer spending. Over the next decade, its significance

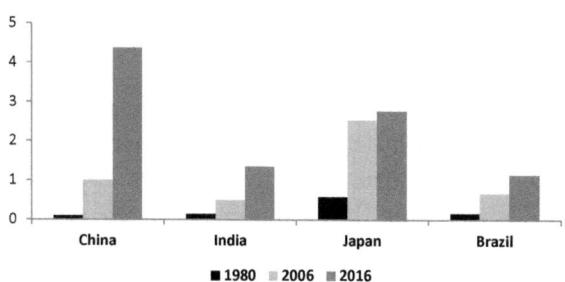

Fig. 2.3 Size of emerging consumer markets versus Japan (USD trillion) (*Source* World Bank data)

for global consumer spending growth is also likely to rise considerably. As with China over the past two decades, the Indian consumer market is expected to become more important as fast-growing export market for both advanced economies as well as developing countries.

ASEAN Consumer Markets

In addition to China and India, the ten member countries of ASEAN are also becoming an increasingly important source of growth for global consumption. The combined total household consumption spending of the ASEAN member countries reached USD 1.4 trillion in 2016, similar in size to Indian household consumption.

Although ASEAN's total population of 635 million persons is less than half the size of India's population, ASEAN's average per capita GDP level is higher than India. Due to this higher average per capita GDP level in ASEAN compared with India, the total size of ASEAN's consumer market is similar to India even though India's population is much larger.

Indonesia, as the largest economy in ASEAN accounting for around 40% of ASEAN GDP, is already a USD 520 billion consumer market, and will be a core driver for future growth in consumer spending growth in ASEAN. With Indonesia's demographic profile very youthful and its working age population set to grow rapidly over the next two decades, the prospects are for rapid future growth in the Indonesian consumer market.

The Philippines is also one of ASEAN's largest consumer markets, with total household consumption of USD 224 billion in 2016. The size of the domestic consumer market has been driven by sustained rapid economic growth since 2012, with GDP growth exceeding 6% each year since that year. Furthermore, household consumption in the Philippines is also underpinned by strong annual remittance inflows from Filipino workers abroad, which provides total annual remittances equivalent to around 10% of the total GDP of the Philippines. With much of these remittance inflows used for household consumption and spending related to the acquisition and improvement of real estate, this helps to lift the level of consumer spending considerably. Another factor driving the future growth of the Philippines consumer market is population growth, with the total population size projected to rise from 102 million in 2015 to 125 million by 2030 and 151 million by 2050. As a result of these factors, the size of the Philippines consumer market accounted for around 73% of GDP in 2016, a very high share of consumption by global standards due to the impact of worker remittances from abroad.

With the Philippines economy having grown at a pace of 6% or more every year since 2012, and sustained rapid growth expected over the medium term, the outlook is for further strong growth in the domestic consumer market over the medium to long term.

Although Vietnam's consumer market is relatively smaller than the Philippines with a size of USD 132 billion in 2016, its fast-growing economy and the rapid growth of household incomes is expected to make the Vietnamese consumer market one of the fastest growing consumer markets in emerging Asia over the medium to long term. With the population of Vietnam projected to grow from 94 million persons in 2015 to 103 million by 2025 and 111 million by 2030, the large size of the total population combined with expected rapid per capita GDP growth will contribute to the rapid expansion of the domestic consumer market (Fig. 2.4).

Thailand is also one of the largest consumer markets in ASEAN, with a total consumer market size of USD 188 billion in 2016. Although the Thai economy has been growing at a relatively moderate pace since 2007 due to the impact of political uncertainty, a major positive factor for the consumer market has been the boom in international tourism, which has become a significant positive factor boosting the growth of the overall consumer market. With 32.6 million tourists visiting Thailand in 2016, international tourism spending is a major contributor to total private consumption expenditure. Total private consumption expenditure including foreign tourism spending rose by 4.1 year-on-year, but when foreign tourism spending is excluded, private consumption spending growth by Thai residents grew at a more moderate pace of 3.1% year-on-year.

In 2016, total consumption expenditure by non-residents in Thailand accounted for around 20% of total private consumption expenditure, highlighting the very significant impact of rapid tourism growth in driving

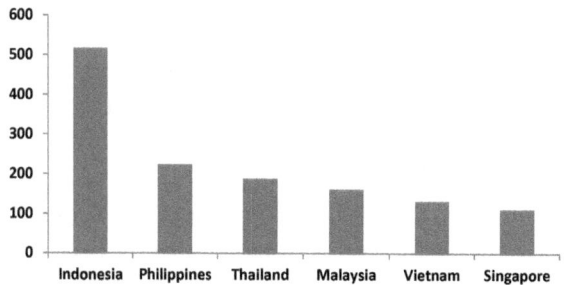

Fig. 2.4 Major ASEAN consumer markets (household consumption, 2016, USD billion) (*Source* World Bank)

the growth of the consumer market. Between 2012 and 2016, consumer expenditure by non-residents grew by 62% overall, whereas total private consumption growth in the Thai economy only grew by 13% over the same period.

Consequently, international tourism has become a key driver for Thai private consumption spending growth, and with the expected further rapid growth of Asian tourism flows to Thailand, the impact of international tourism in boosting the size of the domestic consumer market is likely to continue to increase over the medium term.

The Impact of Asia's Consumer Boom on the Aviation Industry

Rapidly rising household incomes in emerging Asian countries, including China, India and ASEAN, have driven buoyant growth in regional tourism and commercial aviation as the affordability of regional travel has improved for middle-class consumers.

The rapid growth in Chinese tourism has been an important driver of regional international tourism traffic, but other countries such as India, Malaysia and Indonesia are also contributing to rapidly growing regional tourism flows.

The dynamic growth of the regional commercial aviation industry reflects the rapid rise in Asia-Pacific consumer spending power. Fast-growing household incomes in Asia-Pacific economies have driven rapid growth in international and domestic passenger travel, creating rapid growth in the region's commercial aviation industry. In 2016, the International Air Transport Association (IATA) estimated that Asia-Pacific commercial air travel grew by 9.5% year-on-year, compared with global air travel growth of 6.7% year-on-year.

IATA has forecast (IATA 20 Year Forecast, October 2017) that the total number of air passengers travelling on routes to, from or within the Asia-Pacific will increase from 1.4 billion persons in 2016 to 3.5 billion passengers by 2036.

As a result of this rapid growth in commercial air passenger traffic within the Asia-Pacific and on routes to and from the Asia-Pacific, Boeing has forecast that the total size of the commercial jet airliner fleet in the Asia-Pacific will increase from 6380 aircraft in 2016 to 17,520 aircraft by 2036 (Boeing, "Current Market Outlook 2017–2036"). This represents a total increase in the Asia-Pacific jet airliner fleet of 11,140 aircraft, or almost half of the total increase of 23,470 aircraft projected by Boeing for the global jet airliner fleet over the next two decades.

Airbus also forecasts strong growth in total Asia-Pacific new aircraft orders for passenger aircraft over 100 seats and freighter aircraft above 10 tons over the 2017–2036 period. Airbus forecasts project that the size of the Asia-Pacific region's commercial jet airliner fleet will increase by 14,280 aircraft over this period. This is equivalent to 41% of the total global increase in new commercial jet aircraft over the 2017–2036 period.

Therefore, rapidly rising commercial air travel due to rapidly growing Asia-Pacific tourism and business traffic will be the dominant growth driver for the global commercial aircraft manufacturing industry over the next two decades.

Three of the world's five fastest growing aviation markets are forecast by IATA to be in the Asia-Pacific. These are Asia's three most populous nations, China, India and Indonesia.

China is projected by IATA to have a total increase of 920 million passengers between 2016 and 2036, reaching a total air passenger total of 1.5 billion per year by 2036.

India's air passenger numbers are projected by IATA to increase by 337 million passengers over the next two decades, reaching 478 million by 2036. India's domestic commercial aviation market has been leading Asia-Pacific domestic air travel growth rates, reflecting the rapid growth of Indian domestic consumer spending power. In 2016, the Indian domestic air travel growth rate was 23.3% year-on-year, measured in revenue passenger kilometer terms, based on International Air Travel Association (IATA) data. This was more than triple the global growth rate for revenue passenger kilometres, which grew by 7.1% in 2016. The Indian domestic commercial aviation market also grew more quickly than China's, which grew by 16.9% year-on-year in 2016. India's domestic commercial aviation market continued to grow strongly in 2017, with October 2017 domestic revenue passenger kilometers up 20.4% year-on-year, according to IATA statistics.

The Indonesian commercial aviation industry is also forecast to grow rapidly over the medium term. Key factors driving the rapid growth of the Indonesian industry are the strong growth in the size of the Indonesian middle class, the rapid expansion in fleet sizes of Indonesian low-cost carriers such as Lion Air, and increasing air connectivity owing to ASEAN Open Skies implementation, as well as improvement in airport infrastructure. The rapid growth of commercial aviation in Indonesia is also resulting in rapid growth of the Indonesian maintenance, repair and overhaul (MRO) market, with Indonesian MRO value projected to grow at 12.3% per year over 2016–2020, according to forecasts by GMF AeroAsia, which is Garuda Indonesia's MRO subsidiary.

The Indonesian government is currently considering establishing a special economic zone for the MRO industry, with Bintan being a likely location for such an MRO hub. The new special economic zone is being planned in order to accelerate the development of Indonesia's MRO cluster. Indonesia also has an aircraft manufacturing industry, with PT Dirgantara manufacturing the CN235 and N219, and having industrial collaboration with Airbus for production of the NC212i. In addition, PT Regio Aviasi Industri (RAI) is developing the R80 turboprop aircraft for the regional commercial aircraft market, with Indonesian demand for regional commercial aircraft expected to grow rapidly owing to rising middle-class incomes and the airport infrastructure development programme of the Indonesian government to improve connectivity among the 5000 populated islands of the 17,000 island Indonesian archipelago.

The very rapid growth in air passenger traffic in large Asian emerging markets is creating infrastructure bottlenecks, with major expansion in airport capacity required in many major cities across Asia to cope with the fast-growing air passenger numbers. Although many Asian countries have already significantly upgraded their airport infrastructure over the past decade, the very rapid growth of regional air passenger traffic has continued to put pressure on existing airport capacity.

For example, Thailand built the state-of-art new Suvarnabhumi international airport for Bangkok which opened in 2006 with an initial capacity of 45 million passengers per year. However, due to the boom in Chinese and other Asian tourism visits to Thailand since 2012, the airport is already facing bottlenecks due to the large growth in passenger numbers, which reached 61 million in 2017.

To help improve the capacity of airport infrastructure to cope with rapid growth in air passengers, Thailand is planning to redevelop U-Tapao Airport, which is located in Rayong Province and is 150 kilometres east of Bangkok, to make it a major new commercial aviation hub, as well as a new MRO hub for Asia-Pacific airline fleets. Thai Airways International and Airbus are planning to open an MRO facility at the airport, with the new MRO campus planned to open in 2022. The major expansion of this airport will help to increase capacity for international tourism visitors to Bangkok as well as providing an international airport to serve Thailand's Eastern Economic Corridor, a major new regional economic development zone for the nation.

India is planning to build 100 new airports over the next 15 years, of which 70 will be in cities that currently do not have a commercial airport. China is also planning to substantially increase its civil airport infrastructure with 136 new airports to be built by 2025, adding to the 210 airports already operating.

Equally critical for Asian emerging markets will be the task of building human capital for the aviation industry, with a wide range of highly skilled technical staff required to cope with the rapid growth of the industry such as pilots, aerospace engineers and technicians as well as flight controllers. Investing in aviation industry training infrastructure will also be an essential requirement. Another area where substantial upgrading of training is required is in airline management training, to cope with the rapid growth in airline fleet sizes.

Helped by rapid growth in Asia-Pacific air passenger traffic and the rapid expansion of Asian airline fleet sizes, Singapore's role as a leading international aviation hub is expected to continue to grow rapidly over the next two decades. Significant infrastructure expansion plans are being implemented for Changi Airport to handle the strong growth in air passenger traffic expected over the next two decades. Changi Airport handled an estimated 58.7 million air passengers in 2016, with major new infrastructure planned to cope with the projected long-term growth in passenger numbers. The Changi Airport Group has commenced an infrastructure expansion megaproject for Changi Airport that will involve the construction of a new runway, as well as a new Terminal Five building by 2025. Once Terminal Five is completed, the total passenger capacity of Changi Airport is forecast to increase to 135 million passengers per year, with Terminal Five alone projected to have a capacity of 50 million passengers per year.

However, Singapore's role as an international aviation hub is also boosted significantly by its large aerospace engineering sector, as a leading MRO hub for the Asia-Pacific.

Singapore has a 25% share of the Asia-Pacific MRO market, with major global aerospace companies such as Rolls Royce and Pratt & Whitney among over 130 aerospace companies with operations in Singapore.

The Singapore aerospace industry was estimated to have output of SGD 8.3 billion (USD 5.9 billion) in 2014, with over 20,000 employees, dominated by its large MRO industry cluster.

Rolls-Royce has built a major manufacturing, assembly and test facility at its Seletar Campus in Singapore for its Trent family of aero engines, which are used on Airbus A380s, Airbus A330neos, as well as Boeing 787 Dreamliners.

Pratt & Whitney has opened a manufacturing facility in Singapore, which produces fan blades and high-pressure turbine disks for Pratt & Whitney's PurePower® Geared Turbofan™. The Singapore facility is the first Pratt & Whitney aero engine fan blade production facility outside of the United States.

The future growth of Singapore's advanced MRO hub will be boosted by rapid growth in the total fleet size of Asian airlines. The rapid growth in total Asian airline jet airliner fleet size is projected to create very strong growth in demand for Asia-Pacific MRO services. With Singapore already having a leading global cluster of MRO services and key regional MRO facilities established by major global aerospace firms, the outlook is for continued strong growth for Singapore's MRO hub over the next two decades.

With aircraft leasing becoming an increasingly important part of Asian airline strategies for fleet expansion, Singapore has also become a major global aircraft leasing hub, linked to its role as one of the world's largest international financial centres. The aircraft leasing cluster in Singapore has grown rapidly over the last 5 years, and is expected to play a key role in financing for Asia-Pacific airline expansion over the long-term owing to the large expansion in Asian airline fleets projected over the next two decades.

Co-operation and co-ordination among Asia-Pacific governments and the air transport industry is therefore a key priority in order to address these challenges and prepare strategic long-term plans to cope with the rapid growth forecast for the commercial aviation industry.

The strong growth projected for the Asia-Pacific commercial aviation industry will have many positive economic impact effects on the economies of Asia-Pacific countries, through large-scale new investment in industry infrastructure, rapid growth of new employment, and the growth of industry clusters in high-technology sectors such as aerospace manufacturing as well as MRO activities. By boosting air connectivity between Asian cities, the air transport industry will also be a key enabler for further rapid growth in Asian tourism flows, which is a key part of the economy for many Asian countries.

African Consumer Markets

The total size of household consumption in Sub-Saharan Africa amounted to USD 1.13 trillion in 2016 according to World Bank data, which was equivalent to the size of total household consumption of Brazil in the same year. Nigeria is the largest economy in Sub-Saharan Africa, with the size of its consumer market estimated at USD 340 billion, or around 30% of the total Sub-Saharan consumer market. The South African consumer market size totaled USD 177 billion, equivalent to around 16% of total Sub-Saharan African consumption.

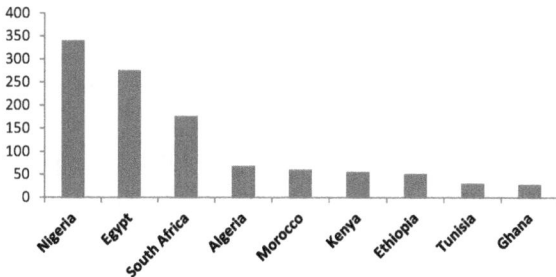

Fig. 2.5 Major African consumer markets (household consumption, USD billion, 2016) (*Source* World Bank)

Consequently, Nigeria and South Africa together have a combined con sumer market size equivalent to around half the total size of Sub-Saharan consumer market spending. In East Africa, Kenya also is a significant consumer market with a total market size of USD 55 billion while Ethiopia is comparable in size with a market size of USD 51 billion (Fig. 2.5).

Due to the rapid pace of GDP growth as well as population growth that is projected for Sub-Saharan Africa, the size of the consumer markets of the region are set to grow rapidly, although the rapid pace of population growth will likely constrain per capita GDP growth rates.

Nevertheless, the rapid growth in the size of Sub-Saharan will make them attractive for a wide range of multinationals in manufacturing, services and construction. With regional demand for food and beverage products and the broader category of fast-moving consumer goods expected to grow rapidly for decades ahead, large global multinationals producing household goods will have considerable market growth opportunities in the region.

In the services sector, rapid growth in demand for services such as communications, retail and wholesale trade, business services and financial services will also grow rapidly. As the total size of the Sub-Saharan consumer markets grow, it will become more attractive for multinationals to boost regional manufacturing production in order to supply Sub-Saharan markets.

The Sub-Saharan African consumer market has already become an important market for South-South exports, as multinationals from India, China and other developing countries are able to enter these markets due to their experience in competing in low-income consumer markets as well as having product ranges designed for developing country markets.

For example, India's Tata Motors opened a truck assembly plant near Pretoria in South Africa in 2011. Africa already accounts for around 18%

of Tata Motors commercial vehicle exports. Total Indian exports to South Africa reached USD 3.5 billion in fiscal 2016–2017, while key Indian exports to Africa as a whole included transport equipment, machinery and pharmaceuticals.

China's Wuxi No. 1 Cotton Mill has signed an agreement with the Ethiopian government in 2017 to establish an integrated textile manufacturing facility with a fabric mill and spinning plant in Dire Dawa, which will produce textiles for both domestic and export markets, including for export to other African markets.

Apart from the fast-growing Sub-Saharan African consumer markets, Africa also has large consumer markets along its Mediterranean coast, with Egypt being one of the largest consumer markets in Africa with a total size of USD 275 billion in 2016. This made Egypt the second largest consumer market on the African continent after Nigeria in 2016. The population of Egypt is also projected to grow rapidly, from 94 million in 2015 to 120 million by 2030 and 153 million by 2050. Consequently, Egypt is expected to be one of the world's fast-growing emerging consumer markets over the next three decades, so long as there is stable governance and no political turmoil that would disrupt sustained economic development.

The North African consumer markets of Algeria, Morocco and Tunisia are also major consumer markets of the African continent, with the combined size of household consumption in these three markets amounting to USD 160 billion in 2016, comparable to the size of the South African consumer market. With the population of all three nations set to rise rapidly over the next three decades, this will also help to drive the expansion of these consumer markets. The population of Algeria is projected to rise from 40 million in 2015 to 49 million by 2030 and 57 million by 2050. Morocco's population is also expected to grow rapidly, from 35 million in 2015 to 41 million by 2030 and 46 million by 2050. Tunisia's population is relatively smaller in comparison with Algeria and Tunisia, and is also projected to less rapidly, from 11 million in 2015 to 13 million by 2030 and 14 million by 2050.

The per capita GDP levels of these North African nations is relatively high compared with most of Sub-Saharan Africa, which boosts the total size of their household consumption. They also benefit from strong trade and investment relationships with the European Union, which is likely to continue to give a high priority to supporting their economic development in the long term for geopolitical reasons in order to try to underpin the economic and social stability of their neighbours. An EU strategy for building co-operation and development with other nations in the Mediterranean was launched in 1995 through the EUROMED initiative, and further strengthened with the Union for the Mediterranean agreement in 2008. However North Africa has subsequently suffered considerable political turmoil since the Arab Spring as well as the impact of the civil war in Libya. This has disrupted the political momentum behind the Barcelona Process, with an eight-year gap in the trade ministerial meetings of the Union for the Mediterranean, which eventually restarted in March 2018.

Although the medium to long-term growth outlook for African consumer markets is for rapid growth due to a combination of expected rapid long-term GDP growth as well as fast-growing populations, the overall size of the total consumer market for the African continent is still relatively small compared with Asian consumer markets. The total size of African household consumption is broadly comparable to total Indian household consumption. Nevertheless, African consumer markets are attractive to multinationals in many different sectors of manufacturing and services as fast-growing markets in contrast to the large, mature markets of the developed nations in North America and Europe.

Middle East Consumer Markets

The consumer markets of the Middle East region exceeded the total size of the Sub-Saharan consumer market in 2016, particularly due to the large size of the Turkish consumer market, which amounted to around USD 517 billion in 2016 (Fig. 2.6). Total Turkish household consumption in 2016 was exactly the same as for Indonesia, even though Indonesia's population was around three times larger than Turkey's population, due to the higher per capita GDP level of Turkey in comparison with Indonesia. Turkey's large tourism economy was an important factor that has helped to boost overall consumer expenditure, with total tourism spending estimated at USD 26.3 billion in 2017. The medium-term outlook for the Turkish consumer market is for continued rapid growth, due to the expected strong GDP growth of the Turkish economy over the next decade, boosted by further population growth from 78 million people in 2015 to a projected 88 million by 2030, a net increase of 10 million persons.

The Saudi Arabian consumer market is the second largest in the region, with a total size of USD 276 billion in 2016. The total population of Saudi Arabia in 2016 was 31.5 million persons, and is projected to grow to 39.5 million by 2030 under the UN Medium Scenario population projections, indicating that the population will increase by 8 million persons over the

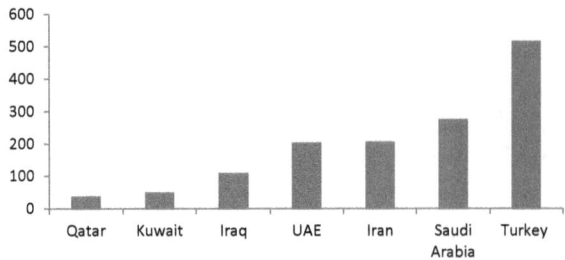

Fig. 2.6 Middle East consumer markets (household consumption, USD billion, 2016) (*Source* World Bank)

next decade. This will help to underpin further rapid growth in the total size of the Saudi Arabian consumer market over the decade ahead.

After Saudi Arabia, the next largest consumer market is Iran, with a total market size of USD 207 billion and a population estimated at 79 million in 2015. Prospects for the future growth of the Iranian consumer market will be highly dependent on geopolitical risks, due to the impact of deteriorating bilateral relations with the US and risk of the US re-introducing sanctions on Iran.

However, the size of the UAE consumer market is comparable to Iran, estimated at USD 204 billion in 2016, although its population is just a fraction of the size of Iran's population, at around 9.2 million people in 2015. The very high level of per capita GDP in the UAE combined with high levels of tourism visitors and tourism expenditure are factors that have made the UAE consumer market one of the largest in the Middle East even though its population size is relatively small. The development of Dubai and Abu Dhabi with high-quality hotel, tourism and commercial infrastructure have contributed to the success of the UAE.

The development of Dubai as a major global aviation hub has also contributed to the nation's success at boosting tourism revenue, with total air passenger traffic at Dubai International Airport reaching 83.6 million in 2016. Dubai has also built a second international airport, Al Maktoum International Airport, with the combined passenger traffic at both airports projected to reach 146 million passengers by 2025.

The Outlook for Emerging Consumer Markets

During the period from the 1950s to 1990s, global economic growth was driven by fast-growing consumer spending in the major developed economies of the US, Europe and Japan. However, over the past 30 years, rapid growth in consumer spending in developing countries has transformed the global economic landscape, making developing countries as a group an increasingly important growth driver for the world economy. Over the next three decades, the growth engines for the global economy will increasingly shift to the emerging markets, with China, India and ASEAN being the key fast-growing consumer markets in the Asia-Pacific region.

For the corporate boardrooms of multinationals worldwide, this will result in a continuing strategic pivot towards emerging markets to build new growth markets that will drive future revenue growth. However, due to the widely varying economic and political risks across developing countries, assessing the risk landscape across emerging markets will be a critical part of the ongoing strategic decision-making process for companies as they evaluate their emerging markets strategies.

3

Emerging Markets Megacities

The Challenges of Urbanization

Since 1950, the world's population has roughly tripled, rising from 2.5 billion people to an estimated 7.4 billion people by 2015, according to United Nations population statistics. By 2050, United Nations medium variant demographic projections indicate that the world's population will have risen to 9.8 billion people, a further increase of 2.4 billion people. The population of developing countries has risen from 1.7 billion in 1950, or around 68% of the world's population, to 6.1 billion by 2015, or around 83% of the global population. By 2050, the population of developing countries is projected to rise to 8.5 billion people in the United Nations medium variant demographic projections.

Furthermore, the 2.4 billion increase in the world population between 2015 and 2050 is very close in total numbers to the overall rise in the total population of developing countries, which is projected to grow by 2.3 billion persons over this time period. The future increase of the world's population over the next three decades will therefore be largely concentrated in the developing world, notably in Africa, South Asia and Southeast Asia.

United Nations projections of urbanization rates also indicate that the global urban population will rise by an estimated 2.4 billion persons between 2014 and 2050 (United Nations, World Urbanization Prospects 2014), with almost 90% of these new urban dwellers expected to be in urban areas of Africa and Asia. The share of the world's population living in urban areas has risen significantly over the past seven decades, from a ratio of 30% in 1950

© The Author(s) 2018
R. Biswas, *Emerging Markets Megatrends*,
https://doi.org/10.1007/978-3-319-78123-5_3

to 54% by 2014. In 1950, only 750 million people lived in urban areas, according to UN estimates, but this figure has risen dramatically, to around 4 billion by 2015, and is projected to rise to 6.4 billion by 2050.

In the developing countries, the rise in urban population has been very dramatic, from an estimated 300 million people in 1950 to 3 billion by 2014, a ten-fold increase. This figure is projected to rise further, to 5.2 billion by 2050, indicating that another 2.2 billion people will be living in urban areas of developing countries by that time. The proportion of the total population of developing countries living in urban areas was estimated at around 18% in 1950, and has risen to around 48% by 2014. By 2050, the UN projects that this ratio will have risen significantly further, to around 63% (Fig. 3.1).

The rapid rate of urbanization for the developing countries as a grouping combined with the large increase projected in actual numbers of persons living in urban areas in developing countries implies that emerging markets cities will face rapidly growing populations, both due to natural increases in population and due to net immigration inflows.

Consequently one of the greatest challenges facing national, state and municipal governments in many developing countries will be to tackle the infrastructure requirements of rapidly growing urban populations. These infrastructure needs will be wide-ranging, including power, sanitation, public transport and urban housing. As urban populations grow, governments will also face rising demand for educational infrastructure as well as healthcare. As many governments of developing countries lack the fiscal resources to finance the necessary infrastructure financing entirely from budget revenues, a key challenge is mobilizing other financial resources for infrastructure development.

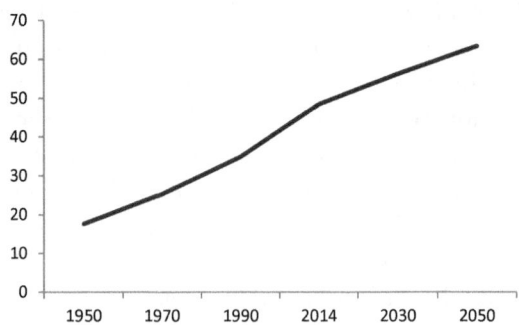

Fig. 3.1 Developing countries: urban share of total population (1950–2050) (*Source* United Nations)

Governments of developing countries face many other challenges as cities continue to grow, including tackling urban crime, environmental pollution and generating sufficient employment growth.

Megacities in Developing Countries

The fast growth of urban populations in developing countries has driven the rapid expansion of major cities. This has resulted in a significant increase in the number of megacities, defined as urban agglomerations with a total population of 10 million persons or more. In 1990, United Nations urbanization statistics show that there were 10 cities worldwide, including in developed countries, which were classified as megacities. By 2014, the number of megacities had almost tripled, to 28 megacities.

By 2030, the UN urbanization projections indicate that there will be 41 megacities globally. The number of megacities in developing countries has risen very rapidly, from just 6 megacities in 1990 to 21 megacities by 2014. By 2030, the number of megacities in developing countries is projected to rise to 34. Furthermore, the number of cities in developing countries with a population between 5 million and 10 million persons is projected to rise from 32 in 2014 to 49 by 2030. The rapid growth in urbanization of developing countries is also expected to drive up the number of cities in developing countries with a population in the range of 1 million to 5 million persons, from 317 in 2014 to 446 by 2030, a net increase of 129 cities in this category.

As a result of the rapid growth in the total number of large cities in developing countries over the next decade, urbanization will be one of the key emerging markets megatrends confronting policymakers. Developing Asia will be at the forefront of this rapid growth of urbanization, with eight additional cities in Asian developing countries expected to enter the ranks of Asian megacities by 2030. Three additional cities in Africa are also expected to become megacities by 2030.

Urbanization in Asia

In Asia, urbanization in China and India are major drivers of rising global urbanization over the next decade and beyond. For Asia as a whole, the share of the total urban population is also projected to increase significantly, from 17.5% in 1950 to 56.3% by 2030. The total size of the urban population in Asia is expected to increase from 2064 million people in 2014 to 2752 million people by 2030, which is a net increase of 688 million people living in urban areas in the Asian region. This will result in another eight Asian cities becoming megacities by 2030, of which four are projected to be in India. The number of cities with a population of 5 million to 10 million in Asia is projected by the UN (UN World Urbanization Prospects, 2014 Revision) to rise from 28 to 35. Meanwhile the number of smaller cities with a size of 1 million to 5 million are expected to grow rapidly, from 212 cities in 2014 to 295 cities by 2050, a net rise of 212 cities which will join this ranking.

China's Rapid Urbanization Path

In China, the share of the total urban population has risen very rapidly, from 11.8% in 1950 to 55.6% by 2015, and is projected to rise to 65.4% by 2030. The rapid industrialization of China since 1980 has been an important driver of urbanization by creating rapid industrial employment growth in urban cities in coastal China, drawing rural migrants from inland provinces into major urban agglomerations such as Shanghai, Tianjin and Guangzhou. By 2014, the total urban population of China had reached 758 million, accounting for around 20% of the world's urban population.

The Chinese government has set out a medium term policy objective to increase the urbanization ratio to 60% by 2020, with Chinese Premier Li Keqiang having stated in policy speeches in 2012 that rising urbanization would help to boost domestic demand.

The number of Chinese megacities is expected to increase by only one between 2015 and 2030, with Chengdu becoming the next Chinese megacity. However the population of existing Chinese megacities is projected to increase significantly, particularly for Shanghai and Beijing, with Shanghai's population projected to reach around 31 million persons while Beijing's population will increase to around 28 million. This will rank China's two largest cities among the top five largest cities in the world by 2030 (Fig. 3.2).

Although only Chengdu is projected to join the ranks of China's megacities between 2015 and 2030, a number of other Chinese cities will approach the megacity threshold by 2030. Nanjing will be on the threshold of becoming a megacity, with its population projected to be around 9.8 million by 2030, while Wuhan, Hangzhou and Dongguan will all have population sizes of around 9 million persons.

However, despite the projected increase in the share of the population living in urban areas over the next decade, the challenges of urbanization for China may not be as severe as for other large populous nations for a number of reasons.

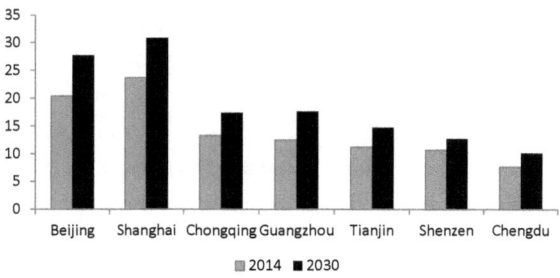

Fig. 3.2 Chinese megacities in 2030 (population in millions) (*Source* United Nations)

Firstly, unlike many other developing countries, China has significant regulatory tools to control the size of population in individual cities. One of the most powerful mechanisms is through the system of resident permits for cities which allow the government to control the number of Chinese migrants from other areas who are eligible to obtain a residency permit in cities. By controlling the allocation of permits, the Chinese government can control the number of migrants from other areas who are allowed to live in a particular city. This policy lever can be used to limit new migrants entering into the largest cities, while it can also be used to encourage migrant flows to other small or medium sized Tier 2, Tier 3 and Tier 4 cities.

One of the other major advantages that China has had during its rapid urbanization path over the past four decades is the considerable fiscal capacity of the central government to finance infrastructure development in co-ordination with state-owned banks and local governments. This has helped to finance large-scale infrastructure development in urban areas, such as road, rail and air transport infrastructure, as well as power generation and transmission infrastructure and affordable housing. This has helped to address the infrastructure challenges of such rapid urbanization, while many other developing countries in Asia and other emerging regions have not had the fiscal capacity to deliver adequate infrastructure development to match urban population growth rates.

Furthermore, due to China's ageing demographic profile, with the total size of China's population stabilizing over the next three decades, the pressure of population growth is no longer such a significant factor impacting on urbanization in future, with rural to urban migration and migration between cities being more important factors over the coming decades. China's total population is projected to decline by 33 million over the period from 2015 to 2050, according to the UN World Population Prospects 2017 Revision in their medium variant demographic projections.

Beyond 2050, the very long-term population projections of the UN indicate that China's population will decline dramatically, falling by 344 million between 2050 and 2100 according to the UN World Population Prospects 2017 Revision medium variant. If these projections are realized, the implications for urban areas will be far-reaching. As Japan is currently experiencing, such large declines in total population will have severe social and economic consequences, implying substantial further contraction in the working age population as well as much-reduced requirements for a wide range of infrastructure such as schools, universities and housing. Such large population declines can also have severe consequences for the fiscal sustainability of smaller towns, as the population base erodes.

One of the most severe implications will be a sustained decline in the size of the domestic consumer market as the total population of China continues to contract over the 2050 to 2100 period. While China is trying to make policy changes to encourage families to have more children, it is unclear whether such regulatory changes will have a significant impact as rising education levels and increasing urbanization are structural trends that have resulted in declining fertility rates in many countries, with similar trends evident in China in recent decades.

Nevertheless, over the next two or three decades, China will still grapple with the consequences of rising populations in its major cities. Despite its considerable investment in infrastructure development, the sheer mass of population in China's largest cities continues to create a wide range of social, economic and environmental challenges. Ever-increasing traffic jams are one of the consequences of increasing consumer affluence, as the rapid growth in total passenger car numbers has resulted in horrendous road congestion in the major cities. While this is not unique to China, as many other Asian cities also have severe traffic congestion problems, the traffic jams in China can reach epic proportions.

I recall going from a central district of Beijing to visit a client in another part of Beijing, with the outbound journey taking over two hours. This was quite a tiring trip, but because this journey took place in the early afternoon, I was told by my Beijing colleagues that the traffic congestion was not as severe as during the rush hour. I learnt what they meant later on after the client meeting was over, when the return journey took over three hours to get back to my hotel. However this was just a normal day in the Beijing traffic.

The ultimate horror story about Chinese traffic congestion took place in August 2010 in the peak of summer, on National Expressway 110 from Inner Mongolia to Beijing, when cars and trucks were stuck in a traffic jam that lasted for 11 days. Vendors set up road-side stalls and sold items to drivers along the way as people had to sleep in their vehicles for many days. This extreme example of gridlock was caused by a combination of large volumes of freight being hauled by trucks on this route, together with a significant road maintenance program that reduced road capacity substantially.

Another major environmental concern in China has been the extreme levels of air pollution in megacities such as Beijing and Tianjin. According to the United Nations World Health Organization (WHO) database of air pollution, the annual mean concentration of particles less than 10 microns in diameter (PM10 measure) was 108 in Beijing and 150 in Tianjin according to latest available WHO data for 2013. The WHO guideline for safe levels of air pollution is for 20 microns per cubic meter based on the PM10 measure, far below the levels in many major Chinese cities. The health consequences of long-term exposure to such high levels of air pollution include increased risk of respiratory diseases as well as diseases such as lung cancer, stroke and heart disease. By comparison, the level of air pollution in Paris based on concentration of particles less than 10 microns in diameter was measured to be 28 in 2014, while in London it was measured to be 22 in 2013 (Fig. 3.3).

China has been giving a much greater policy priority to reducing air pollution in recent years, and has taken major measures such as closing the coal-fired power stations around Beijing and switching to either power generated by natural gas or by supplying power by long-distance power transmission grids. The Chinese government has also implemented policies to reduce air pollution by heavy industries during winter months by restricting output of major industrial products such as steel and aluminium during the winter months when air pollution levels have historically been extremely high.

With China's relatively substantial fiscal capacity to address the problems of urbanization, the outlook for tackling the challenges created by rapid urban growth over the next two decades look relatively more positive than for many other developing countries. A wide range of policy measures, such as the gradual transition towards electric vehicles, switching away from coal towards natural gas for power generation, and managing the emissions of heavy industry will all contribute towards managing the environmental challenges of urbanization.

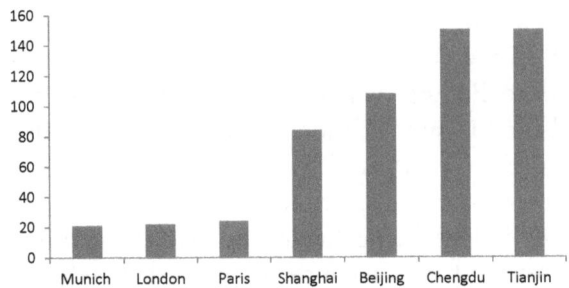

Fig. 3.3 Air pollution in major Chinese cities versus Europe (PM10 measure) (*Source* World Health Organisation)

India's Urbanization

India's pace of urbanization has not been as rapid as China's, although their total population levels are comparable in size. In 1950, only 17% of India's population, around 64 million persons, lived in urban areas, with the nation still being predominantly rural. The rapid growth of Indian cities reflects a number of major drivers.

Firstly, India's total population is projected to continue to rise significantly over the next three decades, unlike China, whose population is projected to be broadly stable over the same period. By 2015, India's urban population amounted to 420 million people, or around 32% of the total Indian population. However, between 2015 and 2050, an additional 395 million persons are projected to live in Indian urban agglomerations, equivalent to an approximate doubling of India's urban population over the next three decades. By 2050, India's urban population is expected to reach 814 million.

A second driver for the growth of Indian cities will be a structural trend of further urbanization of India's population due to rural-urban migration flows. This is expected to continue to be a significant factor contributing to population growth, as migrant workers seek jobs in manufacturing and service sector industries.

As a result of these drivers for future population growth, the size of Indian cities is expected to grow rapidly over the next three decades, with another four Indian cities joining the ranks of Indian megacities by 2030. By 2014, three Indian cities were classified as megacities, namely Mumbai, Delhi and Calcutta. Four more Indian cities, Bangalore, Chennai, Hyderabad and Ahmadabad, are projected to join the ranks of Indian megacities by 2030.

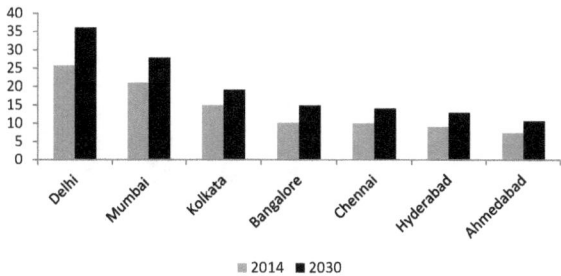

Fig. 3.4 Indian megacities in 2030 (population in millions) (*Source* United Nations)

I recall visiting Bangalore in the 1980's, and my impression was of a sleepy, tranquil Indian backwater where time had stood still. I arrived into a small regional airport with that was not very crowded at all, at least by Indian standards. There was also little traffic congestion in the city center. I remember visiting a local private club in the city centre which had been a former colonial era club from the British Raj, with hardly anybody in the premises. We played snooker in a billiards room which was completely empty apart from me and my friend, with the walls lined with colonial era trophies. However everything changed for Bangalore with the growth of the information technology services industry during the past thirty years. The city has become India's Silicon Valley, with large campuses of Indian and foreign multinational IT firms. Bangalore's population is already at around the 10 million threshold, and by 2030 the population of the city is projected to reach around 15 million people (Fig. 3.4).

In addition to having 7 megacities by 2030, India will also experience rapid growth of other large cities. By 2030, the city of Surat is projected to have a population of 8.6 million persons, while Poona is expected to have a population of 8.1 million. The cities of Lucknow and Jaipur will meanwhile be approaching the 4–5 million mark in terms of their total city populations.

As Indian governments have lacked fiscal resources to invest sufficiently in modernizing urban infrastructure to cope with the rapid growth of urban populations, most Indian cities have dilapidated infrastructure and face a tremendous uphill struggle to retrofit cities with modern transport, communications, power and sanitation.

Latest WHO data from their Global Ambient Urban Air Pollution Database 2016 Update indicates that 14 of the world's 20 worst polluted cities in terms of air pollution levels are in India. These include the cities of Kanpur, Delhi, Patna, Lucknow and Agra.

The environmental challenges facing Indian cities are also great, with air pollution in Indian megacities being extremely high by global standards and

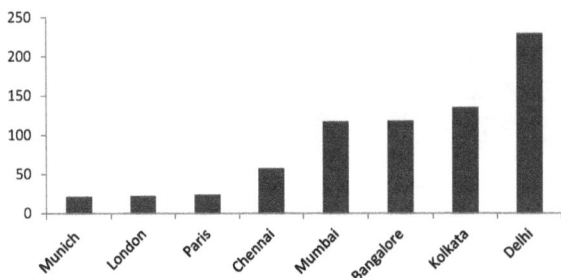

Fig. 3.5 Air pollution in Indian cities versus Europe (PM10 reading) (*Source* World Health Organisation, Global Urban Ambient Air Pollution Database, 2016 update)

posing a significant health risk to the urban populations of many Indian cities. With coal being the main feedstock for power generation for most Indian cities, this contributes to the air pollution problems, particularly because many power stations are old and have not integrated modern clean coal technology to reduce emissions (Fig. 3.5).

However, since Prime Minister Modi was elected to office, new initiatives to modernize Indian urban infrastructure have commenced.

Modi's Smart Cities Initiative

After taking office in May 2014, Indian Prime Minister Narendra Modi made the development of smart cities a key government priority, recognizing that Indian cities had poor infrastructure after decades of neglect and lack of new infrastructure investment. In order to galvanize momentum for his new initiative, Prime Minister Modi created a strategy for building one hundred smart cities, in order to set a vision for modernizing urban infrastructure in India.

The strategy recognized that Indian cities have very poor quality infrastructure, and that the future international competitiveness of India would be critically dependent on having cities with high quality infrastructure that would be attractive hubs for foreign investment by global multinationals to establish R&D centres, manufacturing production facilities and information technology-business process outsourcing (IT-BPO) back offices.

In order for India to compete for foreign direct investment by global multinationals, the strategy recognizes that companies want state-of-art infrastructure for power, water, transport and communications, as well as liveable cities that will be attractive locations for knowledge industry workers.

A number of greenfield smart city projects are already underway in India, including several smart city projects in the state of Gujarat, where

Prime Minister Modi was Chief Minister for many years. The Gujarat International Finance Tec-City (GIFT) is already under construction and is intended to be a new financial centre with modern infrastructure that will provide an alternative new hub to Mumbai's financial centre.

Gujarat is also developing a new smart city precinct called Surat Dream City, which is intended to become India's second diamond exchange after Mumbai. The existing city of Surat, which is projected to have a population of 8.6 million by 2030 and approaching megacity status, will have its commercial competitiveness boosted by the new infrastructure being created for the world's diamond industry with many international as well as Indian diamond merchants having booked floorspace in the new diamond exchange precinct under construction.

Another major new smart city project that has arisen due to the split of an Indian state into two new states is the development of a new capital city for the state of Andhra Pradesh. The state of Andhra Pradesh was split into two states in 2014, with the creation of a new state called Telangana. The former capital city of Andhra Pradesh was Hyderabad, which has become the new state capital of Telangana. Consequently a new capital city was required for the state of Andhra Pradesh, with the Indian federal government having allocated land for a new capital city called Amaravati. Singapore's urban development planner Surbana Jurong won the contract for designing the masterplan for the new city, and the masterplan was completed in July 2015. The new city will be designed for a population size of a megacity of 10 million by 2050.

A Singapore consortium comprising Ascendas-Singbridge and Sembcorp Development has subsequently won the master development rights for developing the new city start-up area, and have created a joint venture firm called Singapore Amaravati Investment Holdings Pte Ltd for the project. Ascendas-Singbridge has already established a strong track record in India with the development of eight industrial parks in five Indian cities.

In the state of Kerala, the state government of Kerala and the UAE's Tecom Investments, a subsidiary of Dubai Holding, have formed a joint venture for the development of a smart city precinct in the city of Kochi, which will be an IT special economic zone. Phase One of this smart city project became operational in 2016, with the project expected to become one of India's major IT parks and industry cluster for the IT sector.

As a result of Prime Minister Modi's new smart cities initiative, a number of foreign governments have offered to help India with its development of new smart cities, recognizing the lucrative commercial opportunities for their own companies in providing the wide range of smart cities technology needed.

Smart cities require state-of-art communications systems, with firms such as Cisco Systems, Microsoft and IBM being global leaders in such smart cities development. Other leading multinationals in development of smart cities technology include GE, Hitachi, Samsung, Siemens, Toshiba and Schneider Electric. A wide range of advanced technologies are required for smart cities, such as advanced urban transport systems that can provide integrated transport infrastructure, as well as modern energy systems that will optimize energy efficiency. Smart cities also have advanced water management systems to ensure efficient use of water resources as well as integrating advanced waste management systems.

If India is able to successfully implement a large number of smart city developments, it will transform the competitiveness of these locations as hubs for foreign direct investment by global multinationals in knowledge industries.

India has already become the leading global hub for IT-Business Process Outsourcing (IT-BPO) service centers for global multinationals as well as Indian IT-BPO service providers, and is also a major international hub for R&D centres for large multinationals. India's Tier 1 and Tier 2 cities have already established strong clusters of knowledge industries. For example, Bangalore is estimated to now be the world's fourth largest technology cluster with around 400 R&D centres located in the city. GE's John F. Welch Technology Centre in Bangalore is estimated to have over 5000 scientists and engineers working in its campus. Microsoft has located its India Development Centers in Bangalore, Delhi, Pune and Hyderabad. In 2015, Huawei opened China's first R&D center located in India in a state-of-art campus in Bangalore, with capacity planned for 5000 engineers.

As India develops better urban infrastructure and smart city precincts, its ability to attract more knowledge industry investments by global multinationals will continue to improve, given its strong human capital in science and technology. The large cities of India will also increasingly need to develop modern public transport systems to cope with the rapidly growing size of urban populations. Japan has been an important partner for India for the construction of metro rail systems, using a combination of Japanese government development finance and Japan's technical expertise in designing and constructing high-quality public transport systems.

Japanese co-operation for the development of Indian mass rapid transit systems in New Delhi was a major step forward for improving public infrastructure in India's most populous city, which was so successful after the first stage that several additional stages have subsequently been built. Other Indian cities have also been developing such public transport infrastructure with Japanese assistance, including in Bangalore, Chennai, Kolkata and Mumbai. Following these successes, India also signed an agreement with Japan for the construction of its first high-speed railway from Mumbai to Ahmedabad with a long-term loan of USD 14.5 billion.

Urban Development in Other Asian Nations

While China and India are the two most populous nations in the world and are the two most significant drivers of future urbanization in developing countries, a number of other Asian nations will also face tremendous challenges from urbanization.

Although China and India will have together have a total of 14 megacities by 2050, a number of other Asian developing countries will also have megacities. These will include a number of Asian nations in ASEAN and South Asia.

In South Asia, Dhaka and Karachi are already megacities, and by 2030 Lahore is expected to also join the ranks of the world's megacities. Meanwhile in the ASEAN region, Jakarta and Manila are already classified as megacities, and two new Southeast Asian megacities will join their ranks by 2030, namely Bangkok and Ho Chi Minh City (Fig. 3.6).

However a number of these megacities face severe environmental problems due to vulnerability to flooding. Bangkok is projected to become a megacity by 2030, but as it is built on swampland with vulnerability to river flooding, Bangkok has a history of being affected by floodwaters. Furthermore, due to the type of soil that Bangkok is built on, the city is facing gradual subsidence each year, due to factors such as pumping of groundwater reservoirs and the broader impact of urbanization and the removal of earlier canal systems that had helped to provide drainage for floodwaters.

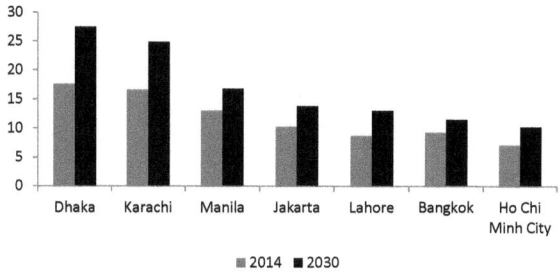

Fig. 3.6 South and SE Asian megacities to 2030 (population in billions) (*Source* UN)

Jakarta also is vulnerable to floods, with many episodes of flooding in the city during recent years. When staying at one of Jakarta's five star hotels in a central area of the city, I discovered from hotel staff that the hotel had suffered from the impact of severe flooding some years ago, and had to be closed for a protracted period as extensive repairs had to be undertaken to repair the flood damage.

The capital of Bangladesh, Dhaka, is also highly vulnerable to floods due to its location on low-lying land on a river delta next to three major rivers. As a result, there have been severe floods that caused tremendous damage to the city in recent years, including in 1987, 1988, 1998 and 2004. Due to the vulnerability of the Bangladesh coastline to cyclones that develop in the Bay of Bengal, flooding due to storm surges is a key risk that has caused severe flooding as well as tremendous loss of life in Bangladesh in recent decades.

Ho Chi Minh City in Vietnam is also built on low-lying river floodplains, and is also vulnerable to flooding events. The impact of climate change remains a risk to Vietnam due to its extensive low-lying river deltas, which are vulnerable to typhoons, with risk of flood damage and storm surges. Ho Chi Minh City and nearby industrial estates are vulnerable to certain extreme weather events such as typhoons, and Hanoi's economy was hit by typhoons Kai-Tak and Son-Tinh in 2012. With Ho Chi Minh City also projected to become a megacity by 2030, its vulnerability to flood events is a significant long-term risk to the fast-growing population and urban infrastructure of the city.

Consequently a key priority for these future Asian megacities will be to invest in urban infrastructure that will help to mitigate the risks from extreme weather events that can cause flooding. The Indonesian government is investing in the Jakarta Urgent Flood Mitigation Project to improve drainage through the dredging of eleven river systems. Bangladesh has made progress by investing in flood warning systems as well as reinforced shelters to help protect inhabitants of low-lying areas from the impact of cyclones and flooding. Another important strategy undertaken by the Bangladesh government is the use of mangrove forests to act as a barrier to storm surges, with such eco-engineering having considerable capability to mitigate the impact of devastating storm surges which have historically been as high as 10 metres during cyclones.

As in China and India, other Asian megacities are also vulnerable to many other environmental problems such as air pollution and the impact of road traffic congestion. One of my worst experiences of traffic jams in Asian cities was in Jakarta on a Friday afternoon, as I tried to get to the airport to catch my flight. When I had arrived in Jakarta, the trip from the international airport to my hotel had taken 45 minutes. The hotel advised me to allow 90 minutes for the time of day I was returning to the airport, and I allowed some extra time, calculating for around 2 hours. However my mid-afternoon departure from the hotel in Plaza Indonesia turned into an epic journey of mounting stress, as we passed the three hour mark for the trip with no end in sight to the continuous traffic jam on the highway to the airport. Finally as I had almost given up hope of catching the flight the car driver managed to use some detours in the vicinity of the airport and get me to the departure terminal in time to make my flight.

As in India, the Japanese government has become a key development partner for a number of other Asian developing countries in helping to build new public transport infrastructure to help mitigate the impact of urban congestion on road systems. In Ho Chi Minh City, the Japan International Co-operation Agency (JICA) has funded the development of a new mass rapid transit system with Line 1 due to be completed by the end of 2018. JICA has also provided loans for the construction of the first phase of Jakarta's first phase MRT system, which will help to alleviate extreme traffic congestion in Jakarta.

Singapore's success at creating a highly efficient city with advanced smart city technology has also created a model for other Asian cities to follow, with a number of Singapore urban development firms having won smart city contracts in a number of Asian countries.

The UAE has also become a leading global cluster of excellence for the development of smart cities and high quality urban infrastructure. Both Dubai and Abu Dhabi have become leading cities of the Middle East, investing heavily in modern urban infrastructure such as urban transport systems, state-of-art airports and advanced ports.

Other major challenges for national and municipal governments across developing Asia will be the provision of essential social infrastructure, such as schools and hospitals, as well as the construction of adequate affordable housing to prevent a social crisis as increasing numbers of urban poor are forced to live in slum dwellings or become homeless. The governments of developing countries have a crucial role to play in providing housing solutions for the low income and lower middle income households of cities, as rising private sector housing prices make such residential properties unaffordable for such households.

Megacities in Africa

In 1950, the population of Africa was mainly rural, with an estimated 32 million living in urban areas, or around 14% of the total population. By 2014, Africa's urban population had risen manifold, to 455 million, with the urban population accounting for 40% of Africa's total population.

Due to the rapid growth of Africa's population projected in coming decades, Africa's urban population is projected to rise significantly over the coming decade, to around 770 million by 2030, and African cities will face severe challenges from fast-growing urban populations and lack of sufficient fiscal capacity for urban infrastructure development. As in Asia, major policy issues facing African governments will include inadequate power, water, sanitation and public transport, as well as lack of hospitals, schools and affordable housing. For example, South Africa's second largest city, Cape Town, faced a severe water crisis in early 2018 due to persistent drought since 2015, forcing severe rationing of municipal water supplies as water supplies in dams depleted. The City of Cape Town government had begun a countdown to Day Zero when the city's taps would run dry, but this was narrowly averted due to rainfall, with the new City of Cape Town timetable for Day Zero shifted to 2019.

By 2050, the urban population of Africa is projected to rise further, to 1339 million, out of Africa's total population of 2393 million. This is equivalent to a further increase of 569 million persons in Africa's urban dwellers between 2030 and 2050.

Three African cities are currently classified as megacities, namely Cairo, Lagos and Kinshasa. By 2030, an additional three African cities, Johannesburg, Dar es Salaam and Luanda will also become megacities (Fig. 3.7).

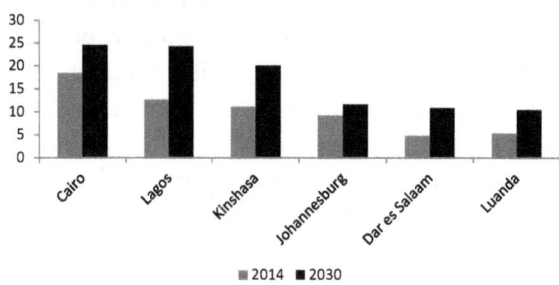

Fig. 3.7 African megacities to 2030 (population in billions) (*Source* UN)

Due to the rapid population growth across much of Sub-Saharan Africa, the number of cities with a population of between 5 million and 10 million is projected to increase from 2 in 2014 to 12 by 2030. Meanwhile cities with a population size of 1 million to 5 million are expected to increase from 50 in 2014 to 77 by 2030.

Urbanization in Latin America

The total urban population of Latin America has risen from 164 million persons in 1970 to 496 million by 2014, and is projected to rise further to 595 million by 2030. Between 2014 and 2030, the number of megacities is projected to increase from 4 to 6. The four existing megacities in Latin America are Mexico City, Sao Paolo, Buenos Aires and Rio de Janeiro. By 2030, the cities of Lima and Bogota are also expected to join the ranks of the world's megacities. Mexico City, with an estimated population of 21 million in its greater metropolitan area, is facing similar long-term water shortage problems as Cape Town in South Africa. Depletion of aquifers and groundwater systems has resulted in subsidence, while the ageing water pipelines also suffer significant losses due to water leakage. Sao Paolo, one of Brazil's megacities, also experienced a water crisis in 2015 when the main reservoir's water supplies fell to just 4% of capacity.

The number of Latin American cities with populations of 5 million to 10 million is expected to remain at 4 between 2014 and 2030, while the number of cities with a population of 1 million to 5 million people are expected to increase from 59 to 78.

Latin American megacities suffer from similar problems to other developing country regions, with traffic congestion, urban crime and the proliferation of slums being among the severe challenges confronting urban policymakers. However the future demographic profile of Latin American countries generally shows less significant population growth over the next three decades than in some other developing country regions, notably Sub-Saharan Africa and South Asia.

Urban Development Challenges in Developing Countries

Financing urban infrastructure development will be one of the key challenges facing emerging markets governments over coming decades, as federal and municipal governments struggle to fund the infrastructure needs of rapidly growing populations in many developing countries. Mobilizing private sector financing for infrastructure development will therefore be an important strategic priority for governments in all developing regions, as they attempt to build adequate urban infrastructure for their urban populations.

Due to decades of underinvestment in most urban agglomerations in developing countries, retrofitting modern infrastructure is particularly challenging. As nations increasingly compete to attract knowledge intensive industries, a number of governments in developing countries are trying to establish greenfields smart cities or smart city precincts in order to create new hubs that can compete for attracting investment from multinationals worldwide. This will help to improve their global competitiveness as locations for foreign direct investment by multinationals in knowledge industries.

As urban populations grow, city planners and municipal governments in developing countries will need to provide a wide range of infrastructure services such as power, urban transport, schooling, hospitals and affordable housing. Severe environmental challenges also face many large urban centres in Asia, including air pollution and depletion of water sources.

Another key challenge will be to generate sufficient employment growth for rapidly growing urban populations, in order to prevent problems relating to rising unemployment, social unrest and urban crime, as well as to prevent the development of inner city slum communities for the poorest and disenfranchised in urban agglomerations.

Therefore for many of the world's developing countries, transforming the infrastructure of cities will be one of the most important priorities over the next three decades. As global cities increasingly compete to attract knowledge industries, high quality infrastructure, strong communications, transportation connectivity and skilled workforces, these will become increasingly important factors driving the success of future cities as growth hubs for the economic development of nations.

4

Reshaping the Global Financial Architecture

Transforming the Post-war International Economic Order

Since the end of the Second World War, global governance and international standards-setting has been dominated by the developed countries, with North America and Europe driving the decision-making structures and voting rights of the Bretton Woods system, notably the IMF and World Bank.

Complementing the role of the Bretton Woods institutions in global standards-setting has been the Organization for Economic Co-operation and Development (OECD) which has assumed the role of a global standards-setting body even though its membership predominantly comprises the developed countries and therefore does not represent the developing countries that account for around 80% of the world's population.

The distribution of voting rights in the IMF and World Bank was originally based on the structure of the global economy that existed at the end of the Second World War when the Bretton Woods system was initially established to create a new international economic architecture for post-war international financial stability and reconstruction. While the Bretton Woods system that was created to build a more stable international economic order following the Second World War has served the world economy well in many ways, a major shortcoming has been that it has not reflected the tremendous geopolitical changes that have occurred since that era.

At the time that the Bretton Woods system was created in 1944, many European countries still had large colonial empires, such as Great Britain,

© The Author(s) 2018
R. Biswas, *Emerging Markets Megatrends*,
https://doi.org/10.1007/978-3-319-78123-5_4

France, Netherlands, Belgium and Portugal. However, seven decades have passed since the creation of the Bretton Woods system, and there have been tremendous political changes in the international economic order. Most of the former European colonies that existed in 1944 have become independent sovereign states that are members of the United Nations and the Bretton Woods institutions in their own right.

When the United Nations first was created in 1945, it had 51 founding sovereign member states. By 2017, the total number of United Nations sovereign member states has increased to 193, reflecting the tremendous changes in the international political order, mainly driven by former European colonies obtaining their independence.

Due to the significant increase in the number of new sovereign nation states as well as the rise in share of world GDP attributable to the developing countries, the global international architecture that was built during the 1940s has become anachronistic. While there has been some gradual adjustment in the voting rights of developing countries in the Bretton Woods institutions since they were founded, the voting rights of developing countries within the IMF governance system are still not representative of their share of world GDP. Despite the reform of IMF voting rights that was proposed in 2010 and finally implemented in 2016, there is still a major imbalance in the gap between China's share of voting rights, at 6.09% of total IMF votes, and its share of world GDP, which is around 15%.

The counterpart of this is the relatively high share of European nations voting rights in the IMF compared to their share of world GDP. As a result, the ability of developing countries to influence the decision-making of the Bretton Woods institutions is still relatively limited, despite the implementation of the IMF voting rights reforms proposed in 2010. The voting rights at the IMF are therefore still dominated by the US and Europe, although the latest round of voting rights reforms did increase the overall share of voting rights of developing countries by 6%.

However, the world has changed tremendously since 1945, with many former European colonies having become sovereign developing nations, while the world share of GDP contributed by developing countries has approximately doubled within the last two decades, rising from 21% of world GDP in 2000 to 40% by 2017. By 2030, the developing country share of world GDP is likely to increase further, to around 50% of world GDP.

Consequently, the old global governance architecture created in the 1940s is no longer relevant, and developing countries are seeking a greater voice in international decision-making at key international institutions such as the IMF and World Bank. While the governance structure of the Bretton Woods institutions has not been cast in stone since its creation in 1944, the pace of change has been glacial compared with the rapid growth in the number of developing countries as well as their rising relative importance in world GDP.

Meanwhile, the OECD has also played a role as an international standards-setting body, although it has only 35 member countries, all of which are developed nations. The origin of the OECD was initially as the predecessor institution, the Organization for European Economic Co-operation (OEEC), to implement the US Marshall Plan for the reconstruction of Europe after the Second World War. The OEEC originally had 18 member countries, all of which were European nations. In 1961, the OEEC was transformed into the OECD with a different charter and an expanded membership to include the US and Canada. Through the OECD, developed nations have created a process of international standards-setting and development of international regulations even though its members are predominantly European nations. Of the 35 OECD members, 25 are European nations and only 4 are emerging markets countries.

As the developing nations have become more numerous and have become increasingly important in the structure of the world economy and international trade, there has been increasing frustration and disappointment that their representation and voice in the global economic architecture has not reflected either their share of the world economy or their share of world population.

Efforts by developing countries to increase their share of voting rights in the IMF were subjected to protracted negotiations and delays, which further upset many developing nations.

Confronted with this glacial pace of change in the existing international economic order and global governance, developing countries have increasingly realized that they need to become masters of their own destiny, rather than appealing to their former colonial masters for a fairer system of international governance.

The momentum for reshaping the international economic architecture has been driven by the formation of a new global grouping of large emerging markets countries, known as the BRICS.

The Role of the BRICS

The creation of a new international forum comprising the BRICS nations—Brazil, Russia, India, China and South Africa—has created a formal mechanism for greater co-operation among some of the largest developing countries. The BRICS nations have been trying to co-ordinate efforts of developing countries to create a fairer system of global governance by working together to change existing governance structures in international bodies such as the IMF as well as to create new international standards-setting bodies that have a modern governance structure with much stronger voting rights for developing countries. The establishment of the BRICS New Development Bank is a key example of such new initiatives.

Although the concept of the BRIC countries has been used by economists to define an economic group of some of the largest emerging market countries, the BRIC countries only decided to actually formalize the concept in 2009, when they established a BRIC Forum that met in Russia in June 2009. In 2011, South Africa was invited to join the BRIC annual meeting, which has subsequently been designated as the annual BRICS Summit.

The five BRICS nations currently account for approximately 23% of world GDP, making these nations an important part of the world economy. China, as the world's second largest economy, has been the key driver for sustained global economic growth since the global financial crisis of 2008–2009, accounting for around 40% of the total increase in world GDP since 2009. The BRICS, led by China, have also been a key driver for growth in world trade and investment flows over the past decade.

However, although the original four BRIC nations are all major economies with national GDP levels that exceed USD 1 trillion, South Africa is a much smaller economy, with a GDP of around USD 350 billion, so does not have the same economic weight as the other BRICS nations in terms of its overall economic size. This is a relevant consideration when assessing the capacity of the individual BRICS nations to support major joint initiatives for co-operation.

While the inclusion of South Africa was important geopolitically to bring the African continent into the BRICS discussions about South–South co-operation, its financial capacity to support major joint initiatives is likely to be considerably less than the other BRICS nations.

There is also a strong argument for bringing Indonesia into the BRICS grouping of nations, as Indonesia has just reached the USD 1 trillion threshold in terms of the USD size of its GDP, and its geopolitical importance is gradually rising due to its membership of the G-20 grouping of nations as well as its lynchpin role within ASEAN as the largest Southeast Asian economy.

As with any international grouping of disparate nations, there have been political and economic challenges to contend with. In 2015–2016, both Russia and Brazil slumped into deep and protracted recessions, which diverted political attention among their government institutions away from international initiatives such as the BRICS Summit. Geopolitical tensions can also pose risks to efforts for strengthening co-operation, with political tensions between China and India having escalated in mid-2017 over a territorial dispute in the Himalayan mountain area where the Chinese, Indian and Bhutanese borders meet.

The BRICS nations began to meet formally in 2009, with the momentum for closer co-operation among BRICS countries gathering momentum during the 2010–2015 period. A major step forward in formalizing the closer co-operation among the BRICS nations was the decision by the five BRICS nations to establish the New Development Bank in 2014.

The New Development Bank

At the BRICS Summit held in 2012 in New Delhi, the BRICS members discussed in detail the concept of establishing a BRICS development bank with a mandate for providing development financing. At that Summit, BRICS leaders mandated their finance ministers to investigate the feasibility of establishing such an institution. Negotiations for the establishment of the bank began after the BRICS Summit in 2013. In July 2014, at the BRICS Summit in Fortaleza, Brazil, the BRICS nations signed a formal agreement to establish the New Development Bank, with equal shareholding and voting rights in the new bank. The initial authorized capital of the New Development Bank was agreed at USD 100 billion, with paid-in capital of USD 10 billion and subscribed capital of USD 50 billion. The BRICS also agreed to establish a reserve currency facility of USD 100 billion at the same meeting.

The objective of the New Development Bank is to finance sustainable infrastructure development in developing countries worldwide and this new multilateral bank became operational in 2016, with the first meeting of the Board of Governors of the bank held in July 2016. The headquarters of the New Development Bank has been established in Shanghai.

The focus of the bank's financing will be on sustainable infrastructure development projects for developing countries, with an initial policy objective of providing 60% of total financing for renewable energy projects. In its first year of operations, the NDB approved USD 1.5 billion of new project loans, with a first green bond valued at USD 450 million also issued.

The NDB will utilize a full range of financing mechanisms, including long term loans, syndicated loans with private sector investors, co-financing with national and multilateral development finance institutions, as well as equity investments. The NDB will have a focus on using local currency financing mechanisms so as to limit risks to borrowers as well as to help recipient countries to strengthen their domestic capital markets.

Initiatives for BRICS Co-operation

Over the medium term, the BRICS nations are likely to further strengthen their joint initiatives for boosting economic development co-operation. The BRICS countries will be likely to act as a core group of emerging markets that will help to build policy frameworks and technological co-operation for a wide range of global South–South development initiatives that will extend to all developing countries. One of the greatest challenges facing developing countries is global climate change and meeting the Paris Climate Change Agreement commitments. Joint co-operation on tackling climate change among the BRICS could create a platform for greater South–South co-operation on a wide range of initiatives such as new technologies for renewable energy, technological co-operation on transition to electric vehicles, joint co-operation on new technologies for smart cities and urban infrastructure development.

Many other joint initiatives for South–South co-operation could also be led by the BRICS, such as co-operation on technological advances in water resource management. In the financial sector, there is also considerable scope for joint initiatives, such as best practice financial system regulation, co-operation in financial technology to assist low-income households to access financial services, or joint forums on developing insurance solutions for farmers to manage weather-related risks to their crops.

Concerns about rising global protectionism have increased significantly among developing countries' governments and corporations following the UK Brexit decision to leave the EU, as well as the Trump Administration's decision to withdraw from the TPP agreement and renegotiate NAFTA and the KORUS FTA with South Korea. BRICS countries can play a key role at the forefront of efforts for greater international trade liberalization and economic development co-operation.

The New Asia-Pacific Economic Architecture

Although the BRICS are at the forefront of efforts to mobilize greater South–South co-operation, there are also other initiatives that have strengthened co-operation among developing countries. The Asia-Pacific region has been at the forefront of initiatives to accelerate regional economic co-operation in trade and development, with Asian developing countries playing a leading role in shaping such initiatives.

Key examples of how Asian developing nations are leading international trade and investment liberalization are the leadership roles of ASEAN and China in advancing Regional Comprehensive Economic Partnership (RCEP) trade negotiations among 16 APAC nations as well as China's strategic plan to boost economic development co-operation through the Belt and Road Initiative. China has also led the initiative for the creation of the Asian Infrastructure Investment Bank (AIIB), which was established in 2014.

Asian Infrastructure Investment Bank

The creation of the AIIB occurred in parallel with negotiations to set up the New Development Bank. However, the creation of the AIIB was led solely by China, rather than by the BRICS nations. While the membership of the AIIB has been open to all nations, the subscription of capital and voting share distribution has been structured so that Asian developing nations have the majority capital subscription and voting rights in the AIIB. Therefore, the AIIB is a very important new institution in the global international economic architecture, creating a new multilateral development finance institution for Asia whose governance is clearly driven by Asian developing countries, which hold a dominant majority in the voting structure and decision-making of the bank. While there are developed country members from Europe as well as members from other developing countries outside of Asia, the focus of the AIIB is to provide development financing for infrastructure projects in developing Asian countries.

Like the NDB, the AIIB became operational in 2016, with its headquarters located in Beijing, and commenced making its first project loans that year.

Chiang Mai Initiative

Another important initiative that has strengthened financial co-operation among Asian countries has been the Chiang Mai Initiative, which established a mechanism for financial co-operation among Asian countries in the aftermath of the East Asian crisis. The Chiang Mai Initiative was initially created in 2000 as a system of bilateral currency swap arrangements among the ASEAN member nations together with China, Japan and South Korea (ASEAN+3), to strengthen regional safety nets for crisis prevention. Discussions for such a regional arrangement were galvanized by the financial and economic contagion effects that created economic crises in many Asian economies during the East Asian crisis in 1997.

While Asian countries undertook many domestic macroeconomic and financial sector reforms in the aftermath of the East Asian crisis, including fiscal consolidation, building up of foreign exchange reserves, strengthening of financial sector prudential supervision and raising capital adequacy ratios for the domestic banking system, East Asian governments also decided to build up regional international financial co-operation for crisis prevention.

An initial proposal in 1997 by Japan to create an Asian Monetary Fund was strongly opposed by the US, which argued that international efforts for crisis prevention and resolution should remain consolidated under the mandate of the IMF. However, further discussions among Asian governments eventually resulted in the establishment of the Chiang Mai Initiative by the ASEAN+3 governments in May 2000 at the ASEAN+3 Finance Ministers Meeting held in Chiang Mai in Thailand. Negotiations on bilateral swap arrangements subsequently ensued, and by 2003 the total size of bilateral currency swaps under the Chiang Mai Initiative had reached USD 35 billion.

At the ASEAN+3 Finance Ministers Meeting held in June 2007, it was agreed that the Chiang Mai Initiative system of bilateral swaps would be multilateralized, to create a single pool of reserve currencies. The new arrangement was named the Chiang Mai Initiative Multilateralisation (CMIM), and had the objectives tackling balance of payments and short-term liquidity difficulties among the ASEAN+3 nations as well as acting as a supplementary reserve pool to assist international support arrangements to address such crises.

In 2008, the size of the reserves pool was set at USD 80 billion, with China, Japan and South Korea agreeing to provide 80% of the total reserves pool. However, due to the onset of the Global Financial Crisis in 2008–2009, the ASEAN+3 Finance Ministers Meeting held in May 2009 decided to expand the total size of the reserves pool to USD 120 billion, with China, Japan and South Korea still providing 80% of the total reserves pool.

Momentum continued to build for further expansion of the CMIM facility as the magnitude of the Global Financial Crisis made Asian nations realize that the scale of reserves required for a future Asian regional crisis would have to be considerably larger. Therefore in 2012, at the annual ASEAN+3

Finance Ministers Meeting, the total size of the reserves pool was doubled to USD 240 billion.

The structure of the CMIM facility has also evolved, with the creation of a separate crisis prevention facility, the CMIM Precautionary Line, and a crisis resolution facility the CMIM Stability Facility. Under the original CMIM arrangements, the CMIM would only disburse funds if an IMF programme was already in place for the requesting country. That IMF conditionality has also been reduced somewhat, with both CMIM facilities able to disburse 30% of the total amount a country is eligible to receive without being conditional upon an IMF programme being in place.

In order to assist with macroeconomic and financial surveillance of the ASEAN+3 countries, the CMIM has established an ASEAN+3 Macroeconomic Research Office (AMRO) which conducts regular analysis on the member countries in order to assist with timely detection of potential balance of payments or liquidity problems. In the event that a member country requests assistance under the CMIM, the decision on whether to provide assistance is to be taken by the CMIM Executive Level Decision Making Body.

Since the initial creation of the Chiang Mai Initiative, its facility has never been tested by crisis, since the ASEAN+3 countries have not experienced a severe balance of payments crisis or liquidity problem that required CMIM assistance. However, due to the considerable strengthening of the facility since its inception, and establishment of better surveillance and decision-making capacity within the CMIM, the CMIM is in a much better position to act in times of crisis than in its earlier years.

With the continued rapid growth of the ASEAN+3 nations, it is likely that the CMIM will continue to grow both in size and capability over the next decade, giving East Asia considerable capacity to help individual ASEAN nations to tackle national balance of payments or liquidity crises through intra-Asian assistance rather than requiring international intervention. However, if a crisis becomes regional in nature and affects multiple countries, particularly the +3 countries, then international programmes will still most likely be required.

The New Champions of Trade Liberalization

Since the end of the Second World War, global trade liberalization was negotiated under the auspices of the General Agreement on Tariffs and Trade (GATT), which came into existence in 1948, and subsequently from

1995 onwards by its successor organization, the World Trade Organisation (WTO). Successive rounds of global trade negotiations achieved considerable progress in reducing tariffs and other barriers for trade between nations. Trade liberalization has been a key driver of global economic and export growth over the past six decades. However, further progress on global trade liberalization has largely stalled during the Doha Round of trade talks which began in 2001, and trade liberalization efforts by many nations have significantly refocused towards negotiating Free Trade Agreements (FTAs) at a bilateral and regional level.

The Asia-Pacific region has been at the forefront of new trade liberalization initiatives over the past decade, as it became increasingly evident that the WTO Doha Round negotiations had become very protracted and that the timing of any successful conclusion to the trade talks was very uncertain.

Over the past decade, Asia-Pacific nations have concluded a large number of bilateral FTAs that have significantly liberalized trade flows within the Asia-Pacific region.

The ASEAN grouping of countries has been at the forefront of these efforts, with the member countries of ASEAN having agreed on the establishment of the ASEAN Free Trade Area (AFTA), which resulted in the removal of tariffs on trade in goods among the first six ASEAN member countries since January 2010, with the remaining four ASEAN members implementing the removal of tariffs on goods over a longer transitional period of time.

ASEAN has also agreed a number of major FTAs with other countries, including the China–ASEAN FTA that was implemented in 2010, and a number of other important FTAs with other Asia-Pacific nations, including India, South Korea, Australia and New Zealand as well as Japan.

This network of ASEAN FTAs with key Asia-Pacific trading partners has significantly enhanced the attractiveness of ASEAN countries as international manufacturing hubs, as manufactures made within ASEAN benefit from low or no tariffs under the FTAs for trade in goods within the ASEAN region, as well as with the largest Asia-Pacific economies.

Trans-Pacific Partnership Agreement

Among the initiatives to push ahead with regional trade liberalization, Asia-Pacific countries had embarked on ambitious trade negotiations among twelve nations, including the North American nations of the US, Canada and Mexico, called the Trans-Pacific Partnership (TPP) Agreement. The scope of this advanced free trade agreement was much wider in its overall scope than any other free trade agreement previously concluded globally. These negotiations for the TPP were successfully concluded in 2016 during the term of the Obama Administration, but had not yet been ratified by the US Congress before the 2016 US Presidential election.

The incoming Trump Administration immediately withdrew from the TPP Agreement upon taking office in January 2017, as one of President Trump's major election campaign pledges had been to take the US out of the TPP Agreement.

Despite the alternative regional trade liberalization initiatives for the Asia-Pacific, the collapse of the TPP Agreement was a blow to the trade liberalization plans of the other 11 Asia-Pacific nations that had been part of that agreement.

Two of the countries that were expected to be the greatest beneficiaries of the TPP were Vietnam and Malaysia, with their manufacturing sectors set to benefit significantly from much-improved market access to the North American market. Under the TPP agreement, tariff barriers for Vietnam's and Malaysia's electronics manufacturing industries would have been significantly reduced. The TPP deal would have also significantly improved market access to North America for Vietnam's textiles exports.

For Malaysia, the US accounted for an estimated 10.3% of total Malaysian exports in 2016, making it the third most important export market after Singapore and China. Exports of electrical and electronic equipment such as electrical equipment, integrated circuits and semiconductors account for around half of total Malaysian exports to the US. Due to the importance of manufactures in the existing structure of Malaysian exports to the US, Malaysia would have been a significant beneficiary of the TPP tariff reduction on manufactured goods, and the US withdrawal from TPP is clearly a negative factor for Malaysia's manufacturing export sector over the medium term outlook. Nevertheless, the competitiveness of the ringgit has also helped to drive the export performance of Malaysian electrical and electronics products during 2015–2016, including to the key US market, which mitigates the negative impact of the US withdrawal from TPP.

For Vietnam, the rapidly growing garments and electronics export industries had been expected to significantly benefit from the TPP agreement implementation, as market access to the US would have significantly improved due to significantly lower tariffs. However, Vietnam is still expected to experience rapid manufacturing export growth due to its relative competitiveness due to significantly lower manufacturing wage costs vis-à-vis coastal Chinese provinces. Another medium to long-term positive factor for

Vietnam's export sector is the EU-Vietnam Free Trade Agreement that was concluded in 2015, which will significantly improve Vietnam's market access to the key EU market once it is implemented. The EU is already Vietnam's second largest export market and a major importer of garments and electronics manufactured in Vietnam.

The TPP Agreement was also important for Japan as it was seen as a key pillar of the Third Arrow structural economic reforms under Abenomics. The US withdrawal from TPP was therefore also a blow to Prime Minister Abe and his economic reform plans for Japan. While President Trump and Prime Minister Abe have agreed on a bilateral path of trade negotiations when they met in the US for a bilateral summit in February 2017, the bilateral US–Japan trade negotiations will need to review the previous terms agreed under the TPP. The incoming US Administration has indicated that is seeking to reduce the bilateral trade deficit with Japan, which was at a level of USD 69 billion in 2016.

Comprehensive and Progressive Agreement for Trans-Pacific Partnership

Despite the decision of the US to withdraw from the TPP Agreement, the other 11 TPP members have pressed ahead with plans to proceed with the TPP. Negotiations have been held among the remaining 11 TPP members to decide on how to proceed.

At the APEC Summit held in Danang in November 2017, the TPP-11 countries agreed on a framework deal to move forward with the TPP agreement without the US. The new version of the TPP agreement was named the Comprehensive and Progressive Agreement for Trans-Pacific Partnership (CPTPP).

The 11 nations that are members of the CPTPP negotiations reached an agreement on the CPTPP deal in Tokyo on 23rd January 2018, with the final agreement signed by trade ministers of the 11 member nations in March 2018. The CPTPP deal will take effect when 6 of the 11 member countries have ratified the agreement through their parliaments.

In order to reach this CPTPP agreement, the TPP-11 nations have agreed to suspend 22 parts of the original TPP agreement, as the relative costs and benefits of the original TPP agreement have changed considerably due to the withdrawal of the US from the TPP Agreement. These suspended provisions include several provisions relating to intellectual property rights as well as a provision relating to Malaysia's state-owned enterprises.

However, the economic benefits will be significantly reduced without US participation. The US accounted for around 65% of the total GDP of the original 12 TPP member countries. The total size of GDP of the 12 TPP negotiating countries with the US included would have been USD 32 trillion or around 40% of world GDP, while CPTPP ex-US will have a combined GDP of USD 12.6 trillion or 15.8% of world GDP, with combined annual trade of USD 356 billion.

Once the new CPTPP takes force after it is ratified by six of the eleven CPTPP member countries, it also will create a multilateral trade liberalization agreement that other Asia-Pacific nations could choose to join. It is possible that other Asia-Pacific countries could eventually join the CPTPP agreement, adding to its economic impact. South Korea and Indonesia had previously signalled their interest in joining the TPP, but that was when the US was still part of the TPP negotiations, and the CPTPP agreement without the US may not be politically or economically attractive for either Indonesia or South Korea. However, Taiwan has signalled its interest in joining the CPTPP as a second wave entrant.

With 22 parts of the original TPP Agreement suspended in the new CPTPP, notably parts of the original deal relating to issues such as intellectual property rights, the hurdles for other APAC countries to join are relatively lower, making the CPTPP more accessible for additional APAC countries wishing to join. South Korea had previously expressed interest in joining the TPP Agreement when the US was still part of the negotiations, and as it confronts a renegotiation of its own Korea–US Free Trade Agreement (KORUS), the possibility of joining the CPTPP could become more attractive.

Other Asia-Pacific Trade Initiatives

The US decision to withdraw from the TPP has accelerated a significant shift in the trade policy landscape in the Asia-Pacific region towards greater leadership by Asian developing countries for further regional trade liberalization. China is likely to play a much stronger lead role in the future Asia Pacific trade architecture through a number of multilateral trade liberalization initiatives, notably the RCEP and FTAAP (Free Trade Area of the Asia-Pacific).

China's President Xi Jinping stated that China would strongly support further global trade liberalization in his speech at the World Economic

Forum in Davos in January 2017, signalling that China would play a much greater role as a champion of international trade liberalization.

The US withdrawal from TPP has already served to strengthen political momentum for the negotiation of the RCEP, an Asia-Pacific trade liberalization initiative led by ASEAN and China. The members of the RCEP negotiations are the ASEAN ten members as well as China, Australia, New Zealand, Japan, South Korea and India. At the APEC Summit held in November 2016 in Lima, Peru, two Latin American TPP member countries, Chile and Peru, also expressed interest in joining the RCEP negotiations on expectations that TPP would stall.

Asia-Pacific Economic Co-operation (APEC) leaders of the 21 APEC member economies have also have reaffirmed their commitment to move forward with a longer term vision of creating a FTAAP, with next steps set out in the APEC Lima Declaration on FTAAP in November 2016. As the FTAAP would be realized outside of APEC, but in parallel with the APEC process, this creates greater flexibility in case some APEC members do not wish to pursue the FTAAP vision.

China has played a leadership role in advancing the APEC discussions for the planning of the FTAAP. The APEC Leaders' Meeting in Danang held on 10–11 November 2017 reaffirmed the commitment of the APEC economies to the FTAAP to further APEC's economic integration agenda.

China has also taken a much greater regional economic leadership role through its initiative to boost the economic development of low-income Asian developing countries with the Belt and Road Initiative and the creation of the AIIB. The US withdrawal from TPP will help to strengthen China's economic leadership position in the Asia Pacific.

Other APAC nations are also continuing to press ahead with an ambitious trade liberalization agenda, including bilateral FTAs between Asian countries as well as FTAs with other major economies, such as the Japan-EU FTA and the Vietnam-EU FTA. Australia and Peru announced the conclusion of a new Peru–Australia FTA on the sidelines of the APEC Leaders' Meeting in Danang on 10 November, in a deal that will eliminate 99% of tariffs faced by Australian exporters in the Peruvian market.

With the APAC share of world GDP forecast to rise from around 34% in 2017 to 46% by 2045, APAC nations have much to gain from further liberalization of Asia-Pacific regional trade. Exports account for a large share of the GDP of many APAC nations, including Malaysia, Singapore and Thailand. The CPTPP deal represents an important victory for advancing trade liberalization in the Asia-Pacific region, with

Asia-Pacific nations increasingly becoming the new champions of global trade liberalization.

The Future International Economic Architecture

Within the last decade, there have been signs of a significant change in the international economic architecture that had previously largely remained intact since the end of the Second World War.

A key driver for the changing international economic architecture has been the increasing economic importance of the Asia-Pacific region, which currently accounts for around one-third of world GDP. Asian countries have been at the forefront of new initiatives, including the Chiang Mai Initiative established by the ASEAN+3 nations, the initiative for the creation of the AIIB by China, the establishment of the New Development Bank by the BRICS nations and China's Belt and Road Initiative for infrastructure development in developing countries.

In addition to these initiatives, Asia-Pacific countries are also pursuing regional trade liberalization negotiations through RCEP with plans for the FTAAP.

The significant momentum behind this range of new initiatives indicates that the international economic architecture that was established at the end of the Second World War is now facing far-reaching transformation as the Asia-Pacific nations force significant changes in the previous status quo established by the former European colonial powers and the US in the 1940s.

With the economic weight of the Asia-Pacific economies expected to rise further to around 50% of global GDP by 2050, and developing countries expected to account for half of world GDP by 2030, it was inevitable that the international economic order built around a model of global governance by Europe and the US would eventually have to change.

Over the next decade, China and the BRICS nations are likely to drive significant further changes in global governance and play a leading role in creating a new international economic architecture that will be much more inclusive for developing countries from all regions. The Belt and Road Initiative, the AIIB and the New Development Bank are key changes that have already transformed the international economic architecture dramatically since 2012.

In the decade ahead, further significant new initiatives can be expected. In Asia, plans for an Asian Monetary Fund were proposed after the East

Asian crisis but scuppered due to US intervention. However, there are strong reasons why such an Asian Monetary Fund could play an important role in Asia-Pacific regional financial stability and financial system surveillance, improving the resilience of the region to financial shocks and regional contagion risks. As the weight of the Asia-Pacific region rises to 50% of world GDP, the political and economic rationale for such a new regional initiative is likely to become more compelling.

5

Financing Infrastructure for Developing Countries

When Argentina set the agenda for its term of presidency in 2018 for the G-20 work programme, it made mobilizing private resources to reduce the global infrastructure deficit one of its three key priorities. In identifying infrastructure as one of the key work priorities for the G-20 in 2018, Argentina has highlighted that the global infrastructure gap between 2018 and 2035 is estimated to be around USD 5.5 trillion while the pool of assets under management by institutional investors worldwide is estimated at USD 80 trillion (G-20 2018 Agenda Priorities, Overview of Argentina's G-20 Presidency, 2018).

The rapid growth of populations in many developing regions makes boosting investment in essential infrastructure a key priority. The quality of infrastructure is also a critical factor that is important for the investment decisions by companies when choosing a suitable location for building a new factory or R&D campus.

It is hard to establish a semiconductors industry which requires continuous reliable electricity supply in a nation which has power blackouts due to inadequate power generation. Multinationals are unlikely to establish production facilities for manufacturing exports if there are long delays and high freight costs due to poor ports infrastructure. Foolish immigration officials may think long queues of foreigners at their airport immigration counters are a sign of their nation's popularity rather than a hallmark of extreme inefficiency. Countries with inadequate, inefficient infrastructure and high logistics costs therefore suffer from a considerable competitive disadvantage compared with competing nations that have high quality, modern infrastructure.

© The Author(s) 2018
R. Biswas, *Emerging Markets Megatrends*,
https://doi.org/10.1007/978-3-319-78123-5_5

The infrastructure needs of developing countries range from critical physical infrastructure such as power generation and transmission, sanitation, public transport and communications to social infrastructure such as schools, universities and hospitals. However, with many developing countries struggling under the burden of high government debt and large fiscal deficits, the ability to finance such infrastructure development from public sector spending alone is well below the estimated required levels needed.

However, latest data from the World Bank on investment commitments into infrastructure projects in energy, transport and water projects in developing countries that involved some element of private sector finance for the first half of 2017 showed that the total amount invested was USD 36.7 billion. Of this total, an estimated 48% was financed by the private sector, with another 23% from the public sector and the remainder from development finance institutions. Although this was higher than for the same period of 2016, the amount was 15% lower than the average for the past five years (Private Participation in Infrastructure, First Half Update, World Bank, 2017).

The United Nations Inter-Agency Task Force on Financing for Development (2017) has estimated that for developing countries, around three-quarters of infrastructure finance is funded from public sector sources, including domestic government budgets, foreign aid and multilateral as well as bilateral development assistance.

Africa's Infrastructure Financing Challenge

The African Development Bank has estimated that the annual infrastructure financing needs of the African continent are currently in the order of USD 130 billion to USD 170 billion per year (African Economic Outlook 2018, African Development Bank, 2018). The actual total investment in African infrastructure in 2016 from all public and private sources was estimated at USD 63 billion, leaving an infrastructure funding gap of around USD 67 billion to USD 107 billion in that year alone.

Infrastructure financing in 2016 did show a significant decline compared to the previous year, reflecting factors such as the global downturn in commodity prices which impacted on the economic outlook for Africa. However, the average annual infrastructure investment level in Africa over the five years from 2012 to 2015 was USD 75 billion per year, which implies an average annual infrastructure investment gap of USD 55 billion to USD 95 billion annually.

Out of this total average annual infrastructure investment over the 2012–2016 period, around 40% of total infrastructure investment was financed by African governments themselves. The bulk of the remaining amount was financed by multilateral and bilateral donors, with China providing 15% of Africa's total infrastructure investment over this period. Japan, India and South Korea were also provided significant infrastructure financing in 2016. However, the role of the private sector has been very limited, accounting for only 8% of Africa's total infrastructure investment over the 2012–2016 period.

The reasons for the very low level of private sector investment in African infrastructure reflects a wide range of factors, including higher levels of country risk in many low-income African countries compared with middle income developing countries in other regions, as well as the difficulties in getting commercial rates of return for many infrastructure projects due to low per capita household income levels. Consequently, emerging market economies with strong sovereign risk ratings and rated at investment grade by the major international rating agencies are often the preferred destinations for international private institutional investors.

Developing Asia's Infrastructure Financing

The infrastructure financing requirements of the developing Asia-Pacific region has been estimated at USD 26 trillion for the 2016–2030 period, according to estimates by the Asian Development Bank. This is equivalent to annual infrastructure spending requirements of USD 1.7 trillion. Of this total, an estimated 68% is required for new capacity expansion, with 32% needed for replacing and maintaining existing infrastructure. (Asian Development Bank, Meeting Asia's Infrastructure Needs, February 2017.)

According to the Asian Development Bank's assessment, the largest share of infrastructure financing is required for the power sector, at around USD 14.7 trillion, or 56% of the total infrastructure financing requirement. The second largest infrastructure financing requirement is for the transport sector, at around USD 8.4 trillion, or 32% of the total.

Due to the large infrastructure funding requirements of the Asia-Pacific region over the next decade, national governments will not have sufficient fiscal resources to fund all of the required infrastructure investment. Therefore, a key economic priority for the governments of the Asia-Pacific region is to co-ordinate strategic initiatives to boost international investment and private capital flows to meet this infrastructure funding gap.

A number of high-level initiatives have already been launched in 2014–2015 that will play an important role in addressing the infrastructure financing gap.

China has led a number of new initiatives to increase infrastructure financing in the Asia-Pacific region (Biswas, R., "Reshaping the financial architecture for development finance: the new development banks", London School of Economics Working Paper, Global South Unit, February 2015). Through the creation of the Asian Infrastructure Investment Bank (AIIB), the Silk Road Fund and the New Development Bank (NDB), significant new infrastructure funding has been mobilized from the public sector that can help to also attract new private sector infrastructure financing through project co-financing.

The AIIB has an initial authorized capital of USD 100 billion, with initial subscribed capital of USD 50 billion, and has commenced operations with planned initial lending to commence during 2016. The Silk Road Fund, with planned capital of USD 40 billion, also has a mandate to invest in infrastructure projects in Asia, and is already operational. The NDB, which was created by the five BRICS countries as founding members, has initial capital of USD 50 billion. Therefore, the combined impact of these three new infrastructure financing organizations provides more than USD 100 billion in funding.

The NDB, AIIB and Silk Road Fund combined have the potential to significantly increase the total multilateral financing available for infrastructure development in the medium term, and will also give developing countries a greater voice in governing global development in the next decade and beyond.

While the initial capital for the AIIB and NDB will be provided by the member governments of each fund as public financing for infrastructure development, these new funds will also help to blend-in additional public and private infrastructure financing flows through co-financing of major infrastructure projects with state-owned development banks as well as with private sector finance.

Japan, which already has played an important role for decades as a source of official development assistance for Asia, has also launched a major new initiative in May 2015 with the Asian Development Bank called the Partnership for Quality Infrastructure to provide USD 110 billion in development aid for developing countries in the Asia-Pacific over a five-year period (Japanese Ministry of Foreign Affairs, 2015).

These new infrastructure financing initiatives are creating considerable positive momentum for significant additional multilateral and bilateral infrastructure financing flows for developing countries in the Asia-Pacific region. However, despite the major new infrastructure financing commitments by China, Japan and other governments worldwide, public sector resources cannot fully fund the large-scale infrastructure financing requirements of Asia-Pacific developing nations. Private sector financing will also need to play an important role in achieving these infrastructure financing targets. A key challenge continues to be mobilizing private capital flows for developing countries.

While the pool of assets held in pension funds, life insurance funds and other collective investment vehicles globally is very large, at an estimated USD 115 trillion (UN Inter-Agency Task Force on Financing for Development, 2017) there are significant obstacles that limit the amount of assets that are invested in infrastructure assets in developing countries. These obstacles include a wide range of issues, including regulatory restrictions on asset allocation by certain types of funds such as pension funds and life insurance funds into infrastructure as an asset class, as well as factors such as the higher risk profile and lack of liquid infrastructure investment vehicles such as listed infrastructure trusts in many emerging markets. Often investment funds in developed countries also have restrictive mandates that limit their ability to invest in sub-investment grade assets, which significantly restricts the number of developing countries that they can invest in.

Therefore, finding new solutions that will unlock the vast global pool of private savings that can be allocated to infrastructure financing in developing countries is a key public policy priority in order to boost private capital flows to finance economic development.

Infrastructure Investment by Pension Funds and Insurance Funds

While investment in the infrastructure asset class has become increasingly acceptable as part of the investment strategy of large global asset managers such as pension funds and insurance funds, there are often regulatory restrictions by governments on the ability of pension funds to invest in such assets.

Many countries do not allow direct investment in real estate or infrastructure by their pension funds, although indirect investment in real estate or infrastructure through listed vehicles is often permitted. In the Asia-Pacific region, Hong Kong, Japan, Thailand and Pakistan do not allow their pension funds to make direct investments in the real estate sector. South Korea does not allow defined benefit pension funds to make direct investments in real estate, but does permit such pension funds to invest in retail investment funds (OECD, 2015). While Hong Kong does not permit its pension funds to invest directly in real estate, they can invest indirectly through bonds and shares of property companies and through approved Real Estate Investment Trusts (REITs). Similarly, Thailand does not allow its pension funds to invest directly in real estate but does allow investment indirectly through REITs and infrastructure trusts.

Therefore, a review of such regulatory restrictions by governments needs to be undertaken in order to assess whether it is possible to allow a small share of total pension fund assets to be invested in the infrastructure asset class. This is a matter for individual governments to undertake such a review and consider whether a small proportion of total asset allocation can be allowed into infrastructure assets. Similar reviews would be needed for insurance funds where government regulations restrict their ability to invest in infrastructure.

Large pools of financial assets are held in global pension funds and insurance funds. According to estimates by the OECD, the total pension fund assets held in OECD countries in both public and private sector funds amounted to around USD 25 trillion at the end of 2014. According to Willis Towers Watson, the total pool of assets held by the world's 300 largest pension funds amounted to USD 15 trillion in 2014.

Therefore, if a small proportion of these total pension fund assets can be unlocked for infrastructure investment, it could potentially provide a significant new source of capital for infrastructure financing. As many investment funds prefer to invest through liquid instruments that are listed on stock markets rather than taking direct equity stakes in projects, the liberalization of regulatory restrictions on pension funds and insurance funds to invest in infrastructure also needs to be accompanied by development of the real estate investment trust and infrastructure investment trust legislation in emerging Asian countries, where such infrastructure investment vehicles do not already exist.

There are many large pension funds worldwide that do invest a significant share of their total assets under management in infrastructure as an asset class, with examples in the Asia-Pacific region including Australian Super, the Retail Employees Super Trust of Australia and the New Zealand Super Fund.

The New Zealand Super Fund is a sovereign wealth fund that has a mandate to fund pension benefits for New Zealand citizens. The fund had an asset allocation in global infrastructure assets of 5% of its total portfolio at the end of June 2015, with a further 5% asset allocation to property assets.

Building the Infrastructure Project Pipeline

There are many hurdles and constraints that limit private capital flows to developing countries for infrastructure projects. One important constraint that limits private sector investment flows into public infrastructure projects relates to inadequate preparation by governments for their infrastructure project pipelines. When governments do not undertake the necessary project approvals and clearances, this can create significant costs for private investors, particularly if there is uncertainty about whether project approvals will be granted by the various government departments involved in the project approval process.

Private sector infrastructure investment can be facilitated by government initiatives to prepare projects for investors by undertaking feasibility studies, preparing priority lists of infrastructure projects, preparing necessary government project approvals and other steps to ensure that the projects are at ready for private sector investment.

The establishment of an infrastructure project pipeline can also be enhanced by better co-ordination among government agencies for the infrastructure project approval process to accelerate the timeframe for obtaining the necessary project approvals. Consultation mechanisms between the government and private sector may also help to improve the infrastructure approval process.

Capital Markets Financing

The use of bonds to finance infrastructure is already very well developed globally. In the United States and Canada, the development of a municipal bond market has played a significant role in infrastructure financing, particularly through the creation of tax-exempt municipal bonds to encourage private sector asset allocation towards municipal bonds. In the United States, the municipal bond market has a total size of USD 3.7 trillion, and is largely bought by US private sector investors through municipal bond funds, providing a large source of low-cost infrastructure financing for a wide range of infrastructure projects. More widely, building deeper and more liquid domestic bond markets will be important for mobilizing long-term domestic private sector financing for infrastructure.

Credit Enhancements

The use of measures to improve the attractiveness of infrastructure projects for private investors includes techniques such as loan guarantees as well as loss reserves on the infrastructure project's balance sheets to provide for lower than expected revenues.

The ADB has worked together with the Indian Infrastructure Finance Company Ltd (IIFCL) in order to create a credit enhancement facility that will guarantee infrastructure bonds. The first such joint ADB-IIFCL bond guarantee was implemented in 2015 for an Indian power company, ReNew Power Ventures Private Ltd.

The effect of having such a credit enhancement guarantee should help to lift the credit rating of the infrastructure bond, which improves its attractiveness for international institutional investors, whose investment mandates often require very high credit ratings to allow them to be included in the investment portfolio.

Insurance Risk Mitigation Products

A range of insurance products help to provide risk mitigation for private sector investors in infrastructure projects in developing countries. These insurance products are provided by both government export credit agencies and by private sector credit and political risk insurers.

Private sector insurers as well as public sector export credit agencies can provide insurance products that facilitate private sector investment in infrastructure projects in developing countries. The spectrum of such insurance and risk mitigation products is very wide, including political risk products, reinsurance for banks and corporates, as well as reinsurance for multilateral development banks such as the World Bank and ADB.

Nippon Export and Investment Insurance (NEXI), the official export credit agency of Japan, helped Japanese private sector companies to invest in a new Myanmar infrastructure development project for the establishment of an industrial park with high-quality infrastructure. NEXI provided Overseas Investment Insurance for the project for a Japanese private sector consortium comprising Mitsubishi Corporation, Marubeni Corporation and Sumitomo Corporation for the Thilawa Industrial Park Development Project. The insurance contract was implemented in December 2014. This project is a crucial step forward in Myanmar's development of its manufacturing sector, as it has created the first industrial park with modern infrastructure.

Co-financing and Blended Finance

The role of co-financing by multilateral development banks as well as national development banks and development finance institutions has already got a well-established track record in catalysing infrastructure financing flows from the private sector for many years. The multilateral development banks already have a long history of working together with national development banks and development finance institutions and export credit agencies to provide financing for infrastructure projects for developing countries, with co-financing by private sector institutions.

However, co-financing is likely to become an increasingly important channel for future infrastructure project financing. Large new funding for infrastructure finance for Asia is now becoming available through the AIIB and the Silk Road Fund, and the co-financing model of financing infrastructure projects will become increasingly important, particularly for developing finance for riskier projects in developing Asian countries.

For large infrastructure projects in developing countries in Asia and the Pacific, co-financing will become an increasing important for large projects, with multilateral development banks such as the World Bank or AIIB playing a lead role in providing project loans, but through a co-financing model with MIGA and national export credit agencies as well as national development banks, as well as private sector financing from commercial banks and credit mitigation products from insurers.

The co-financing of Mongolia's Oyu Tolgoi copper-gold mine project provides a recent example of large-scale project financing amounting to USD 4.4 billion provided by a syndicate of international financial institutions and export credit agencies, together with 15 commercial banks. The project finance facility was funded by Export Development Canada, the European Bank for Reconstruction and Development, the IFC, the US Export-Import Bank, the Export Finance and Insurance Corporation of Australia and 15 commercial banks. The commercial banks were BNP Paribas, ANZ, ING, Société Générale Corporate & Investment Banking, Sumitomo Mitsui Banking Corporation, Standard Chartered Bank, Canadian Imperial Bank of Commerce, Crédit Agricole, Intesa Sanpaolo, National Australia Bank, Natixis, HSBC, The Bank of Tokyo-Mitsubishi UFJ, KfW IPEX-Bank and Nederlandse Financierings-Maatschappij voor Ontwikkelingslanden. MIGA provided political risk insurance for the commercial banks.

Value Capture Systems

The use of value capture systems to boost infrastructure development has been well established in the United States for several decades, and is also used in the EU, with significant infrastructure projects in the UK utilizing such funding approaches. In Asia, Hong Kong has also been a leader in utilizing value capture systems, notably for the Hong Kong Mass Transit Railway.

The basic concept of a value capture system is to tap the additional capital gains and income from new infrastructure investment, generating increased revenue stream opportunities arising as a result of a particular infrastructure project. For example, building a new urban light railway system will usually boost property values for residential and commercial properties located close to the new railway, as well as creating new commercial opportunities in and around the railway stations that are being built. Historically, many governments simply used public finances to invest in these infrastructure projects, with much of the improved value of the land and property as a result of new infrastructure becoming a windfall gain for the property owners.

The Hong Kong Mass Transit Railway has used a value capture system approach for its infrastructure development. The basic formula used by the MTR is a "rail plus property" model. This development model utilizes an integrated development approach through the construction of residential real estate as well as shopping malls and office towers on land acquired by MTR. These real estate developments are built in the vicinity of a railway station. The value created by the railway line helps to boost property prices and rents, allowing the MTR to create substantial revenue streams to fund its infrastructure development.

A key benefit of utilizing value capture systems to raise revenue streams from infrastructure projects is that it creates specific additional revenue streams from an infrastructure project that can be used in a number of ways, including to create more attractive project returns for private sector investors.

The utilization of value capture systems has proliferated widely in Europe, North America and Asia, with many Asian developing countries now having integrated shopping precincts and residential developments alongside or above public transport hubs such as major urban railway stations. Modern airports also integrate retail shopping precincts, restaurants and hotels to maximize revenue from the large volumes of travellers passing through these hubs.

Things have changed considerably from the episode I experienced over a decade ago before the modernization of Mumbai's Chhatrapati Shivaji International Airport, where the only available food outlet seemed to be a small kiosk selling tea and snacks. Following major investment in upgrading and modernization, Mumbai International Airport was completely trans- formed with a large collection of modern shops and restaurants comparable to other leading international airports.

In Asian cities such as Tokyo, Seoul, Beijing and Bangkok, modern inte- grated office, retail and high rise residential developments built near to or above railway hubs are springing up in the inner city area, and proving very appealing for busy urban commuters as traffic congestion problems in large cities continue to escalate.

However, clearly the use of value capture systems has its limitations as a model that may work well for certain types of urban infrastructure projects, but may not be applicable to a significant range of other infrastructure projects.

While the first step in reviewing pension fund regulations can be taken at a national level in order to liberalize investment rules regarding investment into domestic infrastructure assets, a broader and more co-ordinated inter- national approach to allowing pension funds and insurance funds to invest in international infrastructure assets would also be an important aspect of such liberalization measures, to allow pension funds worldwide to invest in infrastructure projects internationally, not just in their domestic economy.

Since the early 1990s, the use of REITs or REITs-type products has boomed worldwide, with considerable success and rapid growth in total assets invested through listed real estate and infrastructure investment vehi- cles in the United States and many EU countries.

In the Asia-Pacific region, REITs and infrastructure trusts have become very well established in most major economies, and play a significant role in mobilizing private capital flows into real estate and infrastructure. The total value of listed REITs in the Asia-Pacific region was estimated at around USD 250 billion in 2015. REITs-type Listed Property Trusts were estab- lished in Australia in the 1970s, and have grown substantially. Japan and Singapore have also had considerable success with REITs legislation and have seen rapid growth in the total investment in these vehicles. As a major international financial centre, Singapore has also been successful in becom- ing a hub for listing of REITs and infrastructure trusts that are invested in real estate and infrastructure assets held in other Asian countries. Taiwan,

South Korea, Thailand and Malaysia have also introduced REITs-type vehicles.

In the new Sri Lankan government's first Budget for fiscal 2016, a range of important measures to deepen domestic capital markets were announced, including the introduction of REITs, with stamp duty exemptions for transfer of real estate assets to a REIT structure that distributes 90% or more of its income to REIT unitholders.

REITs offer considerable advantages for mobilizing capital flows since they are listed vehicles which open up a wider pool of investment from institutional and retail investors who wish to invest in liquid instruments that are traded on stock exchanges but want to invest in real estate and infrastructure as an asset class.

REITs offer a number of advantages for investors, allowing liquidity for real estate and infrastructure investments, as well as greater diversification through investing in a portfolio of properties rather than a single building of infrastructure asset. Diversified REITs invest in a variety of property types, such as shopping centres, apartments, warehouses, office buildings and hotels. Infrastructure REITs are investment vehicles for financing transport infrastructure such as airports, ports and roads, as well as utilities and social infrastructure such as schools and hospitals.

REITs can also be used by the public sector to release capital tied up in government assets such as office buildings, or to de-merge property assets from the balance sheets of public sector corporations.

The Thai listed real estate market commenced in 2003 with the creation of Thai property funds, with rapid growth in the number of listed property funds during 2004–2006. Currently, there are 51 property funds listed in Thailand. In 2013, the Thai Securities and Exchange Commission implemented REITs legislation, and new property funds were no longer allowed to be created since 2014. Five new REITs have been listed on the Stock Exchange of Thailand since the new legislation was introduced. Existing property funds can convert to REITs, and it is expected that eventually there will be a growing number of such conversions which will increase the total number of REITs in Thailand.

Infrastructure Financing in South Asia

South Asia has large-scale infrastructure financing needs over the next decade, with an estimated USD 250 billion per year of infrastructure financing required. A World Bank study ("Reducing Poverty by Closing South

Asia's Infrastructure Gap", World Bank, 2014) estimated that around USD 1.7 trillion to USD 2.5 trillion of infrastructure investment is required to close the infrastructure gap in South Asia over the next decade. This would require annual infrastructure spending of around USD 200 billion to USD 250 billion per year. While a significant proportion of the funding for this infrastructure development will come from national government budgets of South Asian countries, a substantial share will need to be funded by a combination of official development assistance through grants and loans, as well as through private sector financing.

However, there have been many barriers to private sector financing in South Asia, including the limited capacity of domestic commercial banks to fund such large-scale infrastructure funding requirements, high hurdles in terms of required rates of return, as well as other key factors such as credit risk and political risk which have constrained international investment flows from global investment funds and pension funds.

The Indian government has recently undertaken a number of new initiatives to encourage private capital flows into infrastructure that may provide a future model for other developing countries to follow. These include the creation of bond guarantee funds, the creation of a government infrastructure investment fund to inject capital into Indian infrastructure financing companies and the creation of a credit enhancement facility to guarantee infrastructure bonds.

The Indian government plans to create an Indian bond guarantee fund, to provide guarantees for long-term bond issuance for infrastructure development. These guarantees can play a key role in catalysing institutional investment into infrastructure projects, as the guarantee will help to improve the credit rating of the bond. As many international institutional investors require a AAA credit rating for infrastructure bond investments, this will be a significant step in helping to boost international investment flows into infrastructure projects.

The Indian government announced in the 2015–2016 Budget the creation of a National Infrastructure Investment Fund (NIIF), which will be a government fund that will invest in the equity of Indian infrastructure finance companies. This is intended to boost the total financing capacity of Indian infrastructure finance companies.

In the 2014–2015 Budget, the Indian government proposed the introduction of REITs and Infrastructure Investment Trusts. Subsequently, the Indian securities regulator SEBI issued legislation relating to REITs and the Indian Cabinet also approved foreign investment into REITs. However, India's track record with progressing REITs has been extremely weak due to inordinate delays in finalizing REITs legislation that has taken over a decade since SEBI first released guidelines in June 2006 for the establishment of REITs in India.

Despite the recent efforts by the Indian government in the 2014–2015 Budget, not a single REIT has been listed yet on the Indian stock exchanges so far, although one has been registered. Industry views indicate that the slow process of establishing a REITs market is due to the complexity and uncertainty related to the Indian taxation structure for REITs, which has made investors unwilling to move forward with establishing REITs in India.

However, in the 2016–2017 Budget, the Indian government announced that it would exempt the dividend distribution tax for payments made to REITs by special purpose vehicles holding the property assets, removing double taxation of the dividend distribution. This is a key reform that had been viewed as necessary by the Indian real estate industry for REITs to be successful in India.

However, it has been argued by some Indian real estate market analysts that further reforms may also be necessary to improve the efficiency of the tax regulatory regime for REITs, such as exemption from capital gains tax and state government stamp duties. Until the Indian REITs and Infrastructure Trust taxation regime becomes efficient compared to other major financial centres worldwide, the progress of Indian listed property vehicles may be hampered, due to bureaucratic roadblocks to mobilizing private capital flows for Indian infrastructure.

The first Indian REIT was registered by Embassy Office Parks Management Services Pvt. Ltd. with the Securities and Exchange Board of India (SEBI) in 2017, with expectations that it may be listed during 2018.

Market estimates indicate that the total amount of capital that could be mobilized through Indian REITs and Infrastructure Investment Trusts could be in the order of USD 20 billion to 30 billion over the medium term, which would represent a significant amount of new private investment into Indian real estate and infrastructure projects.

Small Island Developing States

Small Island Developing States globally are generally characterized by a high degree of economic vulnerability, and this is particularly true for many of the Pacific Island developing states. Factors that make many of the Pacific

Island states vulnerable include the relatively small size of their economies, often with narrow economic bases heavily dependent on several key industries, such as tourism, agriculture or fisheries. Their vulnerability to climate change and the often devastating effects of natural disasters such as cyclones or tsunamis compound their vulnerability.

Data from the OECD Development Assistance Committee also indicates that Small Island Developing States have a much lower share of external private financing flows from international bank lending and foreign direct investment than other developing countries, and also have much more limited access to international debt capital and equity capital markets. As a result, the Small Island Developing States are more reliant on bilateral and multilateral overseas development assistance as well as remittance flows from their workers abroad.

Research by ESCAP (2010) has indicated that many Pacific Island Developing Countries, including Papua New Guinea, Vanuatu, Tonga, Samoa and Fiji ranked in the lower half of the infrastructure development index for the Asia and Pacific countries. Moreover, the Pacific Regional Infrastructure Facility has estimated that the costs of maintaining existing infrastructure are very high, at an estimated 6% of Pacific Islands GDP per year.

The infrastructure financing problems for Pacific Island Developing Countries are compounded by their high level of vulnerability to natural disasters, which in addition to the devastating human impact, also can result in severe economic damage to key industries such as agriculture and tourism, as well as to critical infrastructure. One recent example is the impact of Cyclone Pam in 2015, which caused tremendous economic losses in Vanuatu and Tuvalu.

Insurance and reinsurance solutions are increasingly being looked at as potential long-term risk mitigation strategies for the economic impact of natural disasters. A number of such catastrophe risk insurance projects have been initiated, including the Pacific Catastrophe Risk Insurance Pilot, which was created as a joint initiative of the World Bank, ADB, and the Secretariat of the Pacific Community, with support from the Japanese government. The risk insurance was provided by private sector insurers comprising Sompo Japan Insurance, Mitsui Sumitomo Insurance, Tokio Marine & Nichido Fire Insurance, Swiss Re and Munich Re. Under this particular scheme, the payouts were linked to the strength of the natural disaster, with the purpose of using insurance to help pay for losses due to a natural catastrophe.

A similar catastrophe risk insurance scheme has also been in operation for the Caribbean since 2007, known as the Caribbean Catastrophe Risk Insurance Facility, providing insurance against natural disasters such as hurricanes and earthquakes.

Table 5.1 Estimated infrastructure damages and losses by Cyclone Pam in Vanuatu (as percentage of GDP)

Sector	Damages	Losses	Total
Infrastructure	8.0	3.7	11.7
Of which			
-Transportation	3.8	2.7	6.5
-Public buildings	0.7	0.0	0.7
-Water	0.5	0.4	0.9
-Communication	2.8	0.4	3.3

Source Government of Vanuatu Post Disaster Needs Assessment (IMF, 2015)

In March 2015, Cyclone Pam caused tremendous economic damage in the Pacific Island states of Vanuatu and Tuvalu. The total damage and lost production in Vanuatu was estimated at around 61% of GDP, while in Tuvalu the total damage and losses were estimated at around 30% of GDP (IMF, 2015) (Table 5.1).

Following the G-7 Leaders' Declaration in June 2015 to increase insurance coverage to help to manage the negative impact of climate change-related disaster risk, the focus on finding insurance solutions to mitigate economic losses from natural disasters is likely to make further significant progress over the next decade.

At the Commonwealth Summit in November 2015, David Cameron, who was then the UK Prime Minister, announced a climate change support package for Commonwealth small island states, including a GBP 15 million disaster risk insurance fund for the Pacific islands to help mitigate the effects of natural disasters.

The G-7 Leaders Declaration in June 2015 pledged to develop insurance solutions to help vulnerable developing countries, to help up to 400 million people to get some form of insurance coverage against climate change risks.

To this end, we will:

a) Intensify our support particularly for vulnerable countries' own efforts to manage climate change related disaster risk and to build resilience. We will aim to increase by up to 400 million the number of people in the most vulnerable developing countries who have access to direct or indirect insurance coverage against the negative impact of climate change-related hazards by 2020 and support the development of early warning systems in the most vulnerable countries. To do so we will learn from and build on already existing risk insurance facilities such as the African Risk Capacity, the Caribbean Catastrophe Risk Insurance Facility and other efforts to develop

insurance solutions and markets in vulnerable regions, including in small islands developing states, Africa, Asia and Pacific, Latin America and the Caribbean.
G-7 Leaders' Declaration to Increase Disaster Risk Insurance Solutions
                                                    Schloss Elmau, Germany, June 8, 2015
From G-7 Leaders' Declaration on Climate Change

At the 2017 UN Climate Conference held in Bonn in November 2017, the InsuResilience Global Partnership for Climate and Disaster Risk Finance and Insurance Solutions was launched to provide a partnership between G20 countries and a group of 49 most vulnerable developing nations to provide risk finance and insurance solutions to manage the risks from climate change.

Beyond the specific challenges of natural disasters, mobilizing domestic private sector capital flows for infrastructure financing is a major hurdle for many small island states. Due to the small size of the economies of many Pacific Island Developing Countries, most lack substantial pools of domestic private savings in the form of bank deposits, pension funds or insurance funds, and domestic capital markets are generally very small or non-existent. Furthermore, international commercial banks have limited credit lines for Small Island Developing States due to the small size of their economies and their often relatively higher risk sovereign credit ratings.

Therefore, bilateral and multilateral donor assistance will continue to play a critical role in infrastructure financing for many Small Island Developing Countries. However, there have been some significant successes for public–private partnership infrastructure financing projects for Pacific Island countries, and co-financing solutions can also contribute to long-term infrastructure financing flows for the Small Island Developing Countries.

One example of private sector participation was led by the IFC, which developed an innovative public–private partnership to inject private capital into a loss-making national flagship airline. This resulted in a public–private joint venture partnership between the Government of Samoa and Australia's Virgin Blue airline. This created a new national airline called Virgin Samoa, which turned around from a loss-making airline to a very profitable airline within two years. Significant savings were estimated to have accrued to consumers due to lower airfares, while total private sector investment in the project was around USD 10.5 million, around twice the amount originally expected. Inbound seat capacity more than doubled within the first four years, yielding significant benefits to the local tourism industry.

With an estimated USD 700 billion to USD 800 billion of infrastructure funding needed each year for the developing countries of the Asia and Pacific region, private sector financing has a crucial role to play in meeting their infrastructure financing needs. Recent initiatives by China and Japan have created new positive momentum to boost infrastructure finance for the Asia-Pacific, and this will play an important role in leveraging greater private sector co-financing for infrastructure projects. However, there are also many additional measures that governments can take to boost private sector financing for infrastructure.

Importantly, the ability of different developing countries to utilize various forms of private sector financing does vary greatly, according to the economic size of the nation as well as the various stages of economic development attained. Therefore, there cannot be a "one size fits all" approach to development financing, and the individual financing approaches for each nation need to be assessed on a case-by-case basis, finding pragmatic solutions to what is best suited to the financing capacity of a nation.

The Outlook for Mobilizing Private Capital Flows for Development

As international financial markets become increasingly sophisticated with an ever-increasing range of financial products and services, the range of private sector solutions that developing countries can consider for mobilizing private capital flows for infrastructure development have grown considerably.

Significant policy focus is turning to the potential role of the vast assets held by pension funds and insurance funds globally, particularly as their own asset allocation strategies have shifted towards a greater role for real estate and infrastructure assets. Although very large pools of savings are held in public and private pension funds and insurance funds worldwide, many of these funds are not yet permitted to invest in infrastructure assets directly, or sometimes not even through indirect investments. Therefore, greater co-ordination and information exchange by governments about the potential scope for liberalizing pension and insurance fund regulations to allow investments into infrastructure asset classes may help to allow a small share of this huge global pool of pension and insurance fund assets to flow into infrastructure asset classes.

The role of REITs and infrastructure trusts in boosting capital markets financing flows for infrastructure and real estate developments also has considerable potential. In parallel with initiatives to unlock pension and insurance fund investments into infrastructure assets, the creation of liquid markets for collective investment vehicles in real estate and infrastructure will also help to enable pension funds and insurance funds to invest in real estate and infrastructure through collective investment vehicles rather than illiquid, direct equity stakes in infrastructure projects. Governments of nations that do not have well-established REITs and infrastructure trusts should undertake assessments of how such investment vehicles can contribute to infrastructure development in their countries.

Co-financing models for mobilizing private sector infrastructure investment will become increasingly important. Co-financing of large infrastructure projects will be particularly critical for developing countries with a higher country risk profile. Multilateral development banks will continue to play a leading role in providing lending, supported by national export credit agencies, which helps to facilitate private sector lending by commercial banks as part of a syndicated project financing deal. The role of national development banks is also expected to become increasingly important in such co-financing deals, with Asian national development banks from China, Japan, South Korea and India expected to be increasingly significant players in project co-financing in Asia.

The further development of domestic bond markets in developing countries also has a significant role to play in raising finance for infrastructure development. Continuing to develop deeper and more liquid local currency bond markets and also building out the yield curves for different bond tenors will continue to be an important strategy for many developing countries for mobilizing greater long-term private capital flows, including for infrastructure financing.

One of the rapidly growing success stories for accelerating private capital flows for infrastructure development relates to the use of value capture systems. Developing country governments are increasingly leveraging upon the international experience and success stories of utilizing value capture systems to enhance private sector investment flows into infrastructure. While the use of value capture systems is limited to certain types of infrastructure projects, it has been effectively utilized for major infrastructure financing projects such as Hong Kong's MTR, and provides a project financing model which has potential applications in many other urban infrastructure projects.

Although the focus of governments is often concentrated upon trying to mobilize greater supply of private sector financing for infrastructure development, there are already large private sector pools of money that are seeking viable projects for investment. In many cases, the private sector investors have significant concerns about the risks related to government approval processes and lengthy approval timetables. Therefore, one potential strategy that national governments as well as state and local governments can take to mobilize such private capital flows is to develop national or regional pipelines of infrastructure projects that already have completed much of the necessary approval processes.

Governments of developing countries therefore need to develop project pipelines that are in an advanced stage of feasibility assessment and with necessary government approvals and permits in place, to reduce the burden on the private sector when making an investment decision in the project. Governments should also develop their own ranking of project pipelines to prioritize projects.

While insurance and reinsurance risk mitigation solutions are a well-established part of infrastructure project financing for developing countries, the use of reinsurance to mitigate the economic impact of natural disasters has become a key policy focus for the G-7. A number of catastrophe risk insurance projects have already been implemented, and further progress in utilizing such innovative solutions may also make an important contribution to protecting infrastructure assets.

Despite the considerable challenges facing developing countries in mobilizing large-scale infrastructure financing flows, the long-term outlook has been boosted by the new strategic initiatives being taken by China and Japan to boost infrastructure financing flows for developing countries. South Korea is also increasing its commitment to development financing. A key positive factor for overall global financing for development is the rapidly growing size of the Asia-Pacific region as a share of world GDP, which is driving strong growth in the size of total financial assets in the Asia-Pacific banking systems, investment funds and pension funds.

This is creating a rapidly growing pool of new financial assets that are available for investing in infrastructure, a significant share of which can be mobilized for financing economic development. The growing importance of Asia-Pacific governments, multilateral development banks, commercial banks, national development banks, asset managers and insurers as key players in global development financing is creating a much brighter long-term outlook for mobilizing capital flows for developing countries.

6

China's Belt and Road Initiative

Building the New Silk Road

The strategic vision for the Belt and Road Initiative was first launched by President Xi Jinping in September 2013 during his state visit to Kazakhstan. During his visit, President Xi gave a speech at Nazarbayev University in which he discussed the concept of a new Silk Road Economic Belt linking China and Central Asia, revitalizing the ancient trade routes of the Silk Road. Historically the Silk Road was the figurative term referring to the overland as well as maritime trade routes that linked Europe and the Middle East with the Far East, with exports of silk having been an important part of the trade flows from China.

> The envisaged economic belt along the Silk Road is inhabited by nearly 3 billion people and it represents the biggest market in the world, with enormous and unparalleled potential for trade and investment co-operation between the countries involved.
>
> Chinese President Xi Jinping, "Work Together to Build the Silk Road Economic Belt", Speech at the Nazarbayev University, Astana, Kazakhstan, 7 September 2013.

Since that time, the original strategic plan has evolved into a much larger blueprint that has become the One Belt, One Road Initiative. China's Belt and Road Initiative, as it is now referred to, is a grand strategy for building infrastructure connectivity among China and 64 other nations by high-speed railways, new highways and modern seaports. The geographic

© The Author(s) 2018
R. Biswas, *Emerging Markets Megatrends*,
https://doi.org/10.1007/978-3-319-78123-5_6

scope of the Belt and Road Initiative extends from China to Southeast Asia, Central Asia, South Asia, the Middle East, Europe and Africa, through overland and maritime connectivity. The scale of this initiative is very large, and has the potential to accelerate infrastructure development in many Asian developing countries, including in ASEAN, Central Asia and South Asia.

In May 2017, China hosted The Belt and Road Forum for International Co-operation in Beijing, with an estimated 28 heads of state having attended, including President Vladimir Putin of Russia, Indonesian President Joko Widodo, Malaysian PM Najib Razak and Philippines President Rodrigo Duterte. This reflected the geopolitical importance of China's Belt and Road Initiative for many Asian developing countries.

The scope of China's One Belt One Road Initiative now extends far beyond developing Asia, to Africa, the Middle East and Europe. China's annual trade with the other 64 Belt and Road countries has already exceeded USD 1 trillion. At a time when forces of nationalism and anti-globalisation have flourished in some parts of the world, China is pursuing an ambitious masterplan to build infrastructure connectivity that will accelerate economic development and strengthen international trade and investment flows across 65 nations, including ASEAN, Central Asia, South Asia and Africa.

The breadth of China's grand strategic vision was reflected in the composition of heads of state who attended the Belt and Road Forum, which included Turkish President Recep Tayyip Erdogan, Spanish Prime Minister Mariano Rajoy, Greek Prime Minister Alexis Tsipras and Kenyan President Uhuru Kenyatta.

Over USD 1 trillion of infrastructure projects are already planned under the umbrella of the Belt and Road Initiative, including transport infrastructure, power infrastructure and industrial parks. While some existing bilateral infrastructure projects that were agreed prior to the official launch of the Belt and Road Initiative in 2013 have been rolled in under its umbrella, nevertheless the new bilateral infrastructure financing commitments that China has made since 2013 are very large.

In tandem with development of the Belt and Road Initiative, China has also led initiatives to create new multilateral development banks to provide infrastructure financing for developing countries, notably the Asian Infrastructure Investment Bank, the New Development Bank and the Silk Road Fund. These institutions have commenced lending activities, and are helping to lift infrastructure financing flows to emerging markets, with Asian countries having access to financing from all three of these institutions.

The New Development Bank created by the BRICS in 2014 and head-quartered in Shanghai, has total authorised capital of USD 100 billion. The Asian Infrastructure Investment Bank has total authorised capital of USD 100 billion and subscribed capital of USD 50 billion, and is headquartered in Beijing. The AIIB has a membership of 57 countries that have joined as founding members, with the AIIB Board having held its inaugural meeting in January 2016. Project lending has commenced during 2016, with financing approved for a range of infrastructure projects in developing Asian countries.

In addition to these new multilateral development financing institutions, China committed to provide USD 40 billion in funding for the Silk Road Fund when it was established, to provide financing for infrastructure projects in central Asia and Southeast Asia. In May 2017, President Xi Jinping committed another USD 14.5 billion in financing for the Silk Road Fund at the Belt and Road Forum in Beijing.

China's strategic masterplan for driving regional economic development across developing Asia will be catalyzed by new infrastructure financing flows for Asian emerging markets. In addition to the Asian Infrastructure Investment Bank, the New Development Bank and the Silk Road Fund, China has made large-scale bilateral infrastructure financing commitments to a number of Asian countries.

Financing for Belt and Road projects will also come from a wide variety of sources within the Chinese financial system, with China Development Bank, China Exim Bank and Bank of China playing important roles. However many other Chinese commercial banks will also be involved in project financing.

President Xi announced at the Belt and Road Forum in Beijing in May 2017 that there would be an additional 250 billion yuan of new loans from China Development Bank and an additional 130 billion yuan of new loans from China Export-Import Bank for Belt and Road projects. China Development Bank has previously stated that it plans to provide financing of around USD 890 billion for the Belt and Road Initiative, prior to the additional new loans announced by President Xi.

The total value of new contracts signed with 61 countries along the Belt and Road during 2016 was estimated at USD 126 billion, with actual Chinese foreign direct investment flows into Belt and Road partner countries in 2016 estimated at USD 14.5 billion.

Role of Insurance Companies in the Belt and Road Initiative

For large infrastructure projects in developing countries in Asia and the Pacific, co-financing is becoming increasing important, with multilateral development banks such as the World Bank or AIIB playing a lead role in providing project loans, but through a co-financing model with MIGA and national export credit agencies as well as national development banks, in addition to private sector financing from commercial banks and credit mitigation products from insurers. With a co-financing approach expected to be important in financing of Belt and Road infrastructure projects, the key role of insurers in mitigating risks related to infrastructure project financing will play a critical role in catalyzing financing flows for the Belt and Road Initiative.

In the National People's Congress Work Reports for 2017, the Chinese government has announced that it will expand the coverage of Chinese export credit insurance. Export financing insurance will be provided for all insurable large sets of manufacturing equipment exports.

China Export & Credit Insurance Corporation (Sinosure) had signed a framework agreement in 2016 with Silk Road Fund Co., Ltd. to provide financial support for Belt and Road projects. Sinosure export credit insurance has so far been provided for Chinese exports of goods and services, although it can extend to projects that are majority-owned by Chinese firms.

With over 1 trillion of infrastructure financing estimated under the umbrella of the Belt and Road Initiative, the role of both government export credit agencies as well as private insurers and reinsurers is likely to become increasingly important to facilitate project co-financing and catalyzing private sector infrastructure financing in many low-income developing countries.

Belt and Road Initiative in ASEAN

With many ASEAN countries being close neighbours of China and with bilateral trade flows having grown rapidly over the past two decades, ASEAN is a key focus for the Belt and Road Initiative. Bilateral trade between China and ASEAN has grown from USD 9 billion in 1991 to USD 346 billion in 2015, making the Belt and Road Initiative a significant geopolitical priority for ASEAN countries, since it will improve transport links with the fast-growing Chinese consumer market for exporting their products.

The political importance of the Belt and Road Initiative for ASEAN countries was evident at the Belt and Road Forum in Beijing, with seven of the ten

ASEAN heads of state having attended. China has already made significant bilateral investment and financing commitments to many of the ASEAN nations.

Since President Duterte took office in the Philippines in May 2016, economic and political relations between China and the Philippines have thawed. During President Duterte's visit to Beijing in October 2016, China and the Philippines agreed on a USD 24 billion package of investment and credit facilities including USD 9 billion of Chinese soft loans for the Philippines.

Malaysian economic ties with China have also strengthened significantly over the past decade, with rapidly growing bilateral trade and investment flows. China and Malaysia agreed on bilateral deals of around USD 34 billion in October 2016, including a USD 13.75 billion Chinese 20-year low interest loan to Malaysia to finance the East Coast Rail Link project. However, Malaysia's incoming new Pakatan Harapan (PH) government led by Prime Minister Dr. Mahathir bin Mohamad that won the national elections on 9th May 2018 had made an election campaign promise to review large infrastructure projects, including a review of the East Coast Rail Link project. A key concern for the new Malaysian government is that the total level of government debt including contingent liabilities is estimated to exceed Ringgit 1 trillion, putting pressure on the government to review major projects that could add significantly to Malaysian government debt.

The Belt and Road Initiative has also provided large-scale infrastructure investment flows for the economic development of Cambodia. Chinese investment in Cambodian infrastructure has included 2600 kilometres of roads and seven hydroelectric power stations. New infrastructure projects under the Belt and Road Initiative include a new airport at Siem Reap and an industrial park in the Sihanoukville Special Economic Zone. The Sihanoukville Special Economic Zone is eventually planned to have over 300 companies and around 100,000 employees, providing a significant boost to the overall industrialization of Cambodia.

Myanmar also plays a strategic role in the Belt and Road Initiative as a key strategic route connecting inland China to the Indian Ocean if new port, rail and highways are built to link Myanmar to southern China.

Myanmar–China Infrastructure

The strategic importance of Myanmar as a gateway to Southern China has been evident since World War Two, when after the Japanese invasion of the coastal Chinese provinces the Allies built a road link that went through northern Myanmar to the southern provinces of China. This land route from Ledo in Assam through to Kunming in southern China was known as the Stillwell Road, name after US Army general Joe Stillwell, known as "Vinegar Joe" for his stoic and acerbic nature. He had walked out of Burma leading his staff all the way to Assam when the Japanese invasion forces had attacked Rangoon, carrying an M1 carbine slung over his shoulder.

Not one to take such a beating lying down, he was the strategist who was the driving force behind the road built from Ledo to Kunming, to provide a land route for Allied supplies to the Chinese army fighting the Japanese forces.

The strategic importance of the Myanmar route to Southern China still remains relevant to this day, as an efficient transportation route connecting the inland Chinese provinces through to the ocean. China has already invested in two major oil and gas pipelines that connect Kyaukpyu port in Myanmar to Yunnan province in southern China. Both pipelines have already been built and are operational, with the natural gas pipeline completed in 2013 and the oil pipeline finished in 2014. The oil pipeline runs through to Kunming, with a total length of 771 kilometres, while the gas pipeline is much longer, with a total length of 2806 kilometres, extending beyond Kunming to Guangxi.

A Chinese consortium led by the CITIC Group has proposed to take a 70–85% stake in the Kyaukpyu port, as well as investing in the development of an industrial park that is part of the port's special economic zone.

As in the Second World War, the transport route from China to Myanmar provides an alternative and shorter transport route to the sea than via the Chinese coastal provinces. Creating transport infrastructure that links southern China to the Indian Ocean will create a more efficient logistics route for inland provinces in southern China to export their products as well as to import commodities such as oil and gas rather than relying on the very long transport routes to the eastern Chinese ports.

Infrastructure Financing for South Asia

South Asia has been a key focus for Chinese bilateral infrastructure financing, with several major port projects in Pakistan and Sri Lanka having been developed with Chinese aid over the past decade. There have also been significant financing commitments made by China for infrastructure development in Bangladesh.

During President Xi's visit to Bangladesh in October 2016, total investment deals of around USD 13.6 billion were agreed for highways, railways and power infrastructure projects.

China Pakistan Economic Corridor

Pakistan has been one of the biggest beneficiaries of Chinese development assistance in the past decade relative to the size of its economy. Under the Belt and Road Initiative, China has made a bilateral commitment of USD 62 billion to Pakistan to finance the China Pakistan Economic Corridor that will connect China with the Arabian Sea through rail and road links, as well as other infrastructure projects including industrial parks and power projects. If these infrastructure projects are completed as expected over the next decade, it will provide a significant boost to Pakistan's economic growth rate as well as accelerating its overall economic development by improving road, rail, port and power infrastructure.

A centerpiece of the China Pakistan Economic Corridor is the port of Gwadar, which has been built with Chinese financial assistance. The Pakistani government announced in April 2017 that Gwadar Port would be operated under a 40 year lease by China Overseas Port Holding Company, which will receive 90% of the revenue from Gwadar's marine operations. It will also develop a special economic zone adjacent to the port.

Gwadar Port will be connected by major new highways to China, to improve connectivity for bilateral trade between China and Pakistan as well as to provide link between inland China and the Arabian Sea. Plans have been discussed for a major new oil pipeline will be built from Gwadar to China, but the economic feasibility of such a pipeline project is still uncertain and such a pipeline would also be vulnerable to security concerns as it would be a prime target for terrorist attacks. However an LNG regasification terminal is planned to be built as part of the Gwadar port expansion plans, in order to provide additional natural gas feedstock for new power stations being built in Pakistan to meet domestic power generation requirements.

A major part of the bilateral infrastructure financing for Pakistan is for energy infrastructure, with Pakistan having suffered severe electricity shortages for many years that have been a major obstacle to industrial development. With major new gas-fired and coal-fired power stations being built under the Belt and Road Initiative, Pakistan will have a significant increase in its overall electricity generating capacity over the next five years, which should help to improve the competitiveness of Pakistan's industrial sector. China will provide financing for 21 new power stations for Pakistan under the Belt and Road Initiative, generating an additional 16 gigawatts of power by around 2021.

However while the massive infrastructure development financing provided by China will help to ramp up economic growth over the medium term, the ability of Pakistan to repay the large-scale loans that have been provided by Chinese banks could be a long term vulnerability for Pakistan if the projects are not able to generate sufficient economic returns to finance the repayments.

Belt and Road to Europe

China's international vision for the Belt and Road initiative also extends to Eastern Europe, with the funding for a high-speed railway between the Hungarian and Serbian capitals of Budapest and Belgrade. A consortium led by China Railway Group (CRG) was awarded a contract to build the Hungarian section of the railway, which is China's first high-speed railway project in the European Union.

A Chinese firm has also taken an investment stake in the Greek port of Piraeus in 2016. COSCO Shipping Corporation Ltd has taken a 51% stake for a total investment of Euro 281 million. Under the purchase agreement with the Greek government, COSCO must invest an additional Euro 300 million in the port in order to proceed with purchasing an additional 16% stake in the port. COSCO has already built a new pier for cruise ships, in order to boost tourism flows through the port.

COSCO plans to transform Piraeus into a major transshipment hub for Asian trade with Europe, with rail links through to other Eastern European countries. COSCO has further built up its strategic positioning in Europe with the acquisition of a 51% stake in Noatum Port Holdings for Euro 228 million. Noatum Port Holdings operates the Spanish ports of Valencia and Bilbao.

Deutsche Bank has announced that it has reached an agreement with China Development Bank to provide USD 3 billion of financing for Belt and Road projects over the next five years.

Western China Growth Pole

The objectives of the Belt and Road Initiative are not only focused on the economic development of other countries, but also on the more balanced development of China's regions. The Chinese government has given a high priority in the past decade to the economic development of inland Chinese provinces, in order to address the significant gap that had been emerging between per capita GDP and overall development standards in coastal China and the inland provinces.

The Belt & Road Initiative will not only accelerate connectivity between China and countries in Central Asia, Southeastern Asia, and even Europe in terms of transportation, trade and finance, but will also push China's vast western region from the fringes to the front line of its opening up drive, thus injecting new vitality into China's comprehensive, large-scale efforts to develop this region. By turning western China into a new growth pole, we will create a fresh pattern of regional development in which China's western and eastern regions develop in unison.

Xu Shaoshi, Minister and Secretary of CPC Leadership Group, National Development and Reform Commission of China, in *Qiushi CPC Journal on China's Governance and Perspectives*, Vol. 8, No. 2, Issue No. 27, April to June 2016.

Land Connectivity

Improving infrastructure connectivity by land routes is a key part of the Belt and Road Initiative. With China's economy already having become the second largest in the world and with China being a key market for other ASEAN countries, improved infrastructure connectivity between ASEAN and China improves the potential for rapid growth in bilateral trade flows. With ASEAN manufacturing companies also having become increasingly integrated into the Asian manufacturing supply chain and with China being a fast-growing consumer market, improved rail and road connectivity will help to accelerate bilateral trade flows.

China is providing large-scale bilateral infrastructure assistance for rail infrastructure projects to many ASEAN countries, including Thailand, Malaysia, Cambodia, Philippines and Laos. China is financing a number of major rail projects in ASEAN, including Indonesia's USD 6 billion Jakarta-Bandung High Speed Rail link, Malaysia's East Coast Rail Link, a USD 5.15 billion China-Thai high speed railway, and a USD 5.9 billion China-Laos-Thailand railway.

Construction work on the Laos section of the China-Laos-Thailand railway commenced in January 2017, with about 14% of the project already completed by the end of 2017. The railway is expected to be completed in 2021.

The Thai government has also planned its own USD 44 billion Eastern Economic Corridor infrastructure megaproject which will be integrated with the new rail infrastructure planned under the Belt and Road Initiative.

In Indonesia, China Development Bank has signed a loan agreement in May 2017 for USD 4.5 billion with the consortium that will build the 142 kilometre high speed railway from Jakarta to Bandung. The new rail link is expected to be completed in 2020 and will reduce the travel time from three hours to around 40 minutes. The joint Indonesian and Chinese consortium, PT Kereta Cepat Indonesia-China (KCIC) comprises China Railway International Co. Ltd, as well as Indonesian companies Wijaya Karya and Jasa Marga. KCIC will finance around USD 1.5 billion of the project cost, with the total cost of the project estimated to be around USD 6 billion. The High Speed Railway Contract Consortium has signed a 50 year contract to design and maintain the railway with the KCIC consortium. The supply of rolling stock has been awarded in a USD 365 million contract to CRCC Qingdao Sifang for the supply of eleven eight-car trains.

In South Asia, China has provided USD 1.8 billion in financing for Bangladesh for a railway between Akhaura and Sylhet.

China's international vision for the Belt and Road Initiative also extends to Eastern Europe, with Chinese funding for a high speed railway between the Hungarian and Serbian capitals of Budapest and Belgrade. A consortium led by CRG was awarded a contract to build the Hungarian section of the railway, which is China's first high-speed railway project in the EU.

The Maritime Silk Road

A key part of the Belt and Road Initiative is to develop maritime connectivity among the Belt and Road countries through a network of ports and economic zones in ASEAN, South Asia and East Africa. Chinese firms have invested heavily in acquiring global ports, with total Chinese investment in port acquisition estimated at USD 20 billion in 2017. The network of Chinese investment in global ports now includes an estimated 68 countries, including the port of Darwin in Australia and Piraeus in Greece. The acquisition by China's COSCO Shipping Holdings of a 51% stake in Spain's container terminal operator Noatum Port Holdings in 2017 has further strengthened China's global network of port ownership by giving COSCO stakes in a number of ports across Europe.

In ASEAN, the Belt and Road Initiative aims to develop port infrastructure in Indonesia, Myanmar and Malaysia. The Melaka Gateway project in Malaysia includes plans for a marina and deep water port that will help to boost cruise ship tourism visits, particularly from China. A port alliance between 11 Chinese and Malaysian ports has also been formed under the Belt and Road Initiative to help improve bilateral co-operation in port operations and technology.

In South Asia, a major port infrastructure construction project financed by China has been undertaken in Pakistan, with the development of Gwadar Port on the Arabian Sea.

In Sri Lanka, China has been involved in development of the Colombo Port City project, although the latter has become embroiled in political controversy and a public backlash against the generous terms granted to the Chinese firms involved. The Sri Lankan government has opened up a tender process to allow international competition for the development of the East Container Terminal.

The South Terminal of the Port of Colombo was built under a 35-year build, operate and transfer public-private partnership agreement with Colombo International Container Terminals, a joint venture between China Merchant Port Holdings Company Limited and the Sri Lanka Ports Authority. Completed in 2013, the South Terminal handled 2 million twenty foot equivalent containers in 2016, representing a 28% increase in cargo volume compared with 2015.

Belt and Road Initiative in Africa

China has provided substantial infrastructure development assistance to Africa over the past decade, with recent infrastructure development projects being included under the umbrella of the Belt and Road Initiative.

A major focus for Chinese infrastructure investment has been East Africa, with China having funded a number of major railway projects with total railway financing of over USD 10 billion. China Exim Bank has financed a Kenyan railway link from the port of Mombasa to Nairobi, and is negotiating new financing for Uganda and Kenya to build a rail link connecting both nations, providing land-locked Uganda with a modern rail link to the port of Mombasa.

Chinese finance has also supported port development in East Africa, often linking up with the new rail infrastructure being developed. In Djibouti, China has helped to finance the new port of Doraleh, a USD 590 million project that was financed by Djibouti Port together with China Merchants Holdings. The port was built by China State Construction Engineering Corporation. The port is expected to provide a major trans-shipment facility for Ethiopia as well as South Sudan.

China has also financed the construction of a 750 kilometre modern electric railway line linking the Ethiopian capital of Addis Ababa with Djibouti, which will increase the importance of the new port as a transshipment hub for Ethiopia. The new railway line was built by CRG and China Civil Engineering Construction Company Limited as a replacement for an antiquated old railway line built in 1917. The new rail service significantly reduces the transportation time between Addis and Djibouti compared to truck haulage, and will help the shipment of Ethiopian exports as well as improving logistics for imports. The total cost of the new railway was USD 4 billion, of which USD 3.4 billion was for the Ethiopian section of the railway, with 30% funded by the Ethiopian government and 70% funded by a project loan by China Exim Bank.

The new railway line has also catalyzed the development of a wider rail network, with Ethiopian Railway Corporation having signed a USD 1.7 billion contract for Turkish company Yapi Merkezi to build a 389 kilometre railway from Awash to Hara Gebeya due for completion in 2018.

However Chinese plans for infrastructure financing for Tanzania have faced difficulties. Significant Chinese infrastructure investment is currently being negotiated for the development of a major new port in Tanzania, but no final agreement has been reached after extended discussions. China Exim Bank had also negotiated an agreement with Tanzania for USD 7.6 billion of financing for 2200 kilometre of rail networks linking major cities. However this financing proposal has not been concluded.

Meanwhile Tanzania has made a separate agreement in early 2017 with Turkish and Portuguese railway construction firms following a public tender competitive process to build a 205 kilometre standard gauge main railway line and six railway stations for USD 1.2 billion. The total railway line planned is for a 1216 kilometre rail link from the Tanzanian capital of Dar es Salaam to Mwanza, with the remaining sections of the railway to be built under a further four phases of tendering that are currently in the bidding process.

Local Content and International Contractors

As the Belt and Road Initiative has progressed, there have been concerns raised by some analysts and commentators that Chinese companies have been the main beneficiaries of the Belt and Road infrastructure construction contracts awarded, and that firms from other countries have not played a significant role in the overall value of construction project work awarded.

From the Chinese economic perspective, the Belt and Road Initiative provides an opportunity for Chinese infrastructure construction firms to win new business for large-scale new infrastructure projects related to the Belt and Road Intiative.

The large number of infrastructure construction projects underway as part of the Belt and Road Initiative have so far been predominantly financed by Chinese banks such as China Development Bank and China Export-Import Bank. Most of the construction projects have been awarded to Chinese engineering, procurement and construction (EPC) contractors. Some of the major Chinese firms that have been key EPC contractors for Belt and Road projects have included China Railway Construction Company, China Railway Corporation, China Merchants Port Holdings Company, China State Construction Engineering, Harbin Electric International Company, China Power Investment Corporation, China Huaneng Group and China Huadian Corporation.

However, international construction and engineering firms that have a good track record of working with the major Chinese contractors have also won substantial contracts for Belt and Road projects, including international firms such as Atkins, GE, ABB, Mott McDonald, ITT, Arup and Honeywell.

With over one trillion dollars of infrastructure projects planned in the 45 Belt and Road nations over the next decade, an increasing number of international construction and other infrastructure-related firms are likely to become involved in these projects, particularly since new multilateral institutions such as the AIIB and New Development Bank ramp up their project lending and work with recipient nations to implement these projects.

A number of nations that are part of the Belt and Road Initiative also have strong domestic construction firms, such as Malaysia and Indonesia, and will likely seek to ensure that their firms are able to take part in the Belt and Road projects in their own countries. For example, the construction of the new high speed rail link between Jakarta and Bandung will be built by a consortium of Chinese and Indonesian construction firms.

Financial Risks Related to the Belt and Road Initiative

China's Belt and Road Initiative is a long-term strategic vision that will involve large-scale Chinese and multilateral financing of infrastructure development in many developing countries, notably in the Asian region, but also extending to Africa, the Middle East and Eastern Europe. The scale of infrastructure financing flows under the Belt and Road Initiative is vast, already exceeding USD 1 trillion over the decade ahead.

Multilateral and bilateral financing flows for infrastructure development projects under the Belt and Road Initiative are already underway in many countries, and are expected to gain momentum over the next three to five years as major new projects enter the construction phase.

However a key medium term risk for China relates to the quality of its loans to Belt and Road nations, and whether some sovereign borrowers may face future difficulties in repaying the large infrastructure financing loans that are being provided. This could pose potential risks of increasing non-performing loans among Chinese banks that have large exposures to infrastructure financing for low income developing countries, particularly for countries that have had previous debt defaults in recent decades.

For example Pakistan, which has received large-scale financing from China for infrastructure projects under the Belt and Road Initiative has had a difficult balance of payments history, and received an IMF Extended Fund Facility of USD 6.6 billion as recently as 2013 to assist with its weak balance of payments position and prevent a currency crisis.

Similarly Sri Lanka, which has also received significant infrastructure financing from China estimated at around USD 8 billion, also agreed an IMF Extended Fund Facility of USD 1.5 billion in 2016 to prevent a balance of payments crisis. One of the Chinese-funded infrastructure projects, the Port of Hambantota, faced debt problems which have resulted in China negotiating to take a large ownership stake in the project as part of the debt restructuring agreement. The port was built at a cost of around USD 1.5 billion, and the Sri Lankan government has been negotiating a debt-equity swap under which it has been proposed that an 80% stake in the port would be exchanged as part of the restructuring of Sri Lanka's debt to China. The proposed arrangement would be that a public-private partnership between China Merchant Port Holdings and the Sri Lankan Port Authority would invest USD 1.4 billion into the port project, with China Merchant Port Holdings to take an 80% stake.

Loans provided by multilateral financing institutions such as the AIIB and NDB are likely to be subject to very stringent loan approval processes given the international nature of the managing boards and experienced global professional staff supported by financial supervision by stakeholder governments. Therefore such loans may be less vulnerable to repayment risks than the bilateral loans provided by Chinese commercial banks and policy banks.

In addition to due diligence and credit risk management by the lending institutions, recipient governments also have a responsibility to assess their repayment capacity when undertaking large new borrowings. Many developing countries have improved their macroeconomic fiscal management considerably over the past two decades, such as Indonesia and the Philippines, which have significantly reduced their government debt as a share of GDP over this period. However governments which do not have such a well-established capacity for undertaking debt sustainability assessments are able to draw on advice from international financial institutions such as the IMF, World Bank and ADB as well as drawing on international fiscal experts to assist them with assessing their capacity to take on additional borrowing for Belt and Road infrastructure projects as well as to assess the economic returns of the projects they are investing in.

In April 2018, the IMF and China opened a new   China-IMF Capacity Development Center that will help to provide developing countries with macroeconomic training as well as training on sovereign debt management, to help countries with assessing their sustainable external debt financing capacity. Drawing on independent international advice from international financial institutions or leading international consultants can also assist with undertaking social and environmental impact assessments to ensure that the projects meet international best practice for assessing the overall costs and benefits of an infrastructure project.

Despite the risks related to additional debt for the Belt and Road infrastructure projects and the need to undertake proper due diligence and cost-benefit analysis, there are significant potential benefits for Belt and Road countries from additional infrastructure financing.

The ADB has estimated that there is an infrastructure financing gap of 5% of GDP for Asian developing countries excluding China. The new infrastructure financing mobilized under the Belt and Road Initiative is expected to play a significant role in helping to boost critical infrastructure development in many low income developing countries in Asia as well as in other developing regions of the world.

For many developing countries that are part of the Belt and Road Initiative, the significant improvements in port, rail and road infrastructure that will be built under the Initiative will provide much improved infrastructure for exports and creates new opportunities to accelerate economic development and boost trade flows.

Outlook for Belt and Road Initiative

During the 19th Communist Party of China National Congress, the Belt and Road Initiative was enshrined into the Chinese constitution in order to ensure China's long-term policy commitment to this strategic goal. This will help to further reinforce the long-term commitment of China to its economic development initiatives and existing commitments to the 68 partner countries that are part of the Belt and Road Initiative.

This is a positive policy development that will help to further reassure the Belt and Road partner countries of China's long-term political and economic commitment to its large-scale infrastructure financing plans, which already exceed USD 1 trillion over the next decade. In addition to large-scale financing from Chinese commercial banks and policy banks such as China Development Bank, China Export-Import Bank, Bank of China and ICBC, additional infrastructure financing flows are expected for Belt and Road projects from the new multilateral development banks, the AIIB and New Development Bank, as well as from commercial banks and development banks in the Belt and Road partner countries.

By enshrining China's political commitment to the Belt and Road Initiative in the constitution, it will also help to strengthen the willingness of other stakeholders such as private sector firms and financial institutions in other countries to taking long-term investment stakes in Belt and Road projects.

China's long term commitment to the Belt and Road Initiative is providing a major boost to infrastructure development for low income developing countries in Asia and Africa, as well as boosting infrastructure financing for other partner countries, including in Eastern Europe and the Middle East. The Belt and Road Initiative is helping to boost infrastructure connectivity through the development of railways, ports and highways, as well as financing other critical infrastructure such as electricity generation and transmission projects.

China's Belt and Road Initiative is therefore set to become the most important development aid initiative being undertaken for developing countries over the decade ahead, with the scope of the financing involved likely to continue to rise as more financial institutions in the partner countries become involved in providing loans for Belt and Road Initiative projects. It has also catapulted China into a global leadership position in providing development assistance to low and middle income developing countries, improving China's political and economic ties with many of the low and middle income nations in Asia, Africa, the Middle East and Eastern Europe.

7

Emerging Manufacturing Hubs

Industrialization in East Asia

Since the 1960s, a succession of developing countries in East Asia have achieved rapid industrial growth, creating what has become known as 'The East Asian Economic Miracle'. Sustained high economic growth rates have succeeded in lifting their economies from among the ranks of low-income developing countries, transforming them into industrial nations with upper middle income or advanced economy status. This has resulted in rapid economic development and rising living standards, creating new hubs of prosperity in Asia among nations that had been very poor and underdeveloped at the end of World War Two.

Compared with other developing country regions, East Asia has been the most successful in achieving rapid industrial growth in the post-colonial era since the end of World War Two. The Japanese economy was the first Asian economy to become an industrial power after recovering from the devastation of its economy during World War Two. Japan's post-war industrial success was followed by a group of other East Asian economies that implemented economic development models based on exports of low-cost manufactured products to the large consumer markets of the US and Europe. These economies included South Korea, Taiwan, Hong Kong, Singapore and Malaysia. Following the economic liberalization and reforms of Deng Xiaoping in 1978, China also joined the ranks of East Asian nations that achieved rapid economic growth driven by a model of low-cost manufacturing for export to the large consumer markets of developed countries.

© The Author(s) 2018
R. Biswas, *Emerging Markets Megatrends*,
https://doi.org/10.1007/978-3-319-78123-5_7

These economies used a wide range of industrial development policies to attract investment in manufacturing, including use of free trade zones and various incentives to attract foreign and domestic investment in manufacturing. However, there was no single industrial development model used by these countries, with each having their own policy mix. Most of these nations did invest heavily in skills development and infrastructure, which also played an important role in improving competitiveness and boosting productivity growth.

However, the success of these economies in achieving industrial development also made them the victims of their own success, as rising wage costs and per capita GDP levels created challenges in maintaining the competitiveness of their low-cost manufacturing industries.

Japan was the first East Asian economy to be confronted by the impact of rising domestic manufacturing wages, which resulted in Japanese multinationals beginning to shift their production abroad and establish manufacturing plants in lower cost location in East Asia. The hollowing out of Japanese manufacturing industry as companies shifted their production to other lower cost Asian countries was followed by similar trends in Hong Kong, Taiwan and Singapore. Multinationals and local manufacturers that had been producing in Taiwan and Hong Kong during the 1960s and 1970s were attracted by the very low wages in mainland China after the 1978 reforms opened up the Chinese economy for global firms to establish manufacturing operations.

Singapore's economy also faced a similar structural transformation as low-cost manufacturing that had been attracted into Singapore during the 1960s and 1970s gradually became less competitive in low-wage segments of manufacturing. The Singapore government responded to the changing competitive landscape by strategic initiatives to develop new industry sectors with higher value-adding, such as more advanced manufacturing clusters for biomedical manufacturing, aerospace engineering and chemicals manufacturing.

China was a major beneficiary of these trends, with its vast pool of surplus labour in the 1980s able to provide a seemingly endless supply of low-cost labor for manufacturing industries that proliferated in the Chinese coastal provinces.

However, by 2010, even China began to face competitiveness pressures. Steadily rising manufacturing wages in coastal China were underpinned by government policies of supporting rapid growth of minimum wages. As a result, multinationals started to consider other emerging markets locations for their new plants and factories. This created new opportunities for other developing countries to attract foreign direct investment flows for establishing low-cost manufacturing.

This model of industrial development whereby countries initially attract low-cost manufacturing and later move up the value-added chain is known as the 'flying geese' model, originally developed by Kaname Akamatsu. As countries build up their low-cost manufacturing industries and wages rise steadily higher, their industrial sector moves into higher value-adding industries while the low-cost manufacturing industries lose competitive advantage. As a result, companies shift their production to other locations with cheaper wages, resulting in the 'hollowing out' of low-cost segments of manufacturing. This results in the 'flying geese' pattern of development, where countries achieve industrial development and rising per capita GDP levels, eventually resulting in low-cost manufacturing production shifting to the next group of low-cost competitors.

This 'flying geese' pattern of economic development has been evident in East Asia, as Japan was the first nation to achieve industrialization, triggering companies to invest in new lower cost locations such as South Korea, Taiwan, Singapore and Hong Kong. As these economies also became successful global manufacturing export hubs, rising labour costs accelerated the shift of low-cost manufacturing production to mainland China.

As China has also faced increasing competitive pressures since 2010 due to rising labour costs, another group of Asian developing countries have also benefited from significant new investment inflows into their manufacturing sectors. These new emerging manufacturing hubs in Asia include Vietnam, Bangladesh and Cambodia, with Myanmar also beginning to attract investment into its low-cost manufacturing sector.

Vietnam's Manufacturing Growth Engine

The Vietnamese economy has emerged since 2010 as one of the world's brightest emerging markets stars, as rapid industrialization continues to transform the economy. Vietnam has achieved sustained strong economic growth since 2000, with the total size of the Vietnamese economy having tripled in the past decade, from USD 66 billion in 2006 to USD 208 billion in 2016. By way of comparison, the Vietnamese economy has already become significantly larger by 2016 than the New Zealand economy, which had a total GDP of around USD 180 billion in the same year.

The Vietnamese economy has the capacity for sustained strong growth over the next decade and beyond, with the potential to grow at over 6% per year. Vietnam's total GDP is projected to reach around USD 450 billion by 2025, with rapid growth in manufacturing exports, international tourism, and fast-growing consumer expenditure being three key growth engines. The fast-growing Haiphong–Hanoi northern industrial corridor is becoming a leading hub for new foreign direct investment, as large-scale infrastructure investment catalyzes industrial development.

After a period of macroeconomic instability during 2009–2011 with high inflation and external account problems, the Vietnamese economy has improved considerably since 2012. During the 2014–2016 period, average annual GDP growth exceeded 6% per year. Foreign investor confidence in Vietnam has also recovered strongly, with foreign direct investment inflows into Vietnam having risen from around USD 11 billion in 2011 to an annual level of USD 16 billion in 2016. Total cumulative inbound FDI inflows between 2011 and 2016 are estimated to have reached USD 66 billion.

After CPI inflation reached a recent peak of 18.7% in 2011, triggering a protracted period of monetary policy tightening, inflationary pressures have moderated, easing to 3.5% in 2017.

External account difficulties have also eased, with the current account position improving from a deficit of 10.9% of GDP in 2008 and 6.2% of GDP in 2009 to sustained current account surpluses between 2011 and 2016. In 2017, Vietnam achieved a trade surplus of USD 2.7 billion, with exports rising by 21% compared to 2016, boosted by strong growth in electronics exports. Worker remittances have also bolstered the balance of payments position, with total remittances estimated at USD 13.8 billion in 2017. The improving external account position has contributed to a significant improvement in foreign exchange reserves, from around USD 12 billion in 2011 to USD 57 billion by February 2018. This has resulted in import cover improving from around 1.5 months cover in 2011 to around 3 months cover by the end of 2016.

The average growth rate in Vietnamese industrial production has been 10% year-on-year between 2013 and 2017. In calendar 2017, industrial production rose by 9.4% year-on-year. A key factor that has driven the economic upturn in Vietnam since 2010 has been the rapid growth of electronics manufacturing. The importance of Vietnam's electronics industry has risen dramatically, with the electronic industry's share of total GDP rising from 5.2% in 2010 to around one-quarter of total GDP in 2016.

The total value of electronics exports rose from USD 6.9 billion in 2011 to USD 43.5 billion in 2016, which has been a key factor supporting the rapid growth in Vietnam's total exports and GDP over the past five years. As a result, the share of electronics in total exports has increased from 5% in 2010 to 34% by 2016.

The Vietnamese textiles and garments export sector has also experienced rapid growth over the past five years, with total exports from the sector reaching USD 31 billion in 2017, up 10.2% compared with 2016.

The strong growth in foreign direct investment flows into the Vietnamese manufacturing sector over the past six years has reflected a number of factors, including low manufacturing wages compared to rapidly rising wage costs in coastal Chinese provinces, a well-educated and skilled Vietnamese workforce, rapidly improving infrastructure and good port logistics for export shipments. The Vietnamese government has also implemented policy changes to encourage foreign direct investment in the electronics and IT sector, as part of a trade strategy to improve the share of higher value-added manufacturing exports, as Vietnam's terms of trade had been structurally deteriorating when their main exports were still agricultural commodities and low value-added manufacturing. South Korea's Samsung has played a key role in Vietnam's industrial development, producing a wide range of electrical and electronics products. In 2017, Samsung products accounted for around 22.7% of total Vietnamese exports.

Manufacturing output growth in 2017 rose by 14.5% year-on-year, with strong growth in output of key industrial products such as electronics, garments, steel and cement. Rapid growth in Vietnam's construction sector is also supporting strong growth in the Vietnamese building products sector for a wide range of construction-related materials such as steel and cement.

In the steel sector, Vietnamese crude steel output reached 5.1 million tons in 2016, up 20.5% year-on-year, while the output of rolled steel reached 5.3 million tons, up 26.8% year-on-year. Production of steel building beams reached 8.5 million tons, up 18.3% year-on-year. A number of Vietnamese steel companies have new projects underway to expand their steel production capacity to meet rapidly growing domestic demand.

In the oil refining sector, Vietnam's second oil refinery project, the Nghi Son Refinery and Petrochemical, is due to begin operations in 2018, involving a total investment of USD 9 billion. The Nghi Son refinery is a joint venture project between Petrovietnam, Idemitsu Kosan, Kuwait Petroleum International and Mitsui Chemicals.

The auto manufacturing sector is also beginning to develop, with a number of auto assembly plants for passenger vehicles and trucks. Total Vietnamese auto sales in 2016 rose by 21.9% year-on-year, reaching 282,756 units. Auto sales remain very low relative to the total size of Vietnam's population due to low per capita GDP levels, as well as very high import taxes on autos.

However, the Vietnamese government is gradually lowering import taxes, and under the ASEAN Free Trade Area agreement, all tariffs on auto imports from other ASEAN countries will be eliminated by 2018. The Vietnamese government is also developing a new masterplan to try to encourage the development of the auto manufacturing sector in Vietnam.

Vietnam's Truong Hai Auto Corporation (THACO) has joint ventures with a number of global automakers for the assembly of knocked down kits in Vietnam, including with Kia, Mazda and Peugeot. Mazda has agreed to build a new USD 522 million auto assembly plant as a joint venture with THACO, with construction having commenced in March 2017. Hyundai Motor has also formed a joint venture with THACO to assemble commercial vehicles in Vietnam with a new USD 100 million assembly plant to be completed in 2017.

South Korea's Daehan Motors having recently commissioned a new truck assembly factory in Ho Chi Minh City. Belarus commercial vehicle manufacturer Minsk Automobile Plant will assemble buses at its plant in Ho Chi Minh City and will construct a truck assembly plant near Hanoi. Belarus commercial vehicle manufacturer Minsk Automobile Plant will assemble buses at its plant in Ho Chi Minh City and will construct a truck assembly plant near Hanoi.

Large-scale infrastructure investment, as well as residential and commercial real estate development is driving strong growth in construction activity. Total construction spending growth has shown strong growth since 2010, due to the large number of industrial and commercial projects being built, as well as significant new public infrastructure construction. Major infrastructure megaprojects include the new JICA-funded MRT system in Ho Chi Minh City as well as the new Lach Huyen International Gateway Port in Haiphong and the construction of Metro Line 3 in Hanoi. Ho Chi Minh City's Tan Sohn Nat International Airport will also be expanded to a capacity of 38 million passengers by 2019 with the addition of a new runway and terminals. Meanwhile, work has commenced on the Long Thanh International Airport for Ho Chi Minh City, which is planned to be operational by 2025. In addition, there are many hotel and industrial construction projects underway which will also contribute significantly to overall construction activity over the medium term outlook.

Large-scale investment in new infrastructure in the Hanoi–Haiphong Industrial Corridor has resulted in strong FDI inflows into the northern region. Major infrastructure development in Haiphong has resulted in a new highway between Haiphong and Hanoi which has cut travel time dramatically. The new Lach Huyen International Gateway Port will create a deep water port that will allow manufactures from Haiphong and its hinterland to be shipped directly to key international markets such as the US and EU. The first two berths at the new port are expected to be completed in 2018. The infrastructure of the Haiphong economic region has also been boosted by the upgrading of Cat Bi International Airport in Haiphong and the Red River Delta Expressway from Hanoi to Haiphong. Large foreign direct investment inflows have been attracted into the Haiphong economic region, including by LG Electronics, Bridgestone ad Kyocera.

The Vietnamese tourism industry is growing rapidly and has become an important growth engine. The total estimated value of tourism increased by 15% in 2016 to reach USD 38.4 billion, or around 20% of total Vietnamese exports. International tourism visitors reached 12.9 million visitors in 2017, up 29.1% year-on-year. China is a major source of tourism visitors, with a total of 4 million Chinese tourists visiting Vietnam in 2017, or around 31% of total international visitors. Total Asian tourism visitors accounted for 9.7 million visits in 2017, with another 1.9 million from the EU.

The rapid growth of tourism is driving significant new construction of new hotels, with an estimated 60 new hotels due to open over 2017–2020, including Four Seasons Hanoi, Hotel Nikko Haiphong, Pullman Haiphong, Melia Ho Tram, Crowne Plaza Phu Quoc, Wyndham Danang and Hilton Saigon.

An important strength for Vietnam's competitive advantage is its extensive framework of free trade agreements (FTAs) with major economies. The centerpiece is Vietnam's membership of ASEAN, under which Vietnam is part of the ASEAN Free Trade Area and will eventually have zero tariffs on trade in goods with other ASEAN countries. As part of the ASEAN FTAs with other countries, Vietnam also benefits from the ASEAN's FTAs with China, India, Japan, South Korea, Australia and New Zealand.

However, the US withdrawal from the TPP Agreement does represent a significant setback for Vietnam's manufacturing export industry outlook. Vietnam's manufacturing export sector was expected to be among the largest beneficiaries from TPP due to the much improved market access to North America. The TPP agreement would have significantly reduced tariff barriers for Vietnam's electronics manufacturing industries, as well as providing a large boost to Vietnam's textiles exports. Due to the significant gains that Vietnam was expected to achieve through the TPP for improving market access for its manufactured exports, the outlook for future export growth, while remaining strong, has been somewhat dampened by the US decision to withdraw from the TPP.

For Vietnam, the rapidly growing garments and electronics export industries had been expected to significantly benefit from the TPP agreement implementation, as market access to the US would have significantly improved. Had the US implemented TPP, average tariffs for Vietnamese exports of garments and textiles into the US would have dropped from 18% to zero. However, even without TPP, the US is already Vietnam's largest export market, with total Vietnamese exports to the US having reached USD 41.5 billion in 2017, or around 1.4% of total Vietnamese exports.

Despite the TPP setback, Vietnam is still expected to experience rapid manufacturing export growth due to its relative competitiveness, reflecting significantly lower manufacturing wage costs vis-à-vis coastal Chinese provinces.

Another medium-term positive factor for Vietnam's export sector is the EU-Vietnam FTA that was agreed in 2015 and is due to be implemented in 2018. The FTA was due to be ratified by the European Parliament in 2017, but the ratification process has been delayed by an opinion of the European Court of Justice, which decided that some elements of the EU-Singapore FTA require that the FTA is ratified by the European Parliament as well as the 28 EU states, which has similar implications for the EU-Vietnam FTA. This new FTA, when eventually ratified, will significantly improve Vietnam's market access to the key EU market, with 99% of tariffs to be eliminated within 7 years of implementation. The EU is already Vietnam's second largest export market and a major importer of garments and electronics manufactured in Vietnam and the FTA is expected to significantly boost bilateral trade flows. In 2017, Vietnamese exports to the EU reached USD 38.3 billion, which was 17.9% of total Vietnamese exports.

The Vietnamese economy is expected to maintain a rapid pace of economic growth over the next decade, with its potential growth rate estimated to be around 6–7% per year. Rapid industrialization, fast-growing domestic consumer spending and buoyant growth in tourism are expected to continue to underpin economic growth momentum, helped by strong investment in infrastructure. Private consumption spending is expected to grow rapidly, with per capita GDP forecast to continue to grow strongly over the next decade, lifting the total size of Vietnam's consumer market as the size of Vietnam's middle class continues to expand quickly.

However, Vietnam's manufacturing hub and fast pace of economic development does also face potential downside risks. Among the key risks and vulnerabilities in the medium term include the potential impact of a Chinese economic slowdown or hard landing, which would have transmission effects on Vietnam through lower Chinese demand for Vietnamese exports as well as declining Chinese tourism visitor flows. Despite significant progress in improving macroeconomic stability, Vietnam is also still vulnerable to risks of rising inflation due to higher external commodity prices as well as external account fragilities, since import cover is still modest.

An important vulnerability for the Vietnamese economy over the next five to ten years is related to the high level of non-performing loans estimated to be in the Vietnamese banking system. Non-performing loans accumulated prior to 2011 during a previous upturn in banking lending. The official non-performing loan ratio significantly underreports the high level of impaired assets on the balance sheets of commercial banks. Due to the high level of government debt and high fiscal deficits, the Vietnamese government has not been able to significantly recapitalize the banks, resulting in a very slow process of reduction of non-performing loans in the banking system since 2012.

However, gradual progress is being made, notably through the creation of the state-owned Vietnam Asset Management Company in 2013 to absorb bad loans from the commercial banks, although the pace at which this has occurred has been very slow during its first five years of operations. The Vietnamese government's regulatory approval in April 2017 for the Saigon Joint Stock Commercial Bank to sell a majority stake to a foreign investor is another positive signal that the government may allow similar foreign capital injections into other domestic banks to help recapitalize its banking sector.

In addition to these economic and financial vulnerabilities, the impact of climate change remains a risk to Vietnam due to its extensive low-lying river deltas, which are vulnerable to typhoons, with risk of flood damage and storm surges. Ho Chi Minh City and nearby industrial estates are vulnerable to certain extreme weather events such as typhoons, and Hanoi's economy was hit by typhoons Kai-Tak and Son-Tinh in 2012. Therefore, investing in flood prevention infrastructure to mitigate the impact of flooding will remain an important priority to reduce vulnerability to climate change and weather events.

Despite some risks and vulnerabilities, the Vietnamese economy is expected to remain one of the world's most attractive emerging markets over the medium term, as rapid growth in manufacturing exports and fast-growing domestic consumer expenditure continue to drive the economy.

Sri Lanka's Manufacturing Sector

Sri Lanka has a substantial garments industry which accounts for around 47% of the nation's exports. The total value of garments exports reached USD 4.8 billion in 2017, with 45% of total garments exports going to the US and 42% to the EU. The ending of the civil war in Sri Lanka in 2009 and commitment of the coalition government led by President Sirisena to strengthening political and economic ties with a wide range of major economies has helped to improve the economic climate. In 2017, foreign direct investment strengthened to USD 1.6 billion, doubling from the 2016 level of foreign direct investment inflows.

A major positive factor supporting the outlook for the manufacturing sector has been the success of the Sirisena coalition in improving relations with the EU. In 2017, the EU decided to restore GSP+ preferences to Sri Lanka, which will significantly improve the competitiveness of Sri Lanka's export sector to EU markets. Due to an existing Free Trade Agreement already in place with India, Sri Lanka has become an attractive manufacturing production hub for Indian garments industry firms, and this will improve further with the improved market access to the EU. Sri Lanka is also negotiating an FTA with China, which will further improve its competitiveness as a manufacturing hub.

China has already invested in a wide range of infrastructure projects in Sri Lanka, including the development of Hambantota Port, with Chinese firms planning to establish an economic zone adjacent to the port, as well as the Colombo Port City project and the Colombo South Harbor container terminal. Japan and India are also investing in Sri Lankan industrial projects, with India's Petronet LNG and Japan's Mitsubishi and Sojitz planning to build a new USD 300 million LNG terminal near Colombo at Kerawalapitiya in order to provide imported LNG feedstock for power stations.

By building high quality, efficient infrastructure, Sri Lanka will improve its competitiveness as a manufacturing hub for export to major markets such as India, the US and EU. However, a key challenge for Sri Lanka over the next decade will be to move up the value-adding chain in manufacturing, as Sri Lankan per capita GDP is already above USD 4000, which has made it an upper middle income country. This will make it increasingly difficult for Sri Lanka to compete for low value-added textiles and garments manufacturing production, requiring the industrial sector to transform significantly towards higher value-added industries such as electronics, auto components manufacturing and other more complex manufacturing segments.

An important competitive advantage for Sri Lanka is its proximity to the vast consumer market of India, which also creates considerable future industrial development opportunities for the food processing sector. A wide range of Sri Lankan processed foods are already exported to the Indian consumer market, which will grow rapidly over the next decade.

Other Asian Emerging Manufacturing Hubs

A number of Asia's least developed countries, notably Bangladesh, Cambodia and Myanmar have also attracted foreign direct investment inflows by multinationals in the textiles and footwear industry seeking to tap into the very low manufacturing wage rates in these countries.

In Bangladesh, exports of textiles and garments accounted for only 3.9% of total exports in 1983–1984 fiscal year, with a value of only USD around 32 million, according to data from the Bangladesh Garment Manufacturers and Exporters Association. However due to the impact of rising labor costs in other Asian manufacturing hubs, Bangladesh was able to lift its garments and textiles exports to USD 624 million by 1989–1990, or around 32% of Bangladesh's total exports. The size of the textiles and garments industry grew very rapidly in the past two decades, as the impact of rising wages in coastal Chinese provinces became an increasingly important factor driving garments manufacturers to source more clothing from Bangladesh. By 2015–2016, Bangladesh's garments and textiles exports had soared to USD 28 billion, accounting for 82% of total exports.

The rapid growth of the textiles industry has been an important growth engine for the Bangladesh economy, which has achieved sustained GDP growth of around 6% per year over the past decade. By 2016, an estimated 4 million workers were employed in the textiles and garments industry, with significant multiplier effects to output and employment from the rapid growth in the total value added of this sector over the past two decades.

The textiles and garments industry has also been an important growth engine for the Cambodian economy, as it gradually recovered from the impact of genocide under the Khmer Rouge. With its technical and professional human capital having been exterminated in the killing fields, the textiles and garments sector has played an important role in creating industrial employment for Cambodia's workforce. The garments industry accounts for around three-quarters of Cambodian exports and directly employs around 700,000 people.

However for both Bangladesh and Cambodia, there have been considerable challenges in trying to transform the industrial sector towards higher value-added manufacturing, with both nations still highly dependent on exports of low-cost textiles for boosting export revenue and generating manufacturing sector jobs.

In Bangladesh, inadequate safety standards for garment workers became an international issue following the Rana Plaza disaster in 2013, when over

1,100 textiles workers were killed when their building collapsed. Although Bangladesh has taken steps to improve regulation of garments industry working conditions since that tragedy, working conditions in the industry are still difficult, with ongoing concerns among international human rights organisations about the use of child labour in the garments industry. In the Cambodian garments industry, workers have benefited from significant increases in minimum wages during the past five years, which has helped to improve living standards for garments industry workers.

Since its economic liberalization, Myanmar has also begun to attract some foreign direct manufacturing investment, although its manufacturing sector is still in the early stages of development. An important competitive advantage for Myanmar is its very low average manufacturing wage costs, which is a key factor attracting manufacturing investment into low value-added manufacturing industries.

Despite a 33% hike in Myanmar's minimum wage in the first quarter of 2018, the new minimum wage was increased to USD 3.5 per day, still very low compared to many other Asian low-cost competitor nations.

Emerging African Manufacturing Hubs

With Africa's population set to rise from 1194 million in 2015 to 1703 million by 2030, its total population will grow by 43% by 2030 under the UN World Population Projections 2017 Revision medium variant projections. This equates to an increase in the size of the population of 509 million over the 2015–2030 period. By 2050, Africa's population will rise further under these projections, to 2527 million, which indicates that Africa's total population will more than double between 2015 and 2050.

During this period, Africa's working age population is projected to increase from 663 million in 2015 to 997 million by 2030, an increase of 334 million over this time period. The working age population is projected to rise to 1565 million by 2050, indicating that Africa's population of working age will increase by 902 million people over the 2015–2050 timeframe.

In Sub-Saharan Africa, the working age population will increase from 522 million in 2015 to 1337 million by 2050, an increase of 815 million persons. This is equivalent to around 90% of the total increase in the African continent's working age population over the 2015–2050 period.

With Africa's working age population set to more than double over the next three decades, a key concern not only for African policymakers but also for governments worldwide is how these additional 902 million Africans joining the working age population will find employment. With Africa's rural economy unlikely to be able to offer significant employment growth opportunities on the scale required by such large increases in population, the growth of the manufacturing and services sectors will be increasingly important as generators of employment growth.

With the manufacturing sector in much of Africa not yet having shown the dynamic growth evident in industrializing Asian countries, the future development of Africa's manufacturing sector will be critical to the progressive economic development of Africa.

If rapid employment growth in manufacturing and services is not achieved in Africa over the next decade ahead, this will already result in significant increases in problems, such as rising unemployment and underemployment, as well as associated social malaise and rising levels of rural and urban poverty. This would inevitably increase pressures for emigration, escalating the challenge of illegal migration flows and associated criminal activity such as organized crime and human trafficking.

Due to the global transmission effects of such an adverse scenario for Africa, it is one of the most pressing global economic concerns for international policymakers. The G-20 has shown a recognition of the importance of industrialization in Africa with its New Industrial Revolution Action Plan, which was launched at the G-20 Summit in Hangzhou, China in 2016 under China's G-20 Presidency. The G-20 instructed its Development Working Group to develop this action plan with a focus on catalyzing the industrialization of Africa and the 47-nation grouping of Least Developed Countries, many of whom are also African countries.

Data from the United Nations Industrial Development Organisation (UNIDO Industrial Development Report, 2016) shows that manufacturing exports from Africa are a small fraction of the manufacturing exports of the Asia-Pacific region, and have been growing relatively slowly in comparison with Asia-Pacific manufacturing exports (Fig. 7.1).

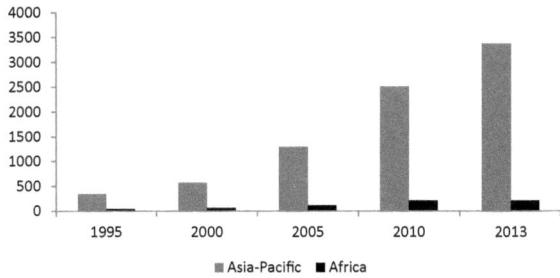

Fig. 7.1 African manufacturing exports compared to Asia (USD billion) (*Source* UNIDO)

UNIDO data (UNIDO Industrial Development Report, 2016) on manufacturing value added in the developing nations and emerging industrial economies indicates that Africa accounts for only 4% of total manufacturing value added by developing countries and emerging industrial nations. In stark contrast, the Asia-Pacific region accounts for 71% of the total manufacturing value added by the developing and emerging industrial economies.

The share of manufacturing value added in total GDP is also much lower for African countries than for many industrializing East Asian economies according to UNIDO data. While South Africa, Egypt and Tunisia do have relatively higher shares of manufacturing value added in their total GDP compared to most other African nations, nevertheless their manufacturing sector share of GDP is still significantly lower than for the East Asian manufacturing hubs such as China, South Korea, Thailand and Malaysia. Tunisia's relatively higher manufacturing value added share compared with many other African nations reflects significant manufacturing of garments and textiles, with the EU being the dominant export market, as well as sub-sectors producing food products, construction products and chemicals.

As a result of the relatively low share of GDP contributed by Africa's manufacturing sector, the share of total employment contributed by manufacturing sector jobs in the Sub-Saharan African region was only 6% during 2010–2013, compared with 19.4% for the East Asian region (Fig. 7.2).

The barriers to Africa's industrial development are wide-ranging, including weak governance, high regulatory burdens, poor critical infrastructure such as power, roads and ports, and relatively weak education and training compared to East Asian economies. Consequently many African countries rank relatively poorly on the World Bank's Ease of Doing Business index, which surveys 190 countries worldwide.

However, it is encouraging that in the World Bank Ease of Doing Business Survey for 2018, a number of African nations were identified as

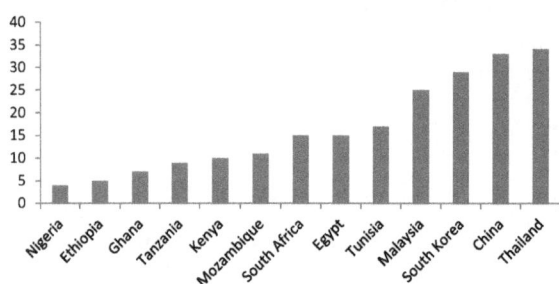

Fig. 7.2 African manufacturing compared to East Asia (manufacturing value added share of GDP) (*Source* UNIDO)

having been among those showing the greatest improvement in their rankings, including Malawi, Zambia, Nigeria and Djibouti.

Some of the future opportunities that may help to catalyze more rapid development in African manufacturing hubs include accelerated infrastructure investment, helped by international development co-operation, notably China's Belt and Road Initiative. An important priority for future policy reform is accelerated regional trade integration through reduction of tariff and non-tariff barriers to intra-African trade. This could significantly strengthen Africa's manufacturing sector growth by boosting intra-regional manufacturing exports.

African intra-regional trade is still relatively low, at only around 10% of total exports, compared with around 25% for ASEAN and 57% for the Asia region as a whole. The new agreement signed by 44 African nations in March 2018 to create an African Continental Free Trade Area is therefore a very important strategic step creating the platform for greater regional trade integration.

The World Trade Organisation Trade Facilitation Agreement which entered into force in February 2017 includes a Trade Facilitation Agreement Facility to provide financing and technical assistance to developing and Least Developed Countries with implementing trade facilitation. According to WTO estimates (WTO World Trade Report 2015, World Trade Organisation, Geneva) the Least Developed Countries and African countries would be the biggest gainers from implementing trade facilitation measures, with full implementation of the WTO Trade Facilitation Agreement potentially lowering their trade costs for manufactured goods by 18%.

The positive outlook for strong growth of GDP in many African countries over the medium term, combined with the large projected growth of population size in Africa, are expected to create fast-growing consumer markets which may attract greater foreign direct investment into manufacturing in the African region in order to produce for regional consumer markets. Initiatives for regional trade integration and trade facilitation will also help to boost the future growth of regional markets for African manufacturing production. This should also catalyze greater foreign direct investment into Africa's manufacturing sector, as firms establish African production facilities for exporting to regional consumer markets.

Latin America's Manufacturing Sector

The Latin American manufacturing sector is significant in size, particularly due to the impact of the large Brazilian and Mexican manufacturing hubs on total manufacturing output for the region. Total Latin American manufacturing exports reached USD 733 billion in 2013, equivalent to around 22% of manufacturing exports by Asia-Pacific developing economies and emerging industrial economies (UNIDO Industrial Development Report, 2016). For Mexico, the US market is extremely important, accounting for USD 314 billion of total Mexican goods exports of USD 409 billion in 2017. Mexican exports to the US include a significant share of manufactured goods, notably USD 84 billion of vehicles and parts as well as USD 62 billion of electrical machinery. The North American Free Trade Agreement implemented in 1994 between the US, Mexico and Canada has been a key factor boosting trade flows, with Mexican exports to the US having increased by 687 per cent since 1993. US and other multinational manufacturing companies have established significant manufacturing plant operations in the Mexican border area to benefit from low Mexican manufacturing wages and its tariff-free access to the US market.

However, when the size of the Brazilian and Mexican manufacturing sector value-added contribution to total GDP is compared to the large East Asian economies, their contribution to GDP is still significantly lower. For the whole of South America, the contribution of manufacturing value added to GDP is 12.5% compared to 19.4% in East Asia in the 2010–2013 period. For Central America, the share of manufacturing value added in GDP is slightly higher than for South America, at 15% (Fig. 7.3).

In terms of the demographic outlook and pressure for the region to create jobs, the population of working age in the Latin American region is projected to increase from 422 million in 2015 to 482 million by 2030, indicating a total rise of 60 million persons over the 2015–2030 period. This is much less relatively than the 334 million increase in working age population projected for Africa over the same period. Nevertheless, it still represents a large expansion in the size of the working age population, making it one of the key economic policy priorities for Latin American governments over the medium term. Therefore the manufacturing sector has an important role to

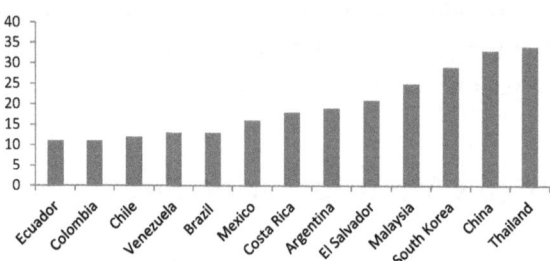

Fig. 7.3 Latin America's manufacturing compared to East Asia (manufacturing value added share of GDP) (*Source* UNIDO)

play in creating future employment growth for the future growth in Latin America's labour force. As in the case of Africa, a key potential reform that could help to boost the growth of Latin America's manufacturing sector will be further initiatives for regional trade integration. Latin America's intra-regional trade accounts for only around 15% of total trade, still very low compared to the intra-regional trade shares for ASEAN and the Asia region as a whole. The 2012 Pacific Alliance trade agreement between Mexico, Colombia, Chile and Peru is an example of Latin American initiatives to improve intra-regional trade flows.

Future Manufacturing Hubs

The industrial development model used by the East Asian economies to accelerate economic development has proven to be very difficult for developing countries in other regions of the world to emulate. Although North Africa and Central America have made significant progress towards building their industrial sectors, the share of manufacturing in overall GDP is still relatively low in Latin America and Sub-Saharan Africa when compared with many East Asian industrial economies.

The future rapid population growth of Africa creates opportunities for accelerated growth of manufacturing hubs in Africa to serve the fast-growing consumer markets of the region. A key policy challenge is the tremendous scale of growth of the working age population of Sub-Saharan Africa, which makes the rapid development of manufacturing employment a crucial economic priority for governments in the region.

However, the manufacturing sectors of developing countries also face new economic challenges from the rapid pace of technological developments and innovation. These forces are creating disruptive change and transforming the global competitive landscape for the manufacturing sector in many industries, favouring nations that are global technology leaders. Despite these challenges, there are significant policy measures that developing countries can implement to boost manufacturing sector output, such as accelerating regional trade integration and implementing trade facilitation measures to reduce the costs of trade in manufactures.

8

Disruptive Change from Robotics, Industrial Automation and the Digital Economy

During a recent visit to Tokyo, I visited the headquarters of a large Japanese bank for a meeting with senior bank executives. As I entered the lobby, I saw a number of robots standing in various corners of the entry hall. One robot looked very friendly, with human features, including a face and hands. Approaching this robot, which was called Pepper, I found that it could engage in reasonable conversation when asked questions. Its purpose was to help visitors get directions to whichever department they wanted to visit in the bank.

However, I also saw several other larger robots without such friendly human features standing in various parts of the hall. When I asked about their functions, I was told that they patrolled the lobby at night using heat and motion sensors, and would relay information about any human movement detected to a central security control station that could respond to security breaches. It reminded me of the futuristic robots depicted in "Robocop", the classic movie released in 1987 that was directed by Paul Verhoeven. Back in 1987, the concept of guard robots was science fiction fantasy, but 30-years later, early forms of such robots clearly are already operational.

A number of companies are already manufacturing security robots and they are being deployed in a wide range of operational roles, such as night patrols in commercial premises and shopping malls after closing hours. Such devices can multiply the ability of companies to monitor the security of premises as well as significantly reducing labour costs for security guards and allowing the human security guards to be deployed more effectively.

What was once science fiction is now the new reality confronting workforces in both developed and developing countries. While during the past few decades workers in the US and EU used to fear that their jobs would

© The Author(s) 2018
R. Biswas, *Emerging Markets Megatrends*,
https://doi.org/10.1007/978-3-319-78123-5_8

be offshored to developing countries, workers worldwide now face increasing challenges from factory automation as well as advances in big data and software technology. Millions of jobs in the traditional retail sector are being lost in both developed and developing countries as the digital economy drives a major shift to e-commerce and online retail sales. The accountancy and bookkeeping professions are also facing tremendous disruptive change from the interface between artificial intelligence and big data.

The backlash against globalization that is becoming increasingly evident in advanced economies such as the EU and US has, among other factors, been linked to fears of jobs being lost through offshoring, as multinationals shifted jobs to countries with lower wage costs. Many developing countries, particularly, East Asian economies, achieved substantial economic progress over the past three decades through the rapid growth of low-cost manufacturing as multinationals invested in factories focused on the exporting to advanced economies.

A key growth engine for many East Asian economies since the 1960s has been the rapid growth of manufacturing, as foreign multinationals invested in establishing low-cost manufacturing plants in sectors, such as garments, footwear, electrical and electronics manufacturing as well as food manufacturing. Many Asian economies experienced waves of industrialization from such investment inflows, including China, Thailand, South Korea and Taiwan. Frontier markets, such as Vietnam, Cambodia and Bangladesh have become new low-cost manufacturing hubs in Asia.

Investment inflows by global multinationals into manufacturing sectors such as garments or assembly of electrical products have often resulted in new industrial equipment being installed in factories, allowing productivity growth to strengthen, resulting in higher wage rises so long as unit labour costs remain constrained.

Eventually, as the stock of capital continues to improve, the marginal productivity gains slow down, resulting in rising unit labour costs and eroding manufacturing competitiveness.

Threats to Emerging Markets Manufacturing Competitiveness

However, the decision by Adidas in 2016 to open a new automated shoe factory in Germany created shockwaves globally, as it heralded a new age of automation in manufacturing that could potentially challenge the competitiveness of many developing countries that are currently dependent on low-cost manufacturing, including many Asian industrial nations. For many years, Adidas had been gradually shifting its manufacturing production to Asia by establishing factories in countries with low-wage costs, such as China and Vietnam. However, due to technological advances in industrial automation, Adidas decided to build a new factory in Ansbach, Germany for the automated production of sports footwear. The new Adidas Speedfactory pilot plant started production in 2015, with the factory having commenced normal production in 2017. A second Adidas Speedfactory has subsequently been built in the US near Atlanta, and this US factory commenced production in early 2018. Adidas plans to ramp up production from both these new factories to one million pairs of shoes per year by 2020.

With many countries in developing Asia having established significant low-cost manufacturing production, these new technological trends in industrial automation create uncertainties about the future competitiveness of low-wage developing nations in such manufacturing industries. For many ASEAN countries with significant manufacturing export sectors, including Malaysia, Thailand, Vietnam, Philippines and Cambodia, this creates new risks and uncertainties about their future industrial development and global competitiveness. It could also undermine aspirations of developing nations that are attempting to industrialize by attracting low-cost manufacturing, such as low-income Asian economies like Myanmar, Bangladesh as well as many developing nations in Africa and Latin America.

Previous historical periods of technological change and innovation had also created tremendous disruption for workforces in many nations. The First Industrial Revolution resulted in disruptive change due to new technologies such as the steam engine and other machines that had far-reaching implications for workforces and industrial production. Further rapid advances in technology such as electricity and telephones resulted in the Second Industrial Revolution that commenced at the end of the 19th Century. The Third Industrial Revolution occurred due to a new technological wave of innovation that included electronics and information technology. All of these Industrial Revolutions created tremendous disruptive change for workforces in many nations. However the Fourth Industrial Revolution that is currently taking place is based on industrial automation and artificial intelligence, which are transforming many manufacturing production processes as well as services organisations. This is generating a new wave of uncertainty among both developing and developed nations about the future impact on their workforces.

Globally, the demand for industrial robots is rising rapidly, with the stock of operational industrial robots having reached 1.8 million by the end of 2016, with the number of industrial robots having increased by 21% that year according to the International Federation of Robotics (IFR). The IFR projects that 1.2 million additional new industrial robots will be installed by 2020. IFR data shows that intensive users of robotics in Asia include South Korea, Singapore and Japan, which are also among the global leaders in the intensity of use of industrial robots, while China, South Korea and Japan were estimated to be the largest markets for sales of industrial robots in 2016.

The IFR has estimated that China has already become the largest market for industrial robots in the world and accounts for around 43% of total Asian demand for industrial robots, with the Asian electrical and electronics (E&E) industry and auto sectors being key sources of demand for industrial robots. Since the E&E sector remains a key segment of the manufacturing industry in many East Asian economies, including South Korea, Japan, Taiwan, Thailand, Singapore and Malaysia, this increasing use of industrial robots could have a significant long-term impact on Asia's E&E industry.

The Fourth Industrial Revolution that is transforming global manufacturing is driven by the Internet of Things and the rapid development of industrial automation. This will create considerable disruptive change in many industries, with a report by Bain & Company having estimated that 20% to 25% of current jobs in the US could be eliminated due to automation by the end of the 2020's ("Labor 2030: The Collision of Demographics, Automation and Inequality", K. Harris, A. Kimson and A. Schwedel, Bain & Company Insights, February 2018). In the global auto sector, there has already been a significant shift towards automation, with robots doing much of the work on modern auto production lines. When I visited a BMW factory in Munich, most of work on the assembly line was being done by robots, with human workers playing more of a role in the final stages of the finishing of the car. Other major industries are also shifting towards greater automation, including pharmaceuticals.

However, it is not only physical industrial robots that challenge the future of the human workforce. Advances in digital technology and artificial intelligence are also creating a significant transformation of society. The financial services industry is at the forefront of such changes, as the traditional client-facing role of bank tellers is being rapidly eroded by automated banking solutions through e-banking, ATMs and mobile phone payments software, allowing banks to reduce the number of physical bank branches. Retail banks in developed countries are at the forefront of such technological changes. The global insurance industry is also undergoing considerable change due to the impact of digital technology.

For example, in October 2017 Sweden's Nordea Bank announced plans to cut 6000 jobs due to a technological shift towards digital services and artificial intelligence. Just a week later, on the other side of the world, Australia's National Australia Bank also announced plans for 6000 job cuts over a period of 3 years, the same size of jobs reduction as Nordea Bank, and again due to a strategy for shifting towards greater automation. However, National Australia Bank also announced that 2000 new jobs would be created in information technology-related roles. The financial sectors in developing countries are also facing similar structural trends, as retail banks are shifting towards digital banking solutions and are also facing increasing competition from new competitors such as telecoms companies that are offering e-banking solutions and convenient digital payments applications through their mobile phones using advanced financial technology.

Although telecoms companies are benefiting from digital technology that enables them to compete in the financial services sector, the telecoms industry is also suffering tremendous disruptive change, particularly for traditional fixed line services due to the structural shift towards mobile and internet telephony. For example, in the UK, the total number of minutes of fixed line voice calls declined by 17.6% year-on-year in Q4 2017. Similar trends globally have resulted in significant job cuts worldwide in many telecoms firms with significant fixed line revenues in recent years.

In the automotive industry, far-reaching disruptive change is also transforming the industry due to the shift towards electric vehicles and the development of driverless cars. If there is widespread adoption of driverless vehicle technology over the medium to longer term, this creates an uncertain outlook for the millions of workers who drive vehicles for their livelihood, including taxi drivers and truck drivers. The development of new electric vehicle technology is also likely to create disruptive change for the global infrastructure of petrol stations as well as potential changes to the nature of the auto maintenance and repair industry.

While developed countries are at the forefront of adopting new electric vehicle technology, developing countries are also in the process of adopting new regulations to shift away from petrol engines towards electric vehicles. The Chinese government is reported to be considering a timetable for the ending of petrol car production, while the Indian government is aiming to have all passenger vehicles powered by electricity by 2030. In 2017, China recorded total sales of new energy vehicles (electric vehicles and hybrids) of 777,000, which was up 53% on 2016, including both passenger vehicles and commercial vehicles. While this was still only 2.7% of total vehicle sales in China, the rapid pace of growth in sales of new energy vehicles signals a rapid transformation of the Chinese auto sector towards new energy vehicles.

Millions of jobs will also be lost over the next decade among white-collar workers worldwide due to advances in software and artificial intelligence creating digital disruption, with repetitive jobs, such as accountants, book-keepers and data entry operators expected to be decimated by the growing capabilities of artificial intelligence.

However, there are also industries and professions that are winners from these far-reaching technological changes. The electronics industry will provide the technological backbone for many key new structural trends, such as the rapid growth of robotics and industrial automation, as well as the increasing use of big data and artificial intelligence. These trends are expected to result in rapidly growing demand for semiconductors and display panels.

The rapid growth of online banking and e-payments has also resulted in a rising wave of cybercrime as sophisticated criminal gangs target online financial systems by hacking into the computer systems of financial institutions, companies and individuals. This is also triggering rapid growth in the cybersecurity industry, as financial firms and companies are forced to invest heavily in cyber defence systems. This is creating rapid jobs growth for IT experts in cybersecurity, in a wide range of institutions ranging from banks and corporates to police and the armed forces.

The rapid development of driverless cars is also resulting in much greater use of electronic components and sensors in autos. As governments increasingly invest in building smart cities and townships, there will be rapid growth in the use of integrated circuits in many smart devices that make cities "smart", such as in street lighting, smart meters and Internet-connected home appliances. There is also rapid growth in the use of chips for wearable devices for healthcare and consumer electronics.

Forecasts by the US government's Bureau of Labor Statistics for industry employment in the United States over the decade from 2016 to 2026 highlight some of the sectors most vulnerable to the impact of technological change. The fixed line telecoms industry is expected to face the most severe job losses amongst US industry sectors, as the communications sector increasingly switches to wireless devices such as smartphones and tablets. Publishers and the printing industry are also facing far-reaching structural changes and large job losses due to the switch towards digital media. Similarly, postal services are also expected to face large job losses as society shifts towards digital communications rather than old-fashioned letters and postcards. The 1978 hit song "Please Mr Postman" by the Carpenters will bemuse Generation Z and future generations if they ever hear the song played as they may never have posted a letter or come across a postman.

In the famous 1967 movie "The Graduate", there is an amusing scene when the young Benjamin Braddock, a 21-year-old graduate, is given career advice by a family friend, Mr. McGuire, who says:

> I just want to say one word to you. Plastics. There is a great future in plastics.
> Source: Mr. McGuire speaking to Benjamin Braddock in "The Graduate", United Artists, 1967.

At the time, the United States was going through the baby boom years and was in the midst of rapid consumer spending growth, which was driving demand for plastics products. However with consumer spending growth having slowed considerably in the United States in recent years, the plastics products manufacturing industry is projected by the US Bureau of Labor Statistics to be one of the US industries with the highest number of job losses over the 2016–2026 period (Fig. 8.1).

However, the US Bureau of Labor Statistics study also forecasts significant job gains in many industries, notably in the services sector. Due to the ageing demographic profile of the United States, some of the largest gains in employment over the next decade are projected to be in sectors related to health care. A wide range of healthcare industry segments are projected to benefit from ageing demographics in the United States over the next decade, with strong jobs growth in nursing and residential homes care, hospitals and home health care. The IT sector is also one of the major winners, with IT systems design also projected to be a major source of jobs growth. There will also be substantial jobs growth in food and drinks outlets, such as restau-

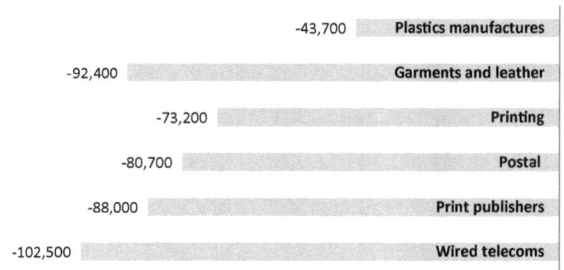

Fig. 8.1 US industries with highest projected job losses, 2016–2026 (number of workers) (*Source* US Bureau of Labor Statistics, Projections of Industry Employment, 2016–2026)

rants, bars and cafes, creating significant new employment growth opportunities (Fig. 8.2).

While the structural trends in the US labor market in terms of industries that are winners and losers for jobs growth will differ to some extent in other countries, some of the broad trends in terms of rising employment in healthcare industries and IT industries are likely to be reflected widely globally, given megatrends of ageing demographics and IT-driven technological change in many nations. The rapid rise of wireless communications as well as digital media also imply large-scale job losses globally in fixed line telephone communications, traditional postal services as well as publishing of printed books, magazines and newspapers.

However, there are also winners in this transition towards digital media. In Singapore, the interactive and digital media industry has grown rapidly, helped by strategic government initiatives to establish local education programmes to provide higher education training in fields such as animation. Singapore's interactive and digital media cluster of industries has grown rapidly, with the flagship for Singapore's industry cluster being Lucas Industrial Light and Magic, which has established a hub in Singapore with around 400 specialist staff, doing work on a broad range of film productions, including the iconic "Star Wars" series of movies.

Other digital media multinationals that have established operations in Singapore include France's Ubisoft, which has around 300–400 people in Singapore, and Japan's Bandainamco, which has around 100 games developers in Singapore. This has created significant growth in digital media jobs in Singapore in fields such as film animation, digital design, games development and digital imaging.

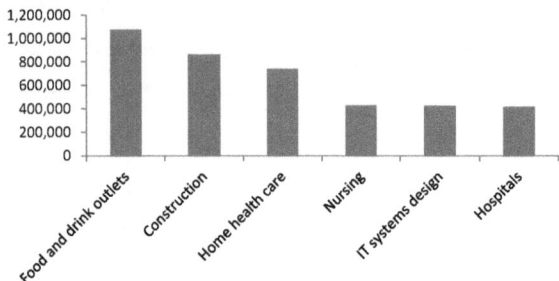

Fig. 8.2 US industries with highest projected job gains, 2016–2026 (*Source* US Bureau of Labor Statistics, Projections of Industry Employment, 2016–2026)

Surfing the Trillion Dollar E-Commerce Wave

Another disruptive technology which is transforming retail and wholesale sales is e-commerce. Physical bricks and mortar retail stores are facing tremendous competition from the rapid growth of e-commerce as millennials use smartphones and tablets to go e-shopping. Major global retail store brands are closing stores as shoppers switch to online purchases. Over 7000 US retail store branch closures were announced by major retailers in 2017, which was approximately double the number of store closures announced in the United States in 2016. These large-scale closures of retail outlets have occurred at a time when US consumer spending growth has been robust. In the UK, an estimated 62,000 job losses occurred in retail stores in 2016, according to the UK government's Office for National Statistics. In June 2018, the famous UK department store company House of Fraser announced that it would close 31 of its 59 stores, with the impact of e-commerce being one of the key factors creating competitive pressures on the firm.

Meanwhile e-commerce is growing rapidly in the United States and Europe, as well as in large developing Asian consumer markets, such as China, India and Indonesia. Developing countries are also facing similar challenges to developed countries in their bricks and mortar retail sectors, as consumers switch to digital shopping for a wide range of goods and services.

In 1993, Wang Wei started a small courier company in China, delivering parcels himself with just one van. From those humble beginnings, he has become the third richest man in China by 2017, with an estimated fortune of USD 27 billion following the listing of his company SF Express on the Shenzen Stock Exchange. Instead of just one van, SF Express now has a fleet of 37 Boeing cargo jets. Five other Chinese entrepreneurs have also become billionaires by setting up their own logistics companies.

These fortunes have been built on a new wave of surging e-commerce sales in China, as consumers are increasingly using their smartphones and tablets to go e-shopping. The total value of online retail sales in China in 2016 reached a staggering Yuan 4.8 billion, equivalent to around USD 750 billion, about the same size as the GDP of the Netherlands.

China is the world's second-largest consumer market, and the total size of China's retail sales reached USD 5 trillion in 2016, bigger than the GDP of any other country in the world except the United States. In 2016, China's retail sales surpassed the total GDP of Japan, the world's third-largest economy.

Online retail sales in China grew by 26% in 2016, more than twice the pace of total retail sales in 2016, which grew at 10.4% year-on-year.

China's boom in online retail sales accelerated further in 2017, with growth in online retail sales for calendar 2017 rising by 32.2% compared to 2016. Online sales of physical goods rose by 29.1% in the first three quarters of 2017 compared to a year ago, accounting for an estimated 14% of total retail sales of consumer goods. However the growth in online sales of services, including fast-growing segments, such as hotel bookings, travel and entertainment, surged by a phenomenal rate of 52.8% growth for the first three quarters of 2017 compared to the same period a year ago.

China has become the world's largest online retail sales market, with Chinese online retail sales reaching USD 1.1 trillion in 2017, more than double the value of US online retail sales, which reached USD 453 billion in 2017. The boom in e-commerce in China has been catalyzed by the rapid growth of e-commerce platforms such as Alibaba, as well as the high level of ownership of smartphones and tablets in China, with an estimated 552 million smartphone users in 2016. China's e-commerce boom is being driven by millennials, who account for an estimated 40% of total online retail sales.

The Chinese government is also encouraging the growth of e-commerce, with the 2017 National People's Congress Work Reports that set out the economic targets for the year ahead highlighting that the government will support the growth of online learning and improve access to e-commerce and express delivery services in rural areas.

In Japan, the world's third-largest economy, consumer spending growth has been very weak over the past 5 years due to the impact of demographic ageing, which has resulted in Japan's population contracting each year. While, this has constrained overall growth in consumer spending to around 0.4% per year in the past decade, online retail sales are growing much more rapidly. In 2015, online retail sales grew by around 7.6% year-on-year, reaching a total estimated value of around USD 115 billion.

China's e-commerce wave is just the beginning of a much larger megatrend that is sweeping across Asia, with the other rising Asian economic giants of India and Indonesia also experiencing very rapid growth in e-commerce, albeit from a much lower level of current online retail sales.

In Malaysia, the government is implementing new policies to accelerate the growth of online retail sales, with the 2017 Budget having announced an initiative to create a Digital Free Zone to be implemented by the Malaysian Digital Economy Corporation. The government has also created a National E-Commerce Strategic Roadmap to accelerate the development of e-commerce and increase its overall contribution to GDP and lift non-tariff barriers to cross-border e-commerce.

The Malaysian government has also appointed Jack Ma, the founder of China's e-commerce giant Alibaba, as Malaysia's digital economy adviser. One early outcome was the launch of Alitrip Malaysia Tourism Pavilion, a new e-commerce tourism booking platform to promote Malaysia for Chinese tourist visitors which is already operational.

Total Asia-Pacific online retail sales are estimated to have exceeded USD 1 trillion in 2016, with rapid growth expected to continue over the medium-term driven by continued rapid expansion in the size of China's online retail e-commerce market as well as the rapid expansion of e-commerce sales in Southeast Asia and South Asia.

The pace of growth of e-commerce in developing Asia will be driven by a number of factors. First, the rapid growth of ownership of mobile devices such as smartphones and tablets and the increasing share of households with Internet access will be a key factor driving retail e-commerce sales.

A second factor will be the increasing adoption of digital payment systems in developing countries, with new financial and communications technology allowing innovative digital payments solutions and wider access to e-banking payments.

Third, the rapid growth of new e-commerce platforms and domestic e-commerce applications customized for the local market will be an important enabler for the growth of domestic retail e-commerce.

Fourth, the growth of logistics companies providing low-cost express delivery solutions will also be important for the growth of retail e-commerce, with China's logistics entrepreneurs having demonstrated the tremendous market growth opportunities for logistics firms due to the growth of e-commerce. At the same time, rapid growth in demand for cross-border e-commerce is also projected, driving growth in demand for delivery services from international logistics companies.

Fifth, the rapid growth of middle-class household incomes and the focus of millennials on digital technology is underpinning the overall growth of e-commerce.

Asia's retail e-commerce boom will create a wide range of new growth opportunities for domestic companies providing e-commerce platforms and logistics solutions. The rapid growth of financial technology will also transform the financial services industry, with new entrants such as telecoms providers also competing to provide e-banking services. The rapid development of financial technology is also accelerating the development of mobile payment solutions for e-commerce transactions.

The e-commerce boom will also transform Asia's retail sales landscape, allowing entrepreneurs with innovative products and services to tap global e-commerce markets without needing to go through conventional wholesale and retail sales channels such as department stores. For example, traditional bookstores have faced tremendous competitive pressure from e-book stores such as Amazon as well as the trend towards buying e-books rather than physical books.

The boom in Asia's e-commerce is a megatrend that will create a wide range of new business opportunities and rapid growth in industries, such as logistics, e-retailing and financial technology for e-commerce. However, together with tremendous new growth opportunities, Asia's e-commerce boom will also bring disruptive change to the retail industry, as traditional retail business models face new forms of competition from online sales.

Other developing country regions have not yet established such deep e-commerce markets, although the pace of growth of e-commerce is also growing rapidly in other developing regions. In the Middle East, where per capita GDP levels are relatively high in the Gulf Co-operation Council (GCC) states and smartphone usage rates are high, e-commerce still accounts for a relatively small share of total retail sales.

In Africa, e-commerce is also relatively small as a share of total retail sales, limited by lack of penetration of smartphones due to relatively low per capita household incomes in many African countries, as well as the need for secure online payments infrastructure.

The Impact of Disruptive Change

Industrial automation, artificial intelligence and big data are transforming the workplace globally, creating tremendous disruption and change for many industries. As a result, millions of jobs will be lost worldwide in the next decade due to the impact of these technological trends. With many nations already struggling with the political repercussions of growing income inequality and a backlash against globalization, these changes herald further increases in economic uncertainty within the workforce.

For governments, companies and individuals worldwide, the impact of robotics, industrial automation and digital disruption will be far-reaching and will create new political and social shock waves in many nations. Redesigning education systems for lifetime learning and career changes and will be a key priority to help to tackle the impact of automation and artificial intelligence on the workforce.

The transformation of industrial competitiveness by digital disruption and robotics also has thrown into question the future relevance of the development model used by many East Asian economies to industrialize. By creating an attractive environment for multinational investment in low-cost manufacturing, many Asian tiger economies were able to transform their agrarian economies through industrialization during the past 50 years, generating higher value-added exports and manufacturing jobs that boosted per capita GDP levels.

Many low-income developing countries in Africa and Latin America still have rural and mineral resources-based economies, and some have tried to adopt development strategies that aim to build competitive advantage in low-cost manufacturing industries. The successful model of East Asian industrialization has become a policy template that many other developing countries have been attempting to follow with varying degrees of success.

However, if industrial automation and the digital economy is shifting competitive advantage in segments of low-cost manufacturing back to higher income economies, then the future development path for low-income developing countries that are still heavily focused on the agricultural and mineral resource exports will become more uncertain.

Developing countries that have industrialized based on attracting low-cost manufacturing industries are also facing a dual competitive threat, as they face competitive challenges from developing countries with significantly lower manufacturing wage costs for attracting low value-added manufacturing industries, while also facing new competition from developed countries using industrial automation to produce manufactures.

9

The New Global Technology Wars

Disruptive technological change in the global economy from the Internet of Things, industrial automation, robotics, digitalization, artificial intelligence and big data is creating new competitive challenges for developing countries. These technological changes are dividing nations worldwide along economic fault lines of technology, with high technology economies far better placed to compete in this rapidly evolving global economic landscape. The new drivers of competitive advantage are increasingly shifting away from natural resource endowments of agriculture, fisheries and minerals, towards knowledge economies built on human talent in information technology and science, as well as global leadership in innovation and research and development (R&D) in industries driving technological change, such as robotics, artificial intelligence, electronics, biotechnology and e-commerce.

Winston Churchill predicted the importance of technological change for the future competitiveness of economies at a time when the world was deep in conflict, as the Axis powers sought to conqueor the world by military force.

> "Let us go forward in malice to none and good will to all. Such plans offer far better prizes than taking away other people's provinces or lands or grinding them down in exploitation. The empires of the future are the empires of the mind."
>
> Winston S. Churchill, 'The Gift of a Common Tongue', Speech at Harvard University, 6th September 1943.

Many developing countries which have focused on exporting agricultural or resource commodities are relatively poorly positioned to compete in this new global economy. Often these nations have not invested sufficiently

© The Author(s) 2018
R. Biswas, *Emerging Markets Megatrends*,
https://doi.org/10.1007/978-3-319-78123-5_9

for decades in their advanced educational infrastructure in key fields, such as information technology, science or biotechnology. Their governments often have not developed industrial or technology policies that are effective in accelerating the growth of technology industries. In addition to lack of human talent pools, the lack of physical infrastructure can also be a significant constraint to attracting technology industries. Many of the developing nations in Africa, Latin America and the Middle East still are in this grouping of nations that are facing a widening technology gap in comparison with the OECD nations and a grouping of technological leaders among developing economies such as China, Taiwan, Singapore, Israel, UAE, Malaysia and India.

The technological divide between nations is also reflected in the location of the world's leading technology firms. Companies which are global technology leaders usually have their headquarters located in advanced economies in the OECD, or rapidly industrializing economies in Asia, rather than in low-income commodity-exporting nations, due to a range of considerations, including educational infrastructure, access to human capital talent pools, and proximity to leading research universities and institutes.

Some developing countries have become knowledge hubs, due to their large pools of highly skilled professionals. India is an attractive location for global technology firms to establish R&D hubs because of the large pool of skilled graduates and postgraduates in leading Indian universities in professions such as physics, engineering, mathematics and medicine. Many Indian companies have become leading multinationals in software and IT services, such as Infosys, Tata Consulting Services, Wipro, Tech Mahindra and Larsen & Toubro Infotech. China is also a leading global hub for R&D, both for global multinationals as well as the fast-growing number of Chinese multinationals that are global leaders in technology, such as Huawei in global telecommunications, Alibaba in e-commerce and Baidu, a leading global internet company.

However, for most developing countries, there is a vast technological gap between their economies and the advanced nations of the OECD or the industrializing nations of Asia, such as South Korea. The new era of disruptive technological change is putting tremendous pressure on developing countries to transform their economies or risk being trapped in the status of low growth economies with weak progress in per capita GDP growth, a slow rate of improvement in human development indicators and potential rising social tensions due to high levels of unemployment or underemployment.

Challenges for Commodity Exporting Nations

For developing countries, one major source of economic vulnerability is exposure to a high share of commodities in total exports. Commodity exporting countries face considerable economic vulnerability to large changes in the value of national exports and their fiscal revenues due to volatile global commodity prices. Around half of developing countries worldwide are still heavily reliant on commodity exports, making economic diversification a key economic development priority (Fig. 9.1).

Amongst the world's developing country regions, East Asia has very limited exposure to commodity exports, due to the rapid industrialization of the region over the past 50 years. Southeast Asia has also significantly reduced its vulnerability to commodity exports, as a number of ASEAN economies have industrialized during the past four decades, including Singapore, Malaysia and Thailand, while the Vietnamese economy has experienced a very substantial economic transformation into an industrial economy within the past decade.

However, most of the other developing regions in the world still have a very high share of commodities in their total exports, including Africa and South America. The export structure of West Africa and Middle Africa is completely dominated by commodity exports, while for East Africa and North Africa, commodity exports still account for a large share of total exports. Despite the industrial development of Brazil, the overall export structure of South America is also has a high share of commodity exports, comparable to the share of commodities in African exports.

Therefore despite decades of economic policy efforts by many African and South American countries to diversify their export base, the recent trade

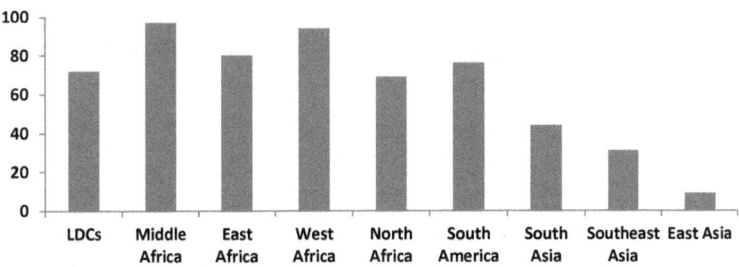

Fig. 9.1 Commodity exports as share of total exports (2014–2015) (*Source* UNCTAD, State of Commodity Dependence, 2016)

statistics continue to show that these developing regions still have an overall export structure that is heavily reliant on commodity exports, making their economies vulnerable to commodity price volatility.

Recent volatility in world commodity prices continues to highlight the considerable macroeconomic vulnerability many commodity exporting nations still face. Following the slump in world oil prices in 2014, many developing countries which are heavily reliant on oil and gas exports faced a sharp slump in oil and gas export revenues as well as significantly reduced fiscal revenues. Developing countries that suffered a substantial negative economic impact due to the slump in world oil prices in 2014 included Saudi Arabia, UAE, Kuwait, Nigeria, Angola, Russia and Venezuela.

Saudi Arabia's Vision 2030 Roadmap

The collapse in world oil prices in late 2014 created a severe economic shock for the Saudi Arabian economy due to its high level of dependency on oil exports both as the dominant source of export earnings as well as fiscal revenue. Sharp declines in oil-related fiscal revenue during 2015 and 2016 resulted in its fiscal balance shifting dramatically from a surplus of 5.8% of GDP in 2013 to a fiscal deficit of 15.8% of GDP in 2015 and an even larger fiscal deficit of 17.2% of GDP in 2016, according to the IMF's Staff Report on Saudi Arabia in October 2017 (IMF Country Report 17/316). The impact of falling oil prices also resulted in the current account shifting from a surplus of 9.8% of GDP in 2014 to a deficit of 8.7% of GDP by 2015.

Saudi Arabia responded to the 2014 oil price shock by launching a major new strategic roadmap called Vision 2030 to transform its economy and diversify the economic structure significantly to reduce its vulnerability to oil. In order to strengthen the capacity of government departments to deliver this long-term roadmap for transforming the economy, a medium-term National Transformation Program has also been launched setting targets for 2020.

Saudi Arabia's main goal is to diversify its economy and reduce its long-term dependency on oil exports. As part of this plan, Saudi Arabia has set an objective of increasing foreign direct investment inflows from around USD 8 billion per year in 2016 to around USD 19 billion per year by 2020. Tax policy reforms have also been implemented to diversify the fiscal revenue base, including the introduction of a new VAT tax from 1 January 2018 and a medium term plan for reducing energy and water subsidies.

Saudi Arabia is seeking to attract East Asian foreign direct investment into Saudi Arabia to help the economic transformation process. In March 2017, His Royal Highness King Salman bin Abdulaziz visited a number of Asian countries, including China and Japan, in order to strengthen bilateral economic ties and attract investment inflows into the diversification of Saudi Arabia's economy.

A key area where Saudi Arabia is seeking greater Chinese investment and technology is in renewable energy, as Saudi Arabia is planning to ramp up its use of solar energy in order to reduce domestic consumption of its oil resources. China is a world leader in the manufacturing of solar panels, and Saudi Arabia is aiming to install around 40 gigawatts of solar energy production by 2030. Saudi Arabia is planning to invest around USD 30 billion to 50 billion in its renewable energy programme by 2030, and China could become a key partner in Saudi Arabia's renewable energy programme.

A key focus of the visit to Japan by His Royal Highness King Salman bin Abdulaziz during his Asia visit programme was to attract investment by Japanese firms into Saudi Arabia. A plan to create special economic zones in Saudi Arabia that will facilitate Japanese trade and investment is under discussion. A joint Saudi-Japanese 2030 Vision Group has already been created earlier, in September 2016, when then Deputy Crown Prince Mohammed bin Salman (who subsequently was appointed Crown Prince of Saudi Arabia in June 2017) and Japanese Prime Minister Shinzo Abe agreed to setup the Joint Group for Saudi-Japan Vision 2030 to develop joint economic projects that would contribute to Saudi Arabia's National Transformation Plan.

Saudi investment ties with Japan have also strengthened significantly following the joint venture setup in late 2016 between the Public Investment Fund of Saudi Arabia and Japan's SoftBank Group Corp. for creating a USD 100 billion technology fund called the SoftBank Vision Fund, with the Public Investment Fund of Saudi Arabia expected to invest USD 45 billion in this new fund. In May 2017, the SoftBank Vision Fund announced it had raised USD 93 billion, with plans for a second Softbank Vision Fund signalled in early 2018.

Saudi Arabia is pursuing these new economic strategies with considerable urgency in order to substantially restructure its economy to reduce its oil dependency and vulnerability to oil price fluctuations as well as to boost the development of technology industries.

Other developing countries that have a high level of dependency on commodity exports also need to increase the diversification of their economies and reduce vulnerability to commodity exports in order to improve their resilience to external shocks that could trigger future economic crises.

However, although such policy goals have been attempted frequently by many developing countries over recent decades, achieving significant diversification has proven to be very difficult for many developing countries, as they have frequently been unable to achieve competitive advantage in exports of manufacturing and services.

Timor Leste: Vulnerability to Depleting Oil and Gas Revenues

In contrast to Saudi Arabia, which has achieved a high level of economic development and institutional infrastructure as a result of decades of large-scale oil revenues, Timor Leste is at the other end of the spectrum, having emerged as an independent nation in 2002 after years of devastating conflict, with a very low per capita GDP and high levels of poverty, as well as weak institutional infrastructure for governance. Like Saudi Arabia, Timor Leste is highly dependent on oil and gas revenues for its export and fiscal revenues.

The outlook for Timor Leste faces many significant challenges. The fundamental structural problem that Timor Leste confronts is that its oil and gas reserves at its major current offshore fields are rapidly depleting, without any agreement for the development of other major oil and gas fields.

After achieving independence, economic growth was accelerated by the development of the Bayu Undan field. The revenues from this field have helped to boost the Timor Leste's annual economic growth rate between 2007 and 2012 to an average double-digit pace per year. However, since then, the pace of growth has moderated as the oil and gas revenues from the field have gradually diminished, partly reflecting the slump in world oil and gas prices since 2014 but also due to the gradual depletion of oil and gas production rates.

Due to the impact of protracted conflict, lack of civil administrative structures and shortages of skilled workers, Timor Leste has faced difficulties in addressing high levels of poverty and malnutrition. Moreover, there have been episodes of renewed civil unrest after independence which have also delayed economic development. However, efforts by the government together with multilateral institutions such as the World Bank and United Nations are gradually resulting in some progress.

Timor Leste has had to rebuild its government institutions, overcome severe shortages of skilled workers as well as tackling issues such as corruption. The quality of physical infrastructure is also still very weak although the government has ramped up efforts to accelerate infrastructure development. All this has resulted in slow progress in achieving economic development goals.

Timor Leste remains heavily dependent on oil and gas, which currently funds around 90% of its annual government revenue. Oil and gas also account for around 80% of GDP and 93% of exports. However, the country is also facing depleting reserves from its major Bayu Undan oil and gas field, with reserves from this field projected to be exhausted by around 2024.

The Timor Leste government has taken the important step of creating a sovereign wealth fund to set aside some of their oil and gas revenues for the future when oil and gas resources are exhausted. An estimated USD 18 billion has been paid into this fund from the oil revenue from the Bayu Undan field, with the fund balance at the end of 2016 being USD 15.8 billion, slightly below the peak level of USD 16.5 billion at the end of 2014. A total of USD 8.5 billion has been withdrawn from the Fund since inception. Return on investment since inception has added USD 3.2 billion to the Fund, although drawdowns for economic development of Timor Leste have resulted in some outflows from the Fund.

In 2016, total drawdowns were USD 1.2 billion while inflows were USD 224 million from petroleum revenues and USD 648 million from investment returns. This indicates that the Fund is no longer receiving significant new inflows from petroleum revenues and has become heavily reliant on investment performance to maintain its asset levels given significant annual drawdowns. Consequently, there is an increasing vulnerability to volatility in international capital markets and any protracted global equities market slump could significantly reduce investment revenues as well as the overall valuation of the Fund.

However, this fund will also rapidly be drawn down once oil and gas revenues from Bayu Undan decline more steeply as reserves diminish. In the meantime, an urgent challenge facing the government is to try to diversify the economy to reduce vulnerability to oil revenues. Key strategic priorities will be to improve physical infrastructure, strengthen human capital, and develop new growth industries such as tourism.

However, due to the depletion of oil and gas reserves at the Bayu Undan field, there is considerable urgency for the development of a major new field called Greater Sunrise, which will help to mitigate the impact of declining production at Bayu Undan. However, this project has been significantly delayed due to a protracted territorial dispute between Timor Leste and Australia that is being considered by the Permanent Court of Arbitration in The Hague.

A major positive breakthrough in the negotiations occurred in August 2017, when the two countries reached an agreement on key elements of a deal to resolve the maritime boundary dispute. A critical part of the deal is an agreement on a special regime for the development and revenue-sharing of the Greater Sunrise field. The new agreement was signed by Australia and Timor Leste at the United Nations headquarters in New York on 6 March 2018.

The oil companies that have the exploration and development rights for the Greater Sunrise field are Woodside Petroleum, ConocoPhillips, Osaka Gas and Royal Dutch Shell. The reserves of this field are estimated at 144 cubic metres of gas and 250 million barrels of condensate, with an estimated value of USD 45–50 billion. Once the field is developed, this will provide a major new source of exports and fiscal revenue for the Timor Leste government. However, this is dependent on a final agreement between Timor Leste and Australia on the joint development of the field, as well as a commercial decision to proceed with bringing the field into production. The commercial negotiations about how the Greater Sunrise field can be developed have also been protracted, as the Timor Leste government has been seeking to have a refinery built in Timor Leste to create additional investment and jobs, while the oil companies have argued that a floating LNG platform is more commercially viable, particularly following the slump in Asian LNG prices since 2014.

Unless the new Greater Sunrise oil and gas project can get the green light soon, the Timor Leste economy could face a rapidly deteriorating fiscal position after 2024 and become highly dependent on donor aid as well as depleting the assets of its sovereign wealth fund, the Petroleum Fund.

In a scenario, where the development of the Greater Sunrise project takes some years to go ahead, this could make economic development in Timor Leste much more dependent on international donor financing as well as significant public sector involvement in public–private partnerships for infrastructure development over the medium to long term. This will be a very different infrastructure financing landscape compared to the other Southeast Asian LDCs, such as Myanmar, Cambodia and Laos.

The relatively high country risk for Timor Leste due political uncertainty and heavy economic reliance on a single depleting oil and gas field is likely to be a major deterrent to private capital inflows for economic development, unless the Greater Sunrise project goes ahead, perhaps with the help of risk mitigation mechanisms. According to the World Risk Report 2016 produced by Bundnis Entwicklung Hilft with the UNU-EHS, Timor Leste was ranked as the 12th highest risk country out of 171 countries ranked due to its vulnerability to natural disasters combined with its weak economic capacity to cope with the impact of such events.

Foreign direct investment inflows have been negligible in recent years, with an estimated USD 50 million per year of inflows between 2013 and 2015, and FDI inflows estimated to have weakened further to only USD 5 million dollars in 2016, according to UNCTAD FDI estimates.

The main opportunity for large-scale new FDI inflows will be if a commercial agreement can be reached on the development of the Greater Sunrise oil and gas project. A key priority will be to attract new private investment into other sectors, with tourism and agriculture having potential opportunities for FDI inflows.

However, unless rapid progress is made with developing the Greater Sunrise project or through accelerated development of other sectors, Timor Leste faces a very challenging economic outlook with risks of declining fiscal revenues, drawdowns of its sovereign wealth fund assets and a vicious cycle of deteriorating fiscal and export revenues, declining living standards and potential rising social tensions that could escalate into internal conflict. The Timor Leste economy highlights the challenges facing low-income developing countries that remain highly reliant on commodity exports and without significant technology industries or human capital resources in technology.

Building Knowledge Economies

Although commodity-dependent nations face considerable challenges due to the volatility of commodity prices and depletion of their finite commodity resources, low-cost manufacturing exporting countries are also facing a perfect storm from disruptive technological change, creating considerable uncertainty about the future of their industrial development strategies.

Despite significant progress by many industrializing nations in reducing their reliance on commodity exports and increasing the share of exports of manufactures in their total exports, there are still significant hurdles to their ability to shift their structure of production to higher value-added industries.

A key differentiating factor between low-income developing countries and the advanced and rapidly industrializing economies is found in the relative standards of higher education. In North America, the tertiary education enrolment ratio for the relevant age cohort in 2015 was 84%, which was the highest ratio among all the regions of the world. This was followed by the EU, which had a tertiary education enrolment ratio of 68%, and then by Latin America with 45% and East Asia, with a ratio of 39%. However, the low-income regions of South Asia and Sub-Saharan Africa had extremely low tertiary enrolment ratios, at 21 and 9%, respectively. This highlights the extreme differences in the level of tertiary education among new cohorts of workers entering the workforce (Fig. 9.2).

When the tertiary enrolment ratios are compared at a country level, even more significant differences become apparent. In South Korea, the tertiary enrolment ratio is very impressive, at 93%, higher than the USA and

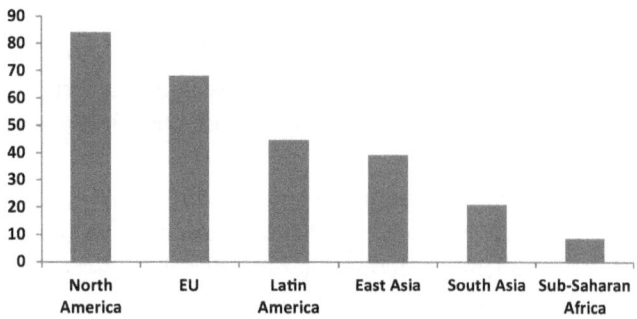

Fig. 9.2 Tertiary education enrolment ratio by region 2015 share (*Source* World Bank Development Indicators)

Germany. Australia and New Zealand also have very high tertiary enrolment ratios compared to most other developed countries. In contrast, many low-income developing countries in Asia and Africa have significantly lower tertiary enrolment ratios, with India at 27%, South Africa at 19%, Bangladesh at 13%, and Rwanda at 8% (Fig. 9.3).

National spending on R&D also is a significant factor that contributes to the technological divide between advanced and industrialized developing economies on one side of the spectrum, in comparison with other developing countries on the other. For example, gross domestic spending on R&D in South Africa was around 0.7% of GDP and in Mexico was around 0.5% of GDP per year, according to the most recent estimate based on the OECD statistics (OECD 2017). In stark contrast, the OECD average spending on R&D was 2.4% of GDP in 2015, with the United States at 2.7%, Switzerland at 3.4% and Germany at 2.9%. Meanwhile, South Korea and

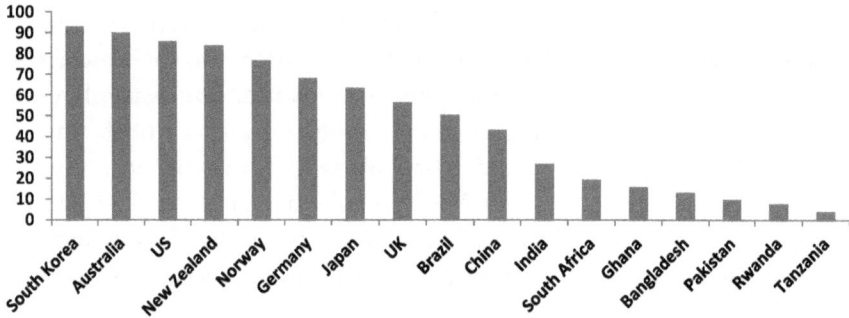

Fig. 9.3 Tertiary education enrolment rate by country share of university age cohort 2015 (*Source* World Bank)

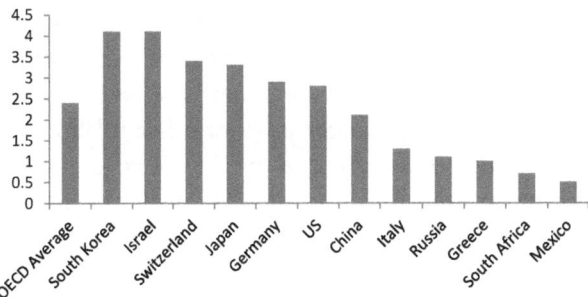

Fig. 9.4 R&D spending as share of GDP (*Source* OECD)

Israel lead the world, with both nations spending around 4.1% of GDP on R&D (Fig. 9.4).

Many developing nations are responding to these challenges by embarking on far-reaching economic transformation strategies, to try to restructure their economies to improve their resilience to these trends.

China's Industrial Economy

Since Deng Xiaoping's economic reforms commenced in 1978, China's rapid economic growth has been based on a model of attracting foreign direct investment into low-cost manufacturing industries. This created very rapid economic growth along China's coastal provinces, as the Pearl River Delta in Guangdong Province and the Yangtze River Delta around Shanghai have become major global manufacturing hubs over the past 40 years.

However, since 2010, rapidly rising manufacturing wages in coastal China have resulted in global multinationals seeking new hubs for low-cost manufacturing for sectors, such as textiles, garments and footwear, as well as some segments of the electrical and electronics industry.

A number of factors have driven the rapid upturn in Chinese manufacturing wages in the coastal provinces that are the major hubs for low-cost manufacturing in China.

First, China is beginning to feel the effects of ageing demographics, due to the impact of China's one child policy introduced in 1980. As a result, the number of youth joining the workforce each year has already begun to decline, and this trend will continue to intensify for future cohorts of workers entering the labour force over the next two decades. Although the Chinese government has reformed its one child policy to allow families to have more children according to various qualifying factors, the impact of these reforms will take many years to impact on the ageing demographic profile of China since the reforms were only recently introduced since 2014.

Second, the coastal provinces of China that have become key hubs of manufacturing have been drawing on large pools of migrant labour from the inland provinces for many years. However, due to Chinese government policies to try to improve economic development in inland Chinese provinces to reduce economic and social inequalities, the availability of migrant labour for coastal Chinese provinces has tightened, as rapid growth in inland Chinese provinces has created rapid growth in employment, reducing the attractiveness of low-wage manufacturing jobs in coastal China. This has been one of the factors contributing to more rapid manufacturing wages growth in coastal China since 2010.

Third, China is facing a significant slowdown in productivity growth as the marginal productivity of capital is declining. During the first three decades of China's rapid economic growth, very high rates of investment resulted in very high productivity growth rates as modern infrastructure as well as plant and equipment was built in China. This resulted in rapid productivity growth in parallel with rapidly rising manufacturing wages, allowing increases in unit labour costs to remain low. However, as the quality of infrastructure and manufacturing equipment has converged towards leading global standards, it has become increasingly difficult to maintain rapid productivity growth, resulting in rising unit labour costs, which in turn have increased pressures on Chinese manufacturers to either pass on higher costs to clients or else to cut down on profit margins.

These factors have driven up Chinese manufacturing wage costs more rapidly since 2010. As Chinese manufacturing wages have been rising rapidly, countries, such as Bangladesh, Vietnam and Cambodia have attracted significant new investment from multinationals into their garments industries, helping to boost their industrial growth.

Faced with this growing challenge from other developing countries with lower labour costs, while also confronted with the risk of increasing competition from industrial automation in developed countries, China has implemented a new manufacturing strategy that sets out a 10-year roadmap to transform the competitiveness of their manufacturing sector called the "Made in China 2025" strategy which was launched in May 2015.

The strategy aims to make China a competitive global manufacturing hub in higher value-added industries over the decade from 2015 to 2025. Some of the key industries identified in the Made in China 2025 strategy are aerospace, new energy vehicles, advanced railway equipment, industrial automation and robotics, advanced medical equipment, new materials, biopharmaceuticals and advanced electronics.

China's advanced manufacturing sector has shown rapid growth since the new strategy was launched, with high tech manufacturing sector showing growth of 13.4% year-on-year in value added during the first three quarters of 2017 compared to the same period a year ago. This was double the growth rate of the value added by the overall manufacturing sector, which grew at 6.7% year-on-year during the same period.

In his speech to the 19th Communist Party Congress on 18 October 2017, President Xi Jinping announced that a key objective of the nation's future economic reform agenda would be to transform Chinese enterprises into world-class, globally competitive firms that are leaders in innovation in areas, such as modern engineering technology and disruptive technology, as well as in leading technology industries such as aerospace.

Chinese firms have significantly ramped up their outbound M&A acquisitions of foreign technology firms since 2014 as they have tried to build up their competitive advantage in advanced manufacturing following the launch of the "Made in China 2025" policy. However this has triggered a political backlash in the US and EU as Chinese firms have acquired various Western technology firms. The acquisition of Germany's Kuka AG by China's Midea Group Co for Euro 3.7 billion in 2016 was met with significant political opposition in Germany and the EU, although the deal was eventually able to be completed.

The European Commission has proposed a new process for reviewing foreign investments that could have security implications, although any recommendations are likely to be non-binding on EU member countries. However in the US, there has been a more severe response to Chinese M&A bids for US firms under the Trump Administration, with the US government's Committee on Foreign Investment in the United States (CFIUS) having blocked a number of major Chinese bids. In February 2018, the bid by China's Hubei Xinyan Equity Investment Partnership for US semiconductors testing firm Xcerra was withdrawn after the CFIUS did not clear the transaction. In September 2017, President Trump also issued an executive order blocking the proposed acquisition of US firm Lattice Semiconductor Corporation by a US incorporated private equity firm Canyon Bridge Capital Partners Inc. owned by China Reform Fund Management Co. US-China frictions over technology escalated further in 2018 when the US Department of Commerce banned US firms from providing products to Chinese telecoms firm ZTE. The US government decision was due to their finding that ZTE had violated an agreement made with the US government arising from earlier violations of US bans on exports of products to North Korea and Iran which had resulted in ZTE paying fines of USD 900 million to the US government. The ban on sales of US components to ZTE crippled their business operations in mid-2018, resulting in high level negotiations as the Chinese government tried to negotiate a deal with the US to allow ZTE to again purchase US products.

Despite the frictions with other nations in regard to Chinese M&A acquisitions of foreign technology firms, China has made rapid progress in developing new strategic industries that are boosting value-added output in the manufacturing sector. China has a considerable advantage in undertaking such far-reaching structural transformation of its economy because the size of domestic demand has grown so large as China has ascended to becoming the world's second-largest economy. Over the past five years, the role of consumption has become an increasingly important growth engine for the economy, replacing the role of investment and exports, which had been the key growth engines between 1978 and 2012. For example, the size of China's domestic auto market has grown tremendously over the past decade, with China has become the world's largest market for passenger vehicle sales since 2010, when it overtook the United States. In 2016, total domestic auto sales in China surpassed the 28 million vehicle mark. This represents a very large increase in annual sales compared to a decade ago in 2006, when Chinese auto sales were 7.2 million cars. This has helped to boost the development of China's new energy vehicles sector, including electric vehicles and hybrids. China has already become the world's largest producer of new energy vehicles, with quarterly production reaching 150,000 vehicles in Q1 2018, which was up 154% year-on-year.

China's GDP data for 2017 clearly demonstrates that China's new growth engine is consumption, which contributed 58.8% of total GDP growth in 2017. President Xi Jinping emphasized the key role that consumption would play in underpinning future Chinese growth during his speech to the 19th Communist Party of China (CPC) National Congress, which is of strategic importance to the sustained strong growth momentum of the Chinese economy over the next decade and beyond and supporting the transition to a higher value-added manufacturing sector.

Malaysia's Economic Transformation Programme

During the period when Malaya was under British colonial rule, the structure of the economy was heavily dominated by commodities, such as tin, rubber and palm oil. Following independence, Malaysia's economy continued to be highly dependent on production and exports of commodities, with commodities accounting for a large share of GDP and exports until the 1970s.

During the 1980s and 1990s, Malaysia achieved rapid economic growth and industrialization by attracting low-value-added manufacturing such as electrical and electronics low-cost assembly to Malaysia. However, as in other East Asian industrializing economies, rising manufacturing wages in Malaysia have made it increasingly difficult for Malaysia to attract new investment into low-cost manufacturing.

Recognizing that historical growth engines were slowing down, in 2010, the Malaysian government announced the launch of an Economic Transformation Programme to restructure the economy towards higher value-added industries, by identifying key industries that would be growth engines for the economy over the long term.

A key focus of the Economic Transformation Programme was transforming Malaysia from a low productivity growth economy towards a higher productivity growth economy. The Malaysian government recognized that a key concern for the medium to long-term economic outlook was that Malaysia could become stuck in a middle-income trap if significant measures were not taken in order to improve Malaysia's competitiveness and shift away from low-wage industries towards higher value-adding.

Eleven priority growth industries were selected through a detailed process of stakeholder consultations between the government and the private sector. The eleven sectors were:

- Financial Services;
- Agriculture;
- Oil, Gas and Energy;
- Electronics;
- Healthcare;
- Education;
- Business Services;
- Tourism;
- Retail and Wholesale Trade;
- Petrochemicals.

The Malaysian economic strategy has resulted in significant foreign direct investment inflows into these strategic priority sectors, helping to accelerate the shift towards higher value-adding industries.

The electrical and electronics sector is already a key segment of Malaysia's manufacturing industry and accounts for around 35% of total Malaysian merchandise exports. Exports of electrical and electronic equipment, such as electrical equipment, integrated circuits and semiconductors accounted for around 50% of total Malaysian exports to the United States.

Strong global growth in demand for smartphones and tablets are an important driver for the Asian electronics manufacturing supply chain, supporting demand for key electronics components produced by the Malaysian electronics sector such as semiconductors.

The upturn in global auto industry momentum is also supporting demand for semiconductors, due to the increasing use of electronics in new auto models. Demand for semiconductors for hybrid and electric vehicles is expected to be the fastest growing segment of the automotive semiconductors market.

Another key structural positive trend is the global growth in demand for electronics due to the Fourth Industrial Revolution and the Internet of Things. As a result, a key source of electronics demand growth will be from industrial demand, for sectors such as industrial automation, smart meters and automated lighting.

An important growth market for electronics will be Internet-connected devices for smart cities. A related underlying global trend supporting the electronics industry is the rapid growth of robotics.

Therefore, Malaysia's electronics industry is an important value-adding growth industry that is leveraged to key global technological trends such as industrial automation and the Internet of Things as well as the rapid growth in use of electronics for wearable devices, electric and driverless cars and for smart city technology.

The Malaysian government is also investing in the development of the digital economy through the creation of infrastructure such as technology parks.

A key challenge facing Malaysia has been to boost productivity and innovation. One measure of Malaysia's relatively weak performance in innovation is that R&D spending as a share of GDP as been relatively low in comparison to the OECD average as well as compared with Asian industrial nations, such as South Korea, Japan and China. Despite a gradual uptrend in R&D spending as a share of GDP, Malaysian R&D spending in 2015 was still at 1.3% of GDP, approximately half the OECD average and considerably below the R&D spending in leading R&D nations such as South Korea and Japan (Fig. 9.5).

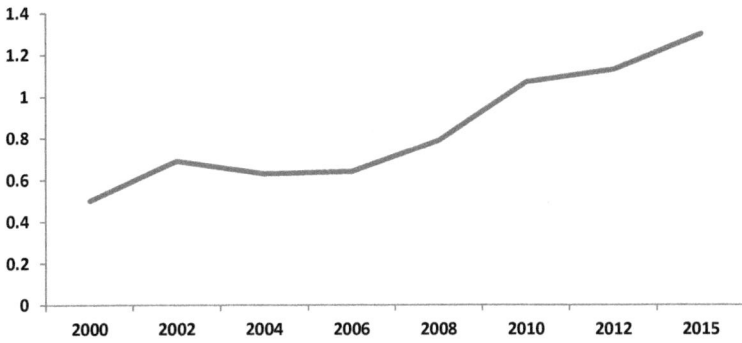

Fig. 9.5 Malaysia's R&D spending as percentage share of GDP (*Source* Malaysian national R&D survey)

Future Industrialization of Emerging Markets

The competitive landscape confronting low-income and lower middle income countries attempting to industrialize their economies is becoming increasingly challenging. While, the vast size of China's domestic consumer market has allowed China to restructure its economy away from export-driven industrial growth towards a new model of manufacturing and service sector growth driven by domestic demand, many other developing countries may face a more difficult path as they often lack the domestic market size to restructure their economies away from export-driven growth.

Many low income developing countries are still heavily reliant on commodity exports, and lack the educational infrastructure to generate the skilled workers needed to build a technology sector. Building such vocational training and tertiary education infrastructure will be a protracted process even if nations invest heavily in new educational infrastructure. Establishing competitive advantage in technology industries will also require increasing R&D spending and creating clusters of excellence in technology research in universities and research institutes. Even if nations are able to embark on such technological transformation programs, the process will require a medium term to long term timeframe.

Due to the rapid pace of technological change, the technological divide between emerging markets with fast-growing technology industries and large talent pools of IT workers and many low-income developing countries that are reliant on primary commodities for exports and fiscal revenue is likely to become wider and deeply entrenched. The path to transitioning out of the low technology grouping of nations could become an increasingly large obstacle over time. This risks creating a deepening divide among developing countries based on the talent pools of science and IT human capital, depth of technology industries and capacity for innovation and R&D.

Therefore an urgent priority for many developing countries will be to accelerate the development and implementation of technology policies. Meanwhile OECD countries and the technology leaders amongst emerging markets are also investing heavily in further strengthening their technological competitiveness, making it increasingly challenging for low technology nations to bridge the technology divide.

10

The Least Developed Countries: Opportunities and Challenges

Among the 193 member nations of the United Nations, there are 47 countries that are still classified as Least Developed Countries (LDCs) by the United Nations. The Committee for Development Policy of the United Nations Economic and Social Council assesses the status of these nations every 3 years in order to determine whether any should be graduated from their status as LDCs.

The status of Least Developed Country is not intended to be a form of punishment or condemnation. The objective is not to classify a nation as an economic failure or to brand a country as having weak economic development prospects. Rather it is intended to give greater economic development assistance and concessional development financing from the international donor community to assist LDCs to accelerate their economic development.

The factors that are taken into account by the United Nations in determining whether a nation can graduate from Least Developed Country Status include low gross national income per capita, weak human assets index scores and extreme economic vulnerability index scores. The ability of a country to maintain sustainable development after graduating from LDC status is also taken into account.

The UN listing of LDCs first commenced in 1971, and since that time, many nations have been added to the list but only five have graduated from LDC status. These five countries are Botswana, Capo Verde, Maldives, Samoa and Equatorial Guinea. Vanuatu was scheduled to graduate in 2017, but due to the impact of a devastating cyclone, the United Nations decided to postpone its graduation to 2020.

© The Author(s) 2018
R. Biswas, *Emerging Markets Megatrends*,
https://doi.org/10.1007/978-3-319-78123-5_10

The inability of so many developing nations to exit from LDC status after many decades highlights the tremendous challenges facing a large number of low income developing nations, many of which are predominantly dependent on commodity exports and exposed to terms of trade shocks when global prices for their key export commodities slump or if weather events destroy their agricultural production.

Many LDCs are also highly vulnerable to natural disasters. Cyclones have recently devastated the economies of Vanuatu (2015) and Haiti (2016), while a massive earthquake and aftershocks caused tremendous destruction and loss of lives in Nepal (2015). Over the past half century, a number of cyclones have also caused catastrophic flooding, tidal surges and millions of deaths in Bangladesh.

The economic and social structure of these 47 LDC nations varies considerably, ranging from small island states with low populations such as Vanuatu and Solomon Islands to very populous nations such as Bangladesh, Ethiopia and Myanmar. The total population of the LDCs is currently estimated at around 12.9% of the total world population but these nations account for only around 1% of world exports (State of the Least Developed Countries 2017, UN-OHRLLS, July 2017).

Conflict is also a major cause of economic and social disintegration in a number of LDCs, including Somalia, Yemen and South Sudan. Some nations such as Timor Leste and Cambodia are also still suffering from the legacy of past conflicts, which have significantly increased the economic development challenges they are facing. The genocide that occurred in Cambodia under the Pol Pot regime destroyed an entire generation of human talent, creating a long process for Cambodia to rebuild its human capital and skilled professional talent that is necessary for economic development.

However despite the tremendous challenges, nine LDCs were assessed by the UN to have reached their graduation thresholds in 2015. These LDCs included Bhutan, Nepal, Sao Tome and Principe, Solomon Islands and Timor Leste, which reached their thresholds for the first time, while Vanuatu is scheduled by the UN to graduate in 2020 and Angola in 2021. Meanwhile Kiribati met its threshold level for the second time in 2015.

The UN Committee for Development Policy has recommended in its 2018 LDC review that four countries should graduate, subject to the approval of the UN Economic and Social Council and then by the UN General Assembly. These four nations are Bhutan, Kiribati, Sao Tome and Principe as well as the Solomon Islands. Bhutan has identified 2023 as the date that it will intend to graduate, as its current five-year plan will be a transition phase towards graduation. Although Nepal and Timor Leste also met the graduation criteria, the UN Committee decided to postpone the decision about their graduation until the next triennial review in 2021, due to the tremendous economic and social challenges both nations are facing. The UN Committee for Development Policy also determined that Bangladesh, Laos and Myanmar met the graduation threshold criteria for the first time in 2018, which would put them on a path for graduation in 2021.

The Challenges of Graduation

The process of graduation from LDC status needs to be carefully planned and managed, in order to ensure that the graduating LDC does not slump back down into LDC status. Consequently the UN assessment process of graduation requires a nation to reach the appropriate thresholds on two consecutive three-yearly reviews, to ensure that the nation is making sustainable development progress in attaining the graduation goals.

When countries graduate from LDC status, they will transition away from international support measures provided for LDCs by advanced economies such as the EU and US as well as from some international organizations.

A number of United Nations organizations, including the UNDP and UNICEF, allocate a proportion of their funding for LDCs. Therefore after graduating, former LDCs will no longer be eligible for this specific pool of funding, although they can still request UN assistance from the non-LDC pool of funding.

The loss of international support measures include reduced access to concessional finance from international donors as well as reduced eligibility for special market access conditions. One of the most important international support measures for LDCs relates to trade. WTO members have agreed to provide LDCs with special and differential treatment (SDT) including duty-free and quota-free preferential market access.

An important preferential market access program is the EU's Everything But Arms (EBA) program. Under the EU EBA scheme an LDC can gain market access to the EU on a duty-free and quota-free basis while it is listed by the UN as an LDC nation.

The US provides preferential trade access through the Generalized System of Preferences (GSP) program, which provides duty-free access to the US market for a large number of developing countries, including 43 LDCs.

Therefore a significant potential economic impact from graduation is the loss of preferential market access privileges which can have a substantial negative impact on the competitiveness of a graduating nation's exports into key markets such as the EU and US.

However the extent to which a nation is impacted by changes in preferential trade access depends on the structure of their export industries. A LDC nation such as Bangladesh which is highly dependent on exports of low wage manufacturing exports could suffer significant loss in competitiveness due to higher tariff barriers following graduation. In contrast, a nation which has a structure of exports which is heavily based on services exports such as tourism will be less impacted by loss of preferential market access for exports of merchandise exports.

In Asia, several LDCs, notably Bhutan, Laos and Nepal, have significant exports of hydroelectric power to their neighboring countries, which would also not be impacted by loss of preferential market access conditions.

Furthermore the World Bank Group does not allocate funding based on LDC categorization but uses per capita measures of national income in order to determine eligibility for various concessional financing programs such as International Development Association (IDA) concessional financing. Therefore graduating LDCs would not be directly impacted by loss of concessional financing from the World Bank Group, although as their per capita income levels rise this will impact upon their IDA eligibility.

Many LDCs still have a high level of reliance on Official Development Assistance (ODA) as a source of external finance, including a number of the LDCs in the Asia and Pacific, notably the Pacific Island LDCs (Kiribati, Solomon Islands, Tuvalu and Vanuatu) and Afghanistan. After graduation, transition away from ODA financing on concessional terms remains a major challenge for many LDCs which may not currently have access to international capital markets or ability to tap significant FDI inflows.

However even where international support measures are impacted directly by graduation, the pathway for transition can be subject to negotiation, with countries able to try to negotiate a timeframe for reducing international support measures.

Nevertheless LDCs on a path towards graduation need to gradually prepare for greater reliance on private capital flows, rather than concessional financing from donor nations. This will result in higher financing costs compared with concessional financing, and graduating countries have to take into account the fiscal implications on their budget of this higher cost of financing.

As part of their transition path towards a greater reliance on private capital flows, graduating countries also need to improve their access to international capital markets. One important step towards this is to ensure that they obtain a sovereign debt rating from an international ratings agency to be able to tap international capital markets.

The loss of international support measures include reduced access to concessional finance from international donors as well as reduced eligibility for special market access conditions such as the EU's EBA program.

Under the EU EBA scheme an LDC can gain market access to the EU on a duty-free and quota-free basis while it is listed by the UN as an LDC nation.

Many LDCs still have a high level of reliance on ODA as a source of external finance, including a number of the LDCs in the Asia and Pacific, notably the Pacific Island LDCs (Tuvalu, Kiribati, Solomon Islands) and Afghanistan. After graduation, transition away from ODA financing on concessional terms remains a major challenge for many LDCs which may not currently have access to international capital markets or ability to tap significant FDI inflows.

Mobilizing Private Capital Flows

The ability of each of the LDC nations to mobilize private capital flows varies considerably, due to different sizes of domestic savings pools and capital markets, as well as wide variations in ability to attract foreign private capital inflows.

LDCs also have varying capacity to tap international capital markets for private capital, depending on their economic and political risk levels and whether they have international sovereign risk ratings from the international rating agencies, as well as what type of sovereign rating they have been assigned.

The examples of a number of LDCs serve to illustrate the wide variation in the opportunities and challenges facing different LDCs.

Bangladesh's Drive Towards Graduation

Bangladesh has the largest population size among the Asian and Pacific LDCs with an estimated population of 160 million persons in 2016. Therefore when Bangladesh graduates from LDC status, it will represent a major achievement for the overall grouping of LDCs, with a large reduction in the total number of people living in LDC status countries.

The UN Committee for Development Policy Secretariat met with Bangladesh government ministries in October 2017 to discuss the prospects of Bangladesh's graduation from LDC status. The Secretariat advised the Bangladesh government that its preliminary calculations indicated that Bangladesh would likely meet the criteria for graduation at the next three-yearly review of LDCs scheduled to be held in March 2018. This was duly confirmed by the UN Committee at their 2018 review, which puts Bangladesh on a timetable for graduation in 2024, if it meets the graduation criteria for a second time when the next three-yearly UN review of LDCs will be held in 2021 and then enters a three year transitional grace period towards graduation in 2024.

Therefore this implies that planning for a transition to graduation is now a high strategic priority for Bangladesh over the next six years, in order to prepare the economy for a gradual shift away from concessional development financing and for catalyzing greater private capital flows for development.

The Bangladesh economy has achieved tremendous economic and social progress in the past decade, with sustained GDP growth rates of over 5% per year ever since 2004. Over the past decade, its annual average growth rate has been even higher, at 6%. Despite periods of significant domestic political turmoil, the sustained rapid pace of economic growth has helped to deliver substantial progress in human development indicators.

The tremendous progress made is reflected in per capita GDP levels, which have risen from extremely low levels of USD 400 in 2000 to USD 1360 by 2016. According to the most recent World Bank thresholds for classifying a nation as low income, the per capita Gross National Income level is set at USD 1025 with Bangladesh now having progressed into the lower middle income grouping of nations.

An important factor that has helped to underpin the rapid economic growth of Bangladesh has been the significant inflows of foreign direct investment into the textiles and garments industry, as rising labour costs in coastal Chinese provinces have driven multinationals to seek alternative locations for production of low-cost textiles and garments. This has helped to significantly transform the Bangladesh economy away from subsistence agriculture and commodity exports towards a higher share of industrial exports.

Sustained rapid economic growth has resulted in a significant increase in the overall size of the Bangladesh economy since 2000, making the fast-growing domestic consumer market more attractive for both domestic and foreign companies seeking to provide goods and services to the local market. With a GDP that reached USD 220 billion in 2016, the size of the Bangladesh economy is large enough to absorb significant inflows of private capital. Foreign direct investment inflows have diversified away from the textiles and garments sector towards other sectors such as banking, telecommunications and energy-related industries.

Foreign direct investment flows into Bangladesh have strengthened over the past 3 years, reaching a level of USD 2.3 billion in 2016. Although FDI into the textiles sector has been a main source of FDI inflows over the past decade, this has diversified significantly in the recent past. Large new FDI inflows have been recorded into the power, gas and petroleum sector as well as into the telecommunications sector over 2015–2016. Reforms to investment regulations have provided new incentives for investors to develop special economic zones.

The rapid economic growth of Bangladesh's manufacturing sector has also created outbound foreign direct investment from Bangladesh to other countries, including to other LDCs. Bangladesh's DBL Group has invested USD 9.5 million in building a garments factory in Ethiopia, and will have several thousand employees in Ethiopia.

A strong advantage for the resilience of Bangladesh for the mobilization of private capital flows as it progresses towards graduation is that domestic capital markets are significant in size.

The Dhaka Stock Exchange had a market capitalization of around USD 45.7 billion in June 2017 with 294 listed companies, while the Chittagong Stock Exchange has a market capitalization of around USD 37.5 billion with 263 listed companies. Altogether the stock market capitalization of Bangladesh amounts to around USD 83.2 billion, at around 37% of GDP.

The well-established stock markets places Bangladesh in a position of relative comparative advantage compared to other Asian and Pacific LDCs to use its stock markets for raising private sector capital for infrastructure financing, using a range of debt capital market and equity capital market mechanisms.

The use of REITs and Investment Trusts offers significant potential for Bangladesh to raise both domestic and foreign capital for infrastructure development. In order for Bangladesh to be able to develop its REITs and Investment Trust market, new legislation will be required in order to make REITs and Investment Trusts attractive for investors.

Overall, Bangladesh has significant capacity to mobilize private capital flows through its well-developed domestic capital markets, banking sector as well as its ability to attract FDI into the garments industry. Compared to many other LDCs, Bangladesh is therefore in a relatively strong position to mobilize private capital flows after it graduates from LDC status.

However, a key challenge is that as manufacturing wages continue to rise in Bangladesh, its ability to compete in the low-wage segment of the global garments industry is likely to suffer.

In addition, Bangladesh's low factory safety standards, highlighted by the Rana Plaza building collapse that killed over 1,100 workers, resulted in the US suspending its access to the US GSP preferences in 2013. Poor air cargo safety standards have resulted in the EU and several other countries banning direct air cargo flights to their airports, adding to costs and transport time due to required screening in major air cargo hubs en route. Accelerating implementation of necessary safety standards is, therefore, an important bottleneck to improving the competitiveness of Bangladesh's manufacturing sector and to attracting new FDI inflows. In its annual report to US Congress, the Office of the US Trade Representative determined in March 2018 that Bangladesh needed to make further progress in protecting worker safety standards before GSP preferences could be restored.

Transitioning to a more diversified manufacturing export base with higher value-adding is also a high priority in order to sustain strong private capital inflows. One of the advantages that Bangladesh has is the large size of its domestic consumer market, with a total population of around 160 million persons creating significant opportunities for domestic manufacturing production for a wide range of goods and services.

Despite the very positive achievements of Bangladesh over the past two decades, it still remains highly vulnerable to natural disasters. According to the World Risk Report 2016 produced by Bundnis Entwicklung Hilft with the UNU-EHS, Bangladesh was ranked as the 5th highest risk country out of 171 countries ranked due to its vulnerability to natural disasters, notably devastating cyclones in the Bay of Bengal which have caused massive loss of life and extensive storm surges often in the past.

Furthermore, Bangladesh is also vulnerable to the impact of climate change, as rising sea levels gradually inundate large low-lying areas of the Bangladesh coastline, reducing the available land for population settlement and agricultural production.

Bangladesh faces these ongoing threats with a high level of vulnerability and limited capacity to cope with such disasters. Therefore improving resilience to such natural disasters will be an important long-term contributor to the sustainability of Bangladesh's economic development achievements.

Bangladesh is also currently providing a safe haven for an estimated 700,000 Rohingya refugees who have fled from Myanmar as a result of escalating ethnic violence. This requires significant annual financing for the refugees, and will add to the overall fiscal burden for the Bangladesh government as it transitions towards graduation. Bangladesh is likely to receive some World Bank IDA funding from the IDA 18 refugee sub-window to help with the financial costs related to the large number of Rohingya refugees. There has also been some discussion of the possibility of issuing "refugee" bonds on international capital markets to provide additional financing for the refugees. Such "refugee" bonds could also be raised as sukuk bonds to tap the Islamic sukuk bond markets.

Myanmar's Economic Transformation

The UN Committee for Development Policy announced in their 2018 triennial review of LDCs that Myanmar had met the graduation criteria for the first time, putting Myanmar on a path towards graduation from LDC status in 2024. The decision reflects the significant economic liberalization of Myanmar, which has accelerated rapidly since 2011. The economy has sustained strong economic growth since 2011, with significant new foreign public and private capital inflows to finance a wide range of projects, including many infrastructure projects. With Myanmar's per capita GDP having risen from around USD 200 in 2000 to USD 1260 by 2017, there has been very substantial progress in improving living standards, with Myanmar now classified as a lower middle income country.

The outlook for Myanmar to graduate from LDC status looks very favorable over the next six years, boosted by its rapidly rising per capita GDP levels and the diversification of its economic base, which will reduce its vulnerability to natural disasters and fluctuating international commodity prices.

The new Foreign Investment Law of 2012 has also made significant reforms to improve the foreign investment climate, although significant regulatory barriers remain for foreign investment. Further reforms have been introduced with a new investment law implemented in 2017.

However, the Myanmar stock market only commenced operations in March 2016 and has only four listed stocks. Myanmar's capital markets are therefore in a very fledgling state of development, and in the medium term are unlikely to provide a significant source of private capital mobilization.

The banking sector is also relatively weak and underdeveloped, with Myanmar retail depositors having low confidence in using the banking system for retail deposits.

Therefore direct investment from foreign and domestic investors is likely to be the main source of private capital financing for economic development.

Foreign direct investment in Myanmar has risen significantly since political reforms commenced in 2011. According to Myanmar government data on investment approvals, total FDI rose from an estimated USD 4.1 billion in 2013/2014 to USD 8 billion in 2014/2015. FDI inflows are estimated by the Myanmar government to have risen further to USD 9.4 billion for 217 projects in 2015/2016.

However there is considerable discrepancy between the Myanmar government data and UNCTAD estimates, which indicate that FDI inflows were USD 2.8 billion in 2015 and USD 2.2 billion in 2016. Nevertheless, even according to UNCTAD figures this represents a very large increase in FDI compared to inflows of around USD 550 billion per year in 2012 and 2013.

Since its political and economic liberalization in 2011, Myanmar has been successful in mobilizing private sector financing flows for key infrastructure projects.

One of the most important examples has been the development of the Thilawa Industrial Park, which was assisted by Nippon Export and Investment Insurance (NEXI), the official export credit agency of Japan. The risk mitigation insurance solutions provided by NEXI helped to catalyze Japanese private sector companies to invest in a new Myanmar infrastructure development project for the establishment of an industrial park with high-quality infrastructure.

NEXI provided Overseas Investment Insurance for the project for a Japanese private sector consortium comprising Mitsubishi Corporation, Marubeni Corporation and Sumitomo Corporation for the Thilawa Industrial Park Development Project. The insurance contract was implemented in December 2014. This project is a crucial step forward in Myanmar's development of its manufacturing sector, as it has created the first industrial park with modern infrastructure.

Zone A of the industrial park opened in September 2015. Construction work for Zone B commenced in February 2017. Over 80 companies have invested in the industrial park, with over USD 1 billion in FDI for manufacturing plants.

Another example of private sector financing flows for infrastructure development has been the Hanthawaddy International Airport project. A framework agreement for a new USD 1.5 billion airport public–private infrastructure project for building Hanthawaddy Airport was signed in 2016 by JGC, a leading Japanese international engineering construction firm together with Singapore's Changi Airports International and Yongnam.

The project will be partly funded by Japanese government overseas development assistance and the first phase of the project is due for completion in 2022. The airport is expected to have an initial capacity of 12 million passengers per year and will be a key infrastructure project for the development of the tourism industry, which is expected to become a leading industry in the Myanmar economy.

Another private sector-funded infrastructure project is Mandalay International Airport. In November 2014, a consortium called MC-Jalux Airport Services comprising Mitsubishi Group, JALUX Inc and the Yoma Development Group signed an agreement with the Myanmar government to operate the Mandalay International Airport for a 30-year term.

The joint venture has commenced operating the airport as well as maintaining the airport facilities and infrastructure. The Japanese investment was facilitated by an insurance facility provided by NEXI.

While Myanmar has achieved significant successes in attracting foreign direct investment, its ability to mobilize private capital through its banking system and capital markets remains weak. Myanmar has a relatively weak banking system and fledgling capital markets, limiting its capacity to use these channels to attract private capital flows. While further policy reforms will gradually help to deepen domestic equity markets and local bond markets, this will likely be over a medium to long-term timeframe.

Since Myanmar has been successful in mobilizing significant FDI capital inflows after its economic liberalization reforms in 2011, with foreign investment into a wide range of sectors, including manufacturing, oil and gas, telecoms, tourism and infrastructure, this remains the most attractive source of FDI inflows for the medium term outlook.

Therefore near-term policy focus should be on further policy measures to encourage foreign direct investment inflows, such as further liberalization of foreign investment regulations and reducing regulatory barriers to foreign investment. While large-scale FDI inflows into projects such as Thilawa Industrial Park are very significant, one of Myanmar's strengths is its attractiveness for small to medium entrepreneurs to invest in a wide range of projects such as textiles, consumer goods and tourism-related projects.

Another important competitive advantage for Myanmar is that its close economic ties and long border with Thailand make Myanmar an attractive location for Thai entrepreneurs to invest in low-cost manufacturing production as Thai wage costs continue to rise, making Thailand less attractive for low value-added manufacturing. Myanmar therefore has the potential to become a significant hub for Thai FDI inflows into low-cost manufacturing, with the ASEAN Free Trade Area allowing Thai firms to produce in Myanmar and export to Thailand as well as other ASEAN nations, as well as to export to China under market access conditions of the China-ASEAN FTA.

Cambodia: Reconstruction and Recovery from the Killing Fields

Cambodia has made considerable progress in its economic recovery from the devastating impact of the genocide that took place under the Khmer Rouge regime led by Pol Pot. It is estimated that around 2 million people were killed by the Khmer Rouge between 1975 and the beginning of 1979 before the Vietnamese army liberated the country and defeated the Khmer Rouge regime, ending the genocide.

With around 25% of the Cambodian population having been killed in the genocide, including most of the people with professional education, the task of rebuilding the nation has been very difficult. Nevertheless, during the past decade, Cambodia has made tremendous economic progress along the path to rebuilding the nation.

Cambodia has maintained strong economic growth over the past decade, with rapid growth of the garments export industry being an important contributor to this sustained pace of expansion.

An important factor that has contributed to Cambodia's recent economic success is the relatively liberal regulatory regime for foreign capital, which has helped to attract foreign capital into the garments industry as well as into other sectors, including Cambodia's real estate sector.

The main source of foreign capital inflows has been foreign direct investment inflows, which have consistently accounted for a high share of GDP. Cambodia has a strong track record of attracting FDI in recent years, into key sectors such as garments and real estate.

Total FDI inflows rose from 9.1% of GDP in 2015 to 10.2% of GDP in 2016, largely offsetting the chronic large current account deficit. Foreign direct investment inflows rose from USD 1.67 billion in 2015 to USD 2.04 billion in 2016.

However, a key challenge is that FDI inflows into the garments industry have slowed down, due to competition from other low wage nations in Asia. FDI into the garments sector has declined from a level of around USD 360 million per year in 2013–2014, down to USD 140 million in 2016. This reflects increasing competition from other low cost garments producing nations, such as Vietnam, as well as labour disruptions in the Cambodian garments industry, notably over protests relating to wage levels.

Despite the slowdown of FDI into the garments sector, this has been more than offset by strong foreign investment inflows into the real estate sector, as foreigners have been purchasing residential and commercial real estate, notably in Phnom Penh. In 2016, total FDI into the real estate sector was estimated at USD 1.3 billion.

The major export markets for Cambodia are the EU, which accounts for 37% of total exports, and the US, which accounts for 20% of total exports. Cambodia as an LDC receives preferential market access to the EU under the EBA initiative, and therefore an important challenge that will face the Cambodian economy will be the loss of preferential market access to the EU under the EBA initiative.

While FDI into the real estate sector has been very strong in 2016, the real estate sector could be vulnerable to correction due to rapidly rising prices in recent years. This could result in a protracted drop in FDI inflows for real estate, leaving Cambodia vulnerable to a widening balance of payments deficit.

Therefore an important priority is for Cambodia to diversify its economy to attract investment into other new manufacturing industries, such as electronics.

As Cambodia also faces infrastructure bottlenecks and is unable to mobilize sufficient domestic public sector financing to meet infrastructure construction needs, policies to accelerate private sector financing flows for infrastructure also need to be strengthened.

Vanuatu: Building Resilience to Natural Disasters

Vanuatu's graduation from LDC status was originally scheduled by the UN General Assembly for December 2017, but this timeframe was extended for an additional 3 year period to December 2020 due to the devastating impact of Cyclone Pam in March 2015.

According to the World Risk Report 2016 produced by Bundnis Entwicklung Hilft with the UNU-EHS, Vanuatu was ranked as the highest risk country out of 171 countries ranked due to its vulnerability to natural disasters combined with its weak economic capacity to cope with the impact of such events.

Vanuatu's per capita income was USD 2540 at the UN 2012 Triennial Review of LDCs, which was significantly above the threshold for graduation of USD 1190. The human development index was also significantly above the graduation threshold.

Data from the OECD Development Assistance Committee indicates that Small Island Developing States have a much lower share of external private financing flows from international bank lending and foreign direct investment than other developing countries, and also have much more limited access to international debt capital and equity capital markets.

As a result, the Small Island Developing States are more reliant on bilateral and multilateral overseas development assistance as well as remittance flows from their workers abroad.

Vanuatu has attracted FDI inflows of around USD 30 million per year in 2015–2016, following the devastating impact of Cyclone Pam which destroyed significant existing private investments such as hotels.

The nation has very limited capacity to mobilize domestic capital due to the lack of domestic capital markets and small domestic savings pools.

The scope for mobilizing private capital inflows will need to be supported by public sector capital to leverage private sector co-financing, combined with risk mitigation through various insurance products due to Vanuatu's vulnerability to natural disasters.

Mobilizing Private Capital Inflows

Most LDCs do not have significant capital markets for equities or local corporate debt. Therefore near to medium term strategies for fostering the development of capital markets to prepare nations for graduation from LDC status can be focused on several LDCs that already have significant existing domestic capital markets. However for those LDCs that do not have well-developed capital markets, there is potential to tap international capital markets for equity and debt capital finance. In order to raise sovereign bonds on international capital markets, nations do need to establish an international sovereign credit rating, as a preliminary step to being able to tap international bond markets.

Bangladesh has the most advanced capital markets among the Asia and Pacific LDCs, and can make the most progress by accelerating capital markets reforms to mobilize both domestic and foreign international capital flows. Major reforms could include the development of REITs and Infrastructure Trusts legislation to enable these types of investment trusts to mobilize private sector capital for infrastructure financing.

Myanmar also has significant potential for development of its domestic capital markets, and further international co-operation to accelerate the development of domestic equity and bond markets will assist the mobilization of private capital flows over the medium term.

LDCs that do not have well developed local equity and debt capital markets can raise capital flows on international capital markets, although the management of such capital raising needs to be carefully managed to avoid building up external debt liabilities that could result in future difficulties in servicing debt repayments.

One of the major advantages for the Asian and Pacific LDCs is that they find themselves in a good neighborhood. The economic ascent of China and Japan into major global economic powers over the past five decades has created large new pools of development finance. Both China and Japan have embarked on long-term development finance assistance programs for developing countries, with Asian and Pacific countries being strategic priorities for their development assistance programs. South Korea is also increasing its policy focus on strengthening economic development co-operation with developing countries.

The strong development finance flows being provided through multilateral and bilateral channels by Asian economic powers is likely to be an important underpinning for the graduation of Asian and Pacific LDCs, as they will likely be able to obtain a combination of public sector development assistance as well as private capital flows to advance their economic development and tackle any tail risk events.

Although LDCs will need to transition away from concessional finance after graduation, public sector development assistance from multilateral and bilateral donor countries will still have a very important role to play for some of the LDCs which are still heavily reliant on overseas development assistance. Such public sector development assistance can also play a key role in helping to catalyze private sector capital flows, through co-financing of projects.

As LDCs transition towards graduation, they need to boost their capacity to attract private capital flows for development since their eligibility for concessional financing and international support mechanisms will gradually diminish after they reach the graduation point. A number of major channels for private capital flows can potentially be tapped, including domestic and international capital markets, foreign direct investment flows, regional funds and private insurance products.

Equity and Debt Capital Markets

Most Asia and Pacific LDCs do not have significant capital markets for equities or local corporate debt. Therefore strategies for fostering the development of capital markets can be focused on several LDCs that have already developed their local capital markets.

Bangladesh has the most advanced capital markets among the Asia and Pacific LDCs, and can make the most progress by accelerating capital markets reforms to strengthen both domestic and foreign international capital flows.

Major reforms could include the development of REITs and Infrastructure Trusts legislation to enable these types of investment trusts to create a new channel for raising private sector capital for infrastructure financing.

Myanmar also has significant potential for development of its domestic capital markets, and further international co-operation to accelerate the development of domestic equity and bond markets will assist the mobilization of private capital flows over the medium term.

Regional Funds

Since most Asia and Pacific LDCs do not have significant domestic capital markets, an alternative form of investment mechanism to generate private capital could be through regional funds that raise capital on international capital markets and invest in different projects across the Asia and Pacific LDCs.

Regional private equity funds that use both public and private sector financing offer a mechanism for leveraging private capital flows into LDCs. Such private equity funds already have a track record in the Pacific Island States, and there is potential for other similar funds to be developed to invest in infrastructure projects in Asia and Pacific LDCs.

Similarly, REITs and Infrastructure Investment Trusts can also be listed on regional stock markets and used to mobilize private capital flows for private infrastructure financing for LDCs.

Other funds that can be listed on regional stock markets to raise finance for LDCs include retail funds that attract investments from retail investors for microfinance for LDCs.

Foreign Direct Investment Flows

Among the Asia and Pacific LDCs, four countries have a strong track record of attracting FDI inflows. These are Bangladesh, Myanmar, Cambodia and Laos.

For these four countries, there are likely to be significant benefits from further reforms to improve the climate for FDI, such as streamlining FDI investment processes, creating portfolios of projects where key government approvals have already been given, and further reducing regulatory hurdles for FDI inflows.

The establishment of industrial parks with foreign developers is an important potential step as it can catalyze FDI inflows, as shown in the case of Myanmar's Thilawa Industrial Park.

Improving the ease of doing business by addressing key barriers to foreign investment that have been identified by the World Bank's Ease of Doing Business Survey as a key priority for many developing countries, particularly LDCs which are often ranked very low in the global ease of doing business global rankings.

Private Insurance for Risk Mitigation

Private sector insurers as well as public sector export credit agencies can provide insurance products that facilitate private sector investment in infrastructure projects in developing countries.

The spectrum of such insurance and risk mitigation products is very wide, including political risk products, reinsurance for banks and corporates, as well as reinsurance for multilateral development banks such as the World Bank and ADB.

Insurance and reinsurance solutions are increasingly being looked at as potential long-term risk mitigation strategies for the economic impact of natural disasters. A number of such catastrophe risk insurance projects have been initiated, including the Pacific Catastrophe Risk Assessment and Finance Initiative (PCRAFI), which was created in 2007 as a joint initiative of the World Bank, ADB, and the Secretariat of the Pacific Community, with support from the Japanese government.

The PCRAFI is administered by the World Bank and financed by donors in order to provide insurance for the Pacific Island States of Cook Islands, Marshall Islands, Samoa, Tonga and Vanuatu. The fifth round of insurance was commenced in November 2016, with total insurance coverage of 38 million against natural disasters, notably cyclones, earthquakes and tsunamis.

The risk insurance is provided by private sector insurers comprising Sompo Japan Nipponkoa Insurance, Mitsui Sumitomo Insurance, Tokio Marine & Nichido Fire Insurance, Swiss Re, and Munich Re. Under this particular scheme, the payouts are linked to the strength of the natural disaster, with the purpose of using insurance to help pay for losses due to a natural catastrophe.

The PCRAFI Multi-Donor Trust Fund has received funding support from Germany, Japan, the United Kingdom, and the United States, with USD 40 million in grant funding under the G7 InsuResilience Initiative.

Outlook for LDCs

Since the first UN listing of LDCs was created in 1971, only 5 LDCs have officially been recognized by the UN as having graduated from LDC status. Despite this poor track record of exiting from LDC status, the outlook for significant further progress over the next decade for LDCs looks more favorable.

In particular, many of the Asian and Pacific LDCs are projected to be able to graduate from LDC status over the next 5 years. Vanuatu is scheduled to graduate in 2020, while The UN Committee for Development Policy has recommended at its three-yearly review of LDCs that Bhutan, Kiribati, Sao Tome and Principe as well as the Solomon Islands should graduate in 2018. Bhutan, Nepal, Solomon Islands and Timor Leste met the graduation thresholds for the first time in 2015, but the UN decision about the graduation of Nepal and Timor Leste has been postponed until the 2021 triennial review due to the severe economic and social problems both nations were facing. Bangladesh met the graduation threshold at the 2018 review, and will therefore be potentially able to graduate by 2021. Therefore within the next 5 years, seven Asia-Pacific LDCs could graduate, significantly reducing the remaining number of LDCs in the Asia and Pacific region.

However the 32 African LDCs face more a more challenging development path, with only Sao Tome and Principe recommended by the UN Committee to graduate in 2018 while Angola is expected to graduate in 2021.

One of the most significant milestones for the LDCs will be when Bangladesh graduates from LDC status, since Bangladesh currently has a population of around 160 million persons out of the total LDC population of 954 million. Consequently when Bangladesh graduates, the total population of persons living in LDC status countries will be significantly reduced. Similarly, when Myanmar graduates, this will also be a major step forward in reducing the total population living in LDC status nations. Since both nations are currently on track to graduate in 2024, this could reduce the total number of people living in LDC status nations by around 230 million, which would represent very substantial progress in the global economic development of the group of LDC nations.

However, many LDCs that are small island states still confront significant challenges in achieving sustainable economic development. The Pacific small island states that are currently in LDC status are Vanuatu, Kiribati, Solomon Islands and Tuvalu. These nations face major difficulties in diversifying their economies towards manufacturing, due to their small domestic consumer market size and geographical remoteness, which escalates logistics costs. Furthermore, these small island states remain highly vulnerable to natural disasters.

Although Nepal and Bhutan are landlocked countries, they are in a comparatively better position than the Pacific Island states to diversify their economies, due to their proximity to the large Indian consumer market. A major opportunity for both these nations will be the growth of tourism, as Indian per capita GDP levels increase to levels that catalyze much stronger Indian international tourism visits, especially to nearby destinations in Asia.

Strategies for Mobilizing Finance

The rapid economic growth of the Asia-Pacific region is helping to push a significant number of the Asian and Pacific LDCs towards their graduation threshold out of LDC status. This represents an important progression in the path of sustainable economic development of these nations.

Over half of the remaining Asia and Pacific LDCs are expected to be able to graduate from LDC status within the next six years. This will require significant preparation for transitioning to greater reliance on private sector capital flows. A number of mechanisms are potentially mobilizing private capital inflows, including portfolio capital inflows, foreign direct investment and debt-financing.

The ability of Asia and Pacific LDCs to mobilize private capital flows varies considerably depending on a range of factors, including country risk ratings, vulnerability to external shocks, domestic savings pools and the depth and liquidity of capital markets.

Strategies to improve mobilization of private capital flows need to be tailored to each country. A "one size fits all" approach is not appropriate as policies that may be relevant for one country may be impractical for other nations.

Some countries will face considerable challenges in attracting significant private capital flows, due to their lack of significant domestic capital markets and inability to tap international capital markets, as well as vulnerability to external shocks such as natural disasters.

Therefore each LDC needs to develop its own transitional roadmap for strengthening its private capital inflows during its path towards graduation and during the early years of transition out of LDC status. This strategic plan for future development financing can be developed together with key development partners such as the UN, World Bank and ADB, in order to create realistic and pragmatic strategies for boosting private capital flows. In the Asia-Pacific region, it is likely that LDCs as well as nations graduating from LDC status will benefit from considerable transitional assistance from other Asian nations such as China, Japan and South Korea, as well as other upper middle income or high income Asian economies.

However, the grouping of 32 African LDCs face a more difficult outlook and will require considerable ongoing assistance from the international financial institutions as well as bilateral donor countries in their future pathway towards exiting from LDC status.

11

Crisis Prevention and Resolution in Emerging Markets

Over the past 50 years, many developing countries have displayed a high degree of vulnerability to economic crises for a number of reasons, including poor macroeconomic management, high and unsustainable levels of external debt, political instability, excessive reliance on commodity exports and lack of fiscal resources to manage economic fluctuations. These vulnerabilities often magnify the transmission effects on the domestic economy and banking sector from external shocks. The consequences have often been severe, and have frequently resulted in protracted recessions with harsh negative economic and social impact effects, including declining living standards that push an increasing share of the population into poverty.

Since 1975, there have been an estimated 200 economic crises in developing countries attributable to either a banking crisis or a sovereign debt crisis or a combination of both (Balteanu and Erce 2014). The frequency with which such crises have occurred highlights the vulnerability of developing countries and the need for economic and financial sector reforms to mitigate such risks.

One of the most significant emerging markets crises that occurred during the 1980s was related to the surge in oil prices during the two major oil price shocks of the 1970s. This resulted in a large accumulation of petrodollar surpluses of Middle East oil exporting nations in the international banking system. As petrodollar deposits accumulated in the international banks, it triggered rapid growth in lending by international banks to emerging markets, in order to recycle the large growth in bank deposits to generate revenue, with international bankers incentivized by commission structures

© The Author(s) 2018
R. Biswas, *Emerging Markets Megatrends*,
https://doi.org/10.1007/978-3-319-78123-5_11

to boost loans. Latin America was at the forefront of this borrowing, with total Latin American debt rising from USD 29 billion in 1970 to USD 327 billion by 1982.

However the emerging markets party on this debt binge ended after 1979, when the US Federal Reserve tightened monetary policy significantly in order to control rising inflation. The sharp increase in US interest rates resulted in rising debt servicing costs for emerging markets borrowers, resulting in a protracted emerging markets debt crisis that hit many developing countries in Latin America and Eastern Europe. By 1982, Mexico teetered on the edge of a debt default as its foreign exchange reserves were exhausted, and only an IMF bailout with an Extended Fund Facility of USD 3.75 billion prevented a Mexican debt default (Clement and Maes 2013).

Similar problems in servicing external debt payments hit many other Latin American countries, resulting in a regional debt crisis that eventually resulted in 16 Latin American countries having to reschedule their external debt repayments. With international financing from capital markets shuttered, many of these Latin American countries were forced to take austerity measures to cut government expenditure, resulting in rising unemployment rates and protracted recessionary conditions. The extent of the regional crisis that hit Latin America was so severe that it was referred to as Latin America's "lost decade" as regional growth stagnated.

The impact of this emerging markets debt crisis was not restricted to Latin America, as other emerging markets borrowers, including in Eastern Europe, also suffered similar problems as the cost of servicing their external debt soared.

The international banks also suffered significantly from the large-scale debt rescheduling and significant debt write-offs that occurred between 1989 and 1994, amounting to an estimated USD 61 billion (Federal Reserve History, The Latin American Debt Crisis of the 1980s).

The only cowboys who rode off into the sunset in this global debt debacle were the international bankers who had arranged the bank loans for the developing countries during the 1970s, pocketing large bonuses and commissions on the new lending deals they had arranged.

Inevitably it was the poorest and most vulnerable segments of the population in developing countries who were hit hardest from the protracted recessionary conditions.

As one economist I knew commented some years later after another emerging markets crisis, '*It is the poor who suffer the most during economic crises – you don't see investment bankers slouching around looking shabby.*'

Recurrent crises have continued to hit emerging markets in subsequent years, including the East Asian crisis in 1997, Russia's debt default in 1998, and a number of economic crises in major Latin American emerging markets. The Mexican Tequila Crisis also known as the Mexican Peso Crisis was triggered by a number of causes, including a widening current account deficit and overvalued peso. Confidence in the peso gradually eroded as a result of deteriorating external account fundamentals and several political shocks, notably the Zapatista uprising in Chiapas state in early 1994 and the assassination in March 1994 of Luis Colosio, a presidential candidate for the 1994 election. Following capital flight and peso devaluation in 1994, Mexico received a USD 50 billion bailout in early 1995 led by the US government and the IMF, with the economy plunging into recession and high unemployment.

In order to fund the Mexican bailout, the US provided USD 20 billion from its Exchange Stabilization Fund, while the IMF provided an additional USD 17.8 billion and the Bank of International Settlements provided USD 10 billion. The bailout package allowed Mexico to avoid defaulting on its debt, although the country experienced a severe recession in 1995 before rebounding in 1996–1997.

In 2001–2002, Argentina experienced a severe economic crisis, caused by factors such as the deteriorating fiscal deficit, falling prices for key commodity exports and the rising current account deficit. During this crisis, the Argentine government defaulting on its sovereign debt and resorting to freezing bank accounts in order to prevent a run on the banking sector, with an international bailout package of around USD 40 billion agreed in 2001, including USD 14 billion from the IMF. Argentina's GDP contracted by 20% between 1998 and 2002. In 2018, it was "back to the future" for Argentina, which again experienced yet another economic crisis, forcing the nation to request an IMF bailout package of around USD 50 billion in the form of an IMF standby facility to stabilise the economy. After a drought hit agricultural exports, this triggered sharp currency depreciation and soaring policy interest rates as the central bank tried to defend the currency. Currency depreciation has increased the burden of external debt repayments, with total external debt estimated at USD 216 billion by the end of 2017. By March 2018, consumer price inflation had risen to 25.4% year-on-year, with the central bank having pushed the policy rate to 27.25%. Venezuela has also been in protracted economic crisis due to gross economic mismanagement, with an inflation rate of 13,779% year-on-year in April 2018, and the economy in a state of collapse, with GDP contracting by an estimated 12% in 2017.

Many of the world's poorest nations have also struggled under external debt burdens, with the IMF and World Bank having launched the Heavily Indebted Poor Countries (HIPC) Initiative in 1996 to provide debt relief for many of the world's poorest nations. Of the 39 nations that were eligible to receive HIPC debt relief, 36 were receiving debt relief from the IMF and other creditors in 2017. Many of the beneficiaries are African low income nations that are classified as Least Developed Countries by the United Nations.

The Impact of the East Asian Crisis

One of the most severe regional economic crises that hit developing countries in the relatively recent past was the East Asian financial crisis. Just over two decades ago, in 1997, East Asia's tiger economies were engulfed by a devastating economic crisis that created deep recessions, financial markets slumps and banking crises in many Asian nations.

Since that time, over the past two decades, East Asia's recovery has been boosted by the rapid economic ascent of China. Led by China, emerging Asia has again shown dynamic growth, and has become the largest growth engine for the global economy since the Global Financial Crisis.

With the Asia-Pacific's share of world GDP having risen from 26% in 2000 to 34% by 2016, the region's importance in the global economy has increased significantly since the East Asian crisis. A key issue confronting developing Asia is whether it is still vulnerable to another regional economic crisis that would be a key risk to global growth momentum.

Two decades ago, in July 1997, the East Asian financial crisis commenced with a currency crisis in Thailand. Speculative pressure against the Thai baht resulted in the depletion of the nation's FX reserves, forcing the nation to abandon its currency peg to the USD and move to a managed float, resulting in sharp currency depreciation, creating severe negative economic shocks within the Thai economy.

Following the Thai currency crisis, many East Asian tiger economies were toppled, one after another, by financial markets contagion, currency crises and capital flight. A number of major Asian economies plunged into protracted recessions, banking crises, major corporate failures and bursting of stock market and property market bubbles, reflecting deep macroeconomic imbalances that had built up.

By August 1997, contagion had spread from Thailand to other East Asian economies with significant macroeconomic imbalances. The case of

Indonesia illustrates the severe nature of the economic shocks that hit East Asia. Indonesia's vulnerabilities included very high levels of external debt and relatively limited foreign exchange reserves. As the regional crisis escalated, the rupiah began to depreciate sharply, creating mounting problems for the large Indonesian corporations which had leveraged their balance sheets with substantial foreign currency borrowings in previous years. As the flight of global capital from East Asia intensified and the economic crisis worsened, the Indonesian economy began to fall into a vicious downward spiral of currency depreciation and rising inflation. The rupiah depreciated from around 2,500 per US dollar in July 1997 to around 14,000 per US dollar by January 1998.

As the Indonesian economy fell into a deep recession and many large corporations were unable to service their debts, a banking sector crisis unfolded which resulted in the closure of 16 commercial banks by November 1997, and a run on banking system deposits during December 1997 that affected many Indonesian banks. The Indonesian financial system became insolvent and came close to total collapse. This was staved off by an emergency financial sector program announced by the government in January 1998 which guaranteed bank deposits, together with a program under which the government would undertake banking sector restructuring. The IMF provided a series of bailouts to Indonesia, with a total of USD 43 billion in IMF loans provided by 1998. Many banks were taken over by the government or recapitalized, and the banking sector went through a protracted period of consolidation and restructuring.

Other East Asian economies were also severely impacted by the East Asian crisis and its contagion effects, including South Korea, Malaysia, Philippines and Thailand. South Korea and Thailand also obtained IMF bailouts, while the Philippines extended an IMF program already in place. However Malaysia rejected the option of an IMF bailout, preferring to set a fixed currency peg against the USD, which helped to maintain macroeconomic stability and facilitated a rapid economic rebound.

Looking back at the East Asian crisis, a key question is whether Asian nations have subsequently built up sufficient resilience to economic shocks and constructed strong enough firewalls to prevent financial markets contagion in the event of another major economic shock.

Undoubtedly, since the East Asian crisis, Asian economies that were at the centre of the economic turmoil have made tremendous progress in addressing the macroeconomic and financial vulnerabilities that contributed to the financial crisis.

Among the major achievements have been significant progress in the sophistication of macroeconomic management, as well as far-reaching banking sector reforms in many East Asian economies that have resulted in stronger prudential regulation of banks, much improved capital adequacy ratios in the banking system, better risk management systems and adoption of macro-prudential measures to manage risks related to real estate lending.

In Malaysia, Dr. Zeti Aziz took the helm as acting Governor of Bank Negara Malaysia in 1998 and then subsequently was appointed as Governor of Bank Negara Malaysia in 2000 and held that office until 2016. She had driven far-reaching reforms to the Malaysian banking system that resulted in banking sector consolidation and substantial strengthening of financial regulation that has made Malaysia a regional leader in commercial banking, with Malaysian banks having become international players with a strong regional footprint in the rest of ASEAN.

Indonesia, Thailand and the Philippines have also implemented substantial banking sector reforms, undertaking banking sector consolidation, improving capital adequacy ratios and strengthening prudential regulation and supervision of their banking systems.

Many East Asian countries have also built up their foreign exchange reserves to improve their resilience to volatile international capital flows as well as strengthening their financial resilience by adopting macro-prudential measures when required.

Indonesian foreign exchange reserves have strengthened from a level of USD 17 billion in 1998 during the peak of the East Asian crisis to USD 126 billion by October 2017. This was equivalent to a level of 8.6 months of import cover and government external debt servicing payments, which represents a very sound level of import cover by emerging markets standards. Thailand's FX reserves had plunged to a level of USD 26 billion in July 1997 during the period of heavy intervention by the Bank of Thailand to defend the Thai baht, but have strengthened considerably in subsequent years, reaching a level of USD 200 billion in October 2017.

Indonesia and the Philippines have also substantially improved their fiscal positions with very substantial reductions in government debt as a share of GDP. Since 2004, the Philippines general government debt-to-GDP ratio has more than halved to a new record low of 34.6% in 2016. In Indonesia, one of the major macroeconomic successes during the two terms of office of President Yudhoyono was that government debt as a share of GDP was reduced from 56% in 2004 to just 26% of GDP when he stepped down from office in 2014.

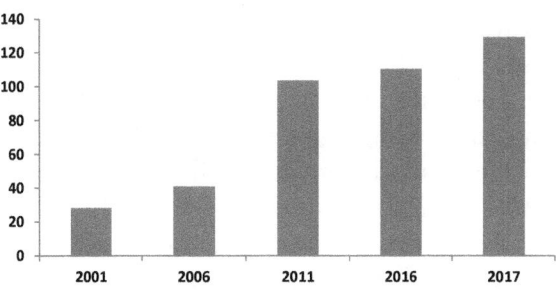

Fig. 11.1 Indonesian foreign exchange reserves (USD billion) (*Source* Bank Indonesia)

In the aftermath of the East Asian Crisis, some of the countries that were heavily impacted by the economic shocks, including Malaysia, Indonesia, Thailand and the Philippines, have also taken steps to deepen their equity and bond markets, improving the diversity and liquidity of their capital markets (Fig. 11.1).

Chiang Mai Initiative

One of the major regional financial sector reforms undertaken after the East Asian crisis has been the Chiang Mai Initiative, which was a key new mechanism for Asian regional co-operation to tackle financial crises that was established soon after the East Asian crisis. The Chiang Mai Initiative, agreed in 2000, has created a regional mechanism for co-operation among the ASEAN countries plus China, Japan and South Korea for financial crisis prevention and resolution, initially built around a network of bilateral currency swaps.

When the Chiang Mai Initiative was initially created in 2000, it was established as a system of bilateral currency swap arrangements among the ASEAN member nations together with China, Japan and South Korea (ASEAN+3), to strengthen regional safety nets for crisis prevention.

At the ASEAN+3 Finance Ministers Meeting held in June 2007, it was agreed that the Chiang Mai Initiative system of bilateral swaps would be multilateralized, to create a single pool of reserve currencies. The new arrangement was named the Chiang Mai Initiative Multilateralization (CMIM), and had the objectives tackling balance of payments and short-term liquidity difficulties among the ASEAN+3 nations as well as acting as a supplementary reserve pool to assist international support arrangements to address such crises.

In 2008, the size of the reserves pool was set at USD 80 billion, with China, Japan and South Korea agreeing to provide 80% of the total reserves pool. However, due to the onset of the Global Financial Crisis in 2008–2009, the ASEAN+3 Finance Ministers Meeting held in May 2009 decided to expand the total size of the reserves pool to USD 120 billion, with China, Japan and South Korea still providing 80% of the total reserves pool.

Momentum continued to build for further expansion of the CMIM facility as the magnitude of the Global Financial Crisis made Asian nations realize that the scale of reserves required for a future Asian regional crisis would have to be considerably larger. Therefore in 2012, at the annual ASEAN+3 Finance Ministers Meeting, the total size of the reserves pool was doubled to USD 240 billion.

Under the original CMIM arrangements, the CMIM would only disburse funds if an IMF program was already in place for the requesting country. That IMF conditionality has also been reduced somewhat with the CMIM facilities able to disburse 30% of the total amount without IMF conditionality.

Creating an Asian Monetary Fund

On 29 August 2017, German Chancellor Angela Merkel endorsed the concept of establishing a new European Monetary Fund for the Eurozone, building on the existing European Stability Mechanism. In Asia, the concept of an Asian Monetary Fund was initially proposed by the Japanese government during the East Asian Crisis in 1997, but was not adopted by Asian countries due to concerns that an Asian Monetary Fund could overlap with the role of the IMF.

Since 1997, the Asian economic landscape has changed very substantially, against a background of rising Asian financial co-operation through the Chiang Mai Initiative, the recent creation of the Asian Infrastructure Investment Bank, as well as increasing regional economic and investment integration.

Consequently, the case for an Asian Monetary Fund could gain renewed traction if the Eurozone proceeds to launch a European Monetary Fund. The functions of a new Asian Monetary Fund could include having a regional role for strengthening financial stability, as well as crisis prevention and supporting Asian countries with balance of payments crises. The role of an Asian Monetary Fund could also include financial system surveillance and helping Asian central banks to co-ordinate regional financial system supervision and tackle supervision of large regional banks.

Is Another Asian Crisis Looming?

Despite the tremendous achievements of many Asian governments in strengthening resilience to economic shocks, the ghosts of the East Asian crisis continue to haunt Asia, with fears that the region could still be vulnerable to another financial crisis. While East Asian governments have made great progress in improving financial resilience, the triggers for the next crisis could be very different to the East Asian crisis.

The greatest change in the East Asian economic landscape since 1997 has been the rapid rise of China as a global economic power, with its share of world GDP having risen from just 3% in 1997 to 15% by 2016 (Fig. 11.2). As a result, the trade and investment ties of many Asian nations with China have increased very significantly. For example, the ASEAN region's bilateral trade with China has increased from USD 24 billion in 1998 to USD 515 billion by 2017. The rapid growth in ASEAN exports to China has been an important growth engine for ASEAN over the past decade, notably helping ASEAN through the global financial crisis in 2008–2009 when the US and EU slumped into recessions. Similarly, China has become the largest export market for South Korea (Fig. 11.3).

However, the risk of a severe Chinese economic slowdown or hard landing in which Chinese GDP growth slows to 4% or less remains a potential key downside risk scenario for the East Asian region due to the significant

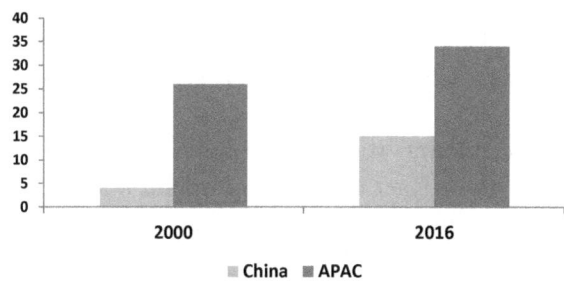

Fig. 11.2   APAC share of world GDP (%, 2000–2016) (*Source* IMF data)

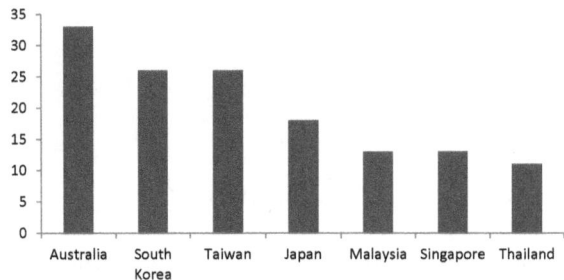

Fig. 11.3 APAC exports to China for 2016 (share of total exports) (*Source* National trade statistics)

increase in the importance of China as a key export market over the past decade.

The risk of a China hard landing remains an important downside risk for the global economy in the medium term because China does face significant economic and financial imbalances. Among these are the high levels of non-performing loans in the Chinese banking system, the rapid growth of the shadow banking sector which has been lightly regulated until very recently, and the large increase in Chinese corporate debt as a share of GDP since 2009. In addition to these financial markets imbalances, the Chinese industrial sector also faces considerable structural reforms due to large excess capacity in key industries such as steel and coal, with millions of job losses expected in these sectors according to the Chinese government's own estimates.

Due to the rapid growth in bilateral trade between China and many other Asian nations over the past two decades, the Asia-Pacific region is particularly vulnerable to a China hard landing shock. Singapore, Taiwan, Hong Kong, South Korea, Malaysia and Thailand are among the most vulnerable to the shock waves of a China economic slowdown. The channels of transmission would be through weakening trade and investment flows, as well as financial markets linkages such as bank balance sheet exposures to Chinese borrowers or loans to other counterparties related to trade and investment flows with China.

If the Chinese economy were to experience a sharp slowdown or hard landing, this could also trigger other macroeconomic vulnerabilities in other Asian countries. For example, the relatively high levels of household debt to GDP in Malaysia and Thailand remain a key source of macroeconomic vulnerability for these countries, and a significant weakening in the economic growth rate for these nations could result in greater stress for highly leveraged households. Similarly, South Korea also has relatively high household debt levels when measured as a share of GDP.

Banks in other Asian countries may also have significant exposure to China-related credit risks if there were to be a sharp slowdown in Chinese economic growth. Therefore stress-testing the impact of a China hard landing is a key risk management task for Asian banks as well as Asian financial regulatory authorities, in order to understand the potential impact of such a downside risk event.

Lessons of the East Asian Crisis

Despite the tremendous progress made by emerging Asian economies since the East Asian crisis in improving macroeconomic management and financial systems, there are still significant economic and financial vulnerabilities in East Asia. Foremost among these vulnerabilities is the much greater vulnerability to a China hard landing due to the rapid economic ascendance of China over the past two decades, as it has become the world's second-largest economy.

In order to further strengthen defences against a future economic crisis and to prevent regional contagion, building stronger regional co-operation for crisis prevention and resolution is an important task ahead for the East Asian region. Improving regulatory co-ordination to manage financial sector risks and building stronger firewalls to prevent regional contagion during future crises will remain key priorities.

For other developing countries, the lessons of the East Asian crisis are also critical for reducing vulnerability to future economic shocks. Two of the major causes of economic crises in developing countries during the past five decades have been banking crises and sovereign debt crises.

Diversification of Exports

In order to manage the risks related to external debt defaults, one of the most important lessons for developing countries is the need to reduce external account vulnerability. This is a complex policy task for most developing countries, particularly because the structure of exports of around half of the world's developing countries still remains heavily dependent on exports of commodities. This creates vulnerability to sharp fluctuations in world commodity prices, with the exports as well as fiscal revenues of commodity exporting nations at risk of greater volatility than countries which have more diversified exports that include a high share of manufactures and services.

Following the slump in world oil prices in 2014, many developing countries which are heavily reliant on oil and gas exports faced a sharp slump in oil and gas export revenues as well as significantly reduced fiscal revenues during 2015–2016. Developing countries which suffered a substantial negative economic impact due to the slump in world oil prices in 2015–2016 included Saudi Arabia, UAE, Kuwait, Nigeria, Angola, Russia and Venezuela.

Many other developing countries that have a high level of dependency on commodity exports also would need to increase the diversification of their economies and reduce vulnerability to commodity exports in order to improve their resilience to external shocks that could trigger future economic crises. However although such policy goals have been attempted frequently by many developing countries over recent decades, achieving significant diversification has proven to be very difficult for many developing countries, as they have frequently been unable to achieve competitive advantage in exports of manufacturing and services.

Increasing Foreign Exchange Reserves

An important lesson from the East Asian crisis has been the need for developing countries to maintain higher levels of foreign exchange reserves, in order to build confidence in international capital markets in ability of a nation to weather external shocks and large, potentially destabilizing capital outflows.

In Asia, there has been a large-scale accumulation of foreign exchange reserves led by China, which built up foreign exchange reserves to USD 4 trillion by June 2014, although subsequent capital outflows during 2015–2016 combined with other factors having resulted in its foreign exchange reserves declining by close to USD 1 trillion between mid-2014 and the end of 2017, to a level of USD 3.1 trillion.

Other Asian nations have also built up their foreign exchange reserves, including India and Indonesia, with both these economies having a history of being vulnerable to capital flight, notably from volatile portfolio capital flows.

Macro-Prudential Measures

As developing countries have continued to liberalize their domestic capital markets to allow international capital flows to boost the depth and liquidity of domestic equity and bond markets, this has also increased risks related to destabilizing speculative portfolio capital flows.

The use of macro-prudential measures by governments and central banks of developing countries has become an important addition to their policy toolkits. This has contributed to creating a more sophisticated system of managing risks related to volatile international capital flows as well as other forms of speculative capital flows which could be destabilizing, such as when signs of property bubbles are developing in real estate markets. While some other emerging markets have utilized such policy tools, greater understanding among other developing countries governments and central banks about the potential costs and benefits of macro-prudential measures could contribute to better crisis prevention.

In order to address these concerns, governments and central banks of developing countries have increasingly added macro-prudential measures to their policy toolkits.

Macro-prudential measures that central banks or governments can draw upon include countercyclical dynamic capital buffers whereby financial regulators can require banks to add additional capital reserves in response to conditions of rapid credit expansion, or also can use dynamic provisioning which requires banks to set aside greater reserves provisioning for bad debts during times of good profitability.

Use by banking regulatory authorities of caps on loan-to-value ratios or loan-to-income ratios for lending to sectors with excessive growth in credit have also become an important tool of policymakers, notably by increasing collateral requirements for residential property loans when rapidly rising residential home prices signal potential property bubbles are building up. This helps to improve the resilience of the financial system to housing sector downturns as well as reducing default risk for mortgage loans. As real estate crises can be an important potential source of systemic risk to the financial system and a potential trigger for economic crises, using macro-prudential tools to prevent real estate crises can play an important role in crisis prevention.

There have been a large number of cases where developing countries have used such macro-prudential tools in the past decade, with loan-to-value ratios used to control potential risks from property bubbles in Brazil, Chile, Indonesia, Turkey, Malaysia and India over the past decade. While most countries use some form of loan-to-value ratio as a standard risk management tool for property loans, the use of higher loan-to-value ratios to manage rising risks during property cycle upturns has been relatively heavily used by Asian central banks, including in Japan, South Korea, Singapore, Malaysia and Thailand.

Conversely, when property cycles turn down, such macro-prudential measures can be relaxed in order to boost demand for mortgage lending. Another instrument that has been used by central banks to manage risks related to mortgages and consumer credit is by varying capital weights for bank regulatory capital.

Overall the evidence indicates that the use of macro-prudential measures can provide significant benefits in helping to manage cyclical risks in a targeted way to prevent crises.

Capital Flow Management Measures

A key destabilizing factor for developing countries has been volatile capital flows, particularly as measures for liberalization of the capital account have been increasingly adopted by many developing countries in order to encourage international capital inflows and boost the pace of economic development. Many developing countries have also taken steps to deepen domestic equity and bond markets, including allowing liberalizing rules to allow greater foreign ownership of domestic equities and bonds.

However volatile international capital flows can potentially destabilize the economy of a developing country. For example, large foreign portfolio capital inflows can build up the foreign ownership share of a domestic stock market or bond market over several years, as well as driving local currency appreciation. However such portfolio capital flows can also be vulnerable to sudden reversal and capital flight due to adverse domestic political or economic developments, or due to external shocks such as the global financial crisis of 2008–2009. Capital flight can be very destabilizing for a developing country as it can cause sharp declines in domestic equity markets as well as causing significant depreciation of the local currency.

Previous emerging markets crises such as the East Asian crisis highlight the significant destabilization that can be caused to an economy due to sharp currency depreciation, including rising import price inflation, higher external debt servicing burdens for corporate and sovereign borrowers, higher overall import costs and potential depletion of foreign exchange reserves as central banks attempt to smooth local currency depreciation.

In order to better manage volatile capital flows, developing countries have increasingly used capital flow management measures to try to address volatile flows through more targeted measures. The IMF has indicated that the temporary use of such measures can be appropriate within the context of a long-term strategy of capital liberalization when a country faces large capital outflows or inflows that are potentially destabilizing (IMF 2012).

There are a wide range of capital flow management tools available for regulatory authorities. The use of reserve requirements for bank external credit lines with foreign residents that have relatively short terms of less than 3 years is one tool that helps to reduce foreign exchange lending and also helps to limit currency mismatches for the domestic banking sector.

In the aftermath of the global financial crisis with the US and EU experiencing recessionary conditions, banking crises and ultra-loose monetary policy, emerging markets attracted significant capital inflows as the large stimulus measures in China as well as in the OECD countries boosted world commodity prices and resulted in stronger economic growth in many developing countries, as well as much more attractive yields in debt markets than in the US, EU and Japan.

In order to stem potentially disruptive capital inflows, some developing countries have utilized capital flow management tools to discourage speculative capital inflows.

Probably the most controversial episode of capital controls in recent times was Malaysia's decision to implement capital control policies during the East Asian Crisis. The decision by the Malaysian government to adopt limited capital controls on 1 September 1998 generated tremendous controversy and fierce criticism from governments of some developed countries and from international financial markets, as well as the rebuke of the IMF at the time. The measures Malaysia adopted were very targeted and intended only to deter short term speculative capital flows, whereas more stable foreign direct investment flows were not impacted and foreign exchange transactions related to the current account continued to be permitted (Kaplan and Rodrick 2001).

After the international financial community observed the impact of the Malaysian measures, the Malaysian capital controls were generally accepted to have been successful, and many of the critics later changed their assessment. This helped to reinforce the case for the future selective use of capital controls to manage volatile capital flows.

I recall being at the Commonwealth Finance Ministerial Meeting in September 1999 when one of the key topics under discussion was the management of volatile capital flows during the East Asian Crisis. Many of the finance ministers of developing countries voiced their strong support for adopting capital controls as a policy tool and acknowledged their effectiveness in the Malaysian case. Two years later, I attended a speech by Mervyn King, then the Deputy Governor of the Bank of England, where he also acknowledged that limited use of capital controls could have a role to play in managing episodes of volatile capital flows.

In a subsequent speech that he made in New Delhi in August 2001, Mervyn King highlighted the impact of volatile capital flows during the East Asian crisis.

> The costs of recent crises have been large. Between 1996 and 1998, the reversal of private capital flows to the five Asian countries primarily affected (Indonesia, Korea, Malaysia, the Philippines and Thailand) was almost $150 bn, equivalent to about 15% of the pre-crisis level of GDP. Changes in the capital account imply equal and opposite swings in the current account. Inevitably, a change in the current account on that scale is likely to mean a deep recession. And during the Asian crisis, real GDP fell by 1% in the Philippines, 7% in Korea and Malaysia, 11% in Thailand and by 13% in Indonesia.
>
> Speech by Mervyn King, Deputy Governor, Bank of England at the Indian Council for Research on International Economic Relations, August 2001, New Delhi, India.

The dangers of capital account liberalization have been well understood by some of the largest developing countries. Due to their concerns about the potential disruptive impact on their economies from volatile international capital flows, both China and India have taken a very gradual approach to capital account liberalization in order to manage these risks. Due to their conservative approach to capital account liberalization, China and India did not suffer significant capital outflows or economic disruption during the East Asian Crisis.

Brazil has also been among the emerging markets at the forefront of regulatory policies for capital flow management. During the global financial crisis of 2008–2009, Brazil utilized a financial transaction tax on certain types of capital inflows as well as on short USD positions. A tax of 2% was introduced on portfolio capital inflows into equities and fixed income on October 2009 (IMF 2014). The following month, a 1.5% tax was also imposed on depository receipts, to prevent such instruments being used as a loophole to avoid the financial transaction tax. In October 2010, the tax on fixed income capital inflows was raised to 6% to deter speculative inflows.

Brazil also adopted other measures such as more stringent capital adequacy ratios for foreign exchange liabilities and reserve requirements for foreign exchange short positions. A reserve requirement was imposed on banks foreign exchange liabilities in excess of USD 3 billion in January 2011, and in March 2011 new rules required Brazilian firms to pay a 6% tax on short term foreign exchange loans from abroad with a maturity of less than one year. As capital flows into Brazil slowed by 2012, many of these capital flow management measures were gradually withdrawn.

The use of capital flow management tools has become part of the policy toolkit of governments and central banks in developing countries, and is likely to remain part of their armoury against volatile capital flows.

Regional Co-operation Mechanisms

The East Asian experience also indicates that there may be a role for regional co-operation mechanisms such as the Chiang Mai Initiative in other emerging market regions to strengthen financial co-operation and improve regional economic stability. In Asia, discussions for such a regional arrangement were galvanized by the financial and economic contagion effects that created economic crises in many Asian economies during the East Asian crisis. The experience of Asia in developing a regional co-operation mechanism for crisis prevention and resolution through the Chiang Mai Initiative may offer lessons for other emerging markets regions to establish or strengthen regional co-operation mechanisms.

Banking Supervision

A key lesson of the East Asian crisis as well as many other economic crises in both developed and developing countries is the need for high quality supervision of domestic banking systems by the national bank regulatory authority. Baltenau and Erce (2014) have identified 113 banking crises in emerging markets since 1975. Even the banking systems of the US and many major European countries were facing meltdown during the global financial crisis of 2008–2009, exposing considerable weaknesses in the financial regulation and supervision in place in these advanced economies.

Banking sector crises contributed to the economic slump in a number of nations during the East Asian crisis, including Indonesia, Malaysia and Thailand, reflecting the impact of sharp exchange rate depreciation, capital flight and underlying problems with the commercial banking sector in terms of weak risk management, concentration of risks on bank balance sheets, and inadequate bank capital reserves.

In Malaysia, the banking system had an estimated non-performing loan ratio of around 2% on the eve of the East Asian crisis in June 1997, but this rose sharply to an estimated 11.5% just a year later. A number of negative factors contributed to this large negative shock to bank balance sheets. These included the impact of large ringgit depreciation on foreign currency debts of companies, a sharp downturn in the local real estate market and financial difficulties for some property developers, and a broad economic slowdown that affected companies in many sectors of industry. In Indonesia, the banking sector crisis that occurred in 1997 resulted in a run on banking system deposits that brought the financial system close to collapse.

Therefore a key focus for developing countries must be on strengthening their domestic banking system through high quality financial regulation and supervision, to ensure that banks have good quality risk management systems in place and also that bank capital adequacy ratios meet international standards in order to cope with economic shocks. Progressive implementation by banks in developing countries of the evolving international capital adequacy standards recommended by the Basel Committee on Capital Standards has been critical for reducing vulnerability to future banking crises. Nevertheless, despite the Basel capital adequacy standards, many developing countries still have troubled banking systems with high levels of non-performing loans, highlighting the importance of strengthening banking supervision and meeteing international capital standards.

Another key priority to improve the resilience of nations to economic crises is to improve the regulation of the corporate sector, to ensure that large companies are complying with international accounting standards and that public companies are following high quality reporting standards for their annual company accounts.

Prevention of Future Emerging Markets Crises

During the last 50 years, there have been frequent economic crises in developing countries, due to a number of factors, including banking crises and external debt crises.

While the international financial institutions such as the IMF and World Bank have worked closely with developing countries to try to improve resilience to crises, many developing countries remain vulnerable due to a range of factors, including dependence on commodities for fiscal and export revenues, vulnerability to volatile international capital flows and high levels of country risk due to geopolitical instability and domestic political risks.

A range of strategies can be adopted by countries to improve resilience to external shocks. Firstly, economic diversification of developing countries can help to reduce reliance on commodity exports, given around half of developing countries worldwide still rely on commodities as a key source of export revenue and as a major contributor to fiscal revenue.

Secondly, nations can build resilience by improving the regulation and prudential supervision of their financial system, as well as strengthening corporate governance to improve transparency and comply with international accounting standards.

Thirdly, deepening domestic capital markets can help to improve resilience and reduce dependency on international debt markets, which can be a potential source of instability for nations that have a high level of short term foreign loans.

Fourthly, sound macroeconomic management of fiscal and monetary policy is also important for building confidence for global and domestic investors.

Fifthly, management of foreign exchange reserves and use of foreign exchange swap facilities among central banks can play an important role in maintaining economic stability.

However even with skilful management of economic and financial risks developing countries remain vulnerable to the impact of political risks, notably the risk of conflict.

The devastating impact of conflict has often resulted in tremendous economic damage and human suffering across many developing countries in different regions, such as the killing fields of Cambodia, genocide in Rwanda and years of brutal war in Syria. Consequently, political risk also remains a key factor that has held back the economic development of many developing countries worldwide, and can be an important factor triggering economic and financial crises. Prevention and resolution of conflicts is therefore also critical to crisis prevention and resolution in developing countries.

One of the most promising areas of progress in crisis prevention and resolution has been the considerable progress in regional economic and financial co-operation in Asia, which should allow much stronger co-ordinated regional responses to economic crises in individual Asian countries.

However the spectre of a China hard landing continues to haunt the region, with downside shock from such an event having the potential to create regional contagion effects similar to the East Asian crisis. As the size of the Chinese economy continues to grow each year, the vulnerabilities of the Asia-Pacific region to such a shock continue to grow. The armoury of defensive tools and financial firewalls that have been built up since the East

Asian crisis could easily be torn down by a China hard landing, depending on its severity. Other emerging markets regions may learn valuable lessons from the crisis prevention and resolution strategies adopted in Asia, notably by the strengthening of East Asian regional co-operation through the Chiang Mai Initiative.

12

The Impact of Climate Change

The mountain train journey from Interlaken to Grindelwald in the Bernese Oberland of Switzerland is one of the most beautiful and scenic rail trips in the world. As the train winds its way up the steep Alpine mountainside and approaches Grindelwald, the spectacular view of three of the most famous Swiss mountains, Eiger, Jungfrau and Monch, comes into sight. If you look on the right-hand side of the train facing forward, you will see the lower Grindelwald glacier far in the distance, the blue glacial ice visible high on the slope of the mountainside.

Some years ago, I came across an antique print of the lower Grindelwald glacier, dated from about a 100 years ago. I was astonished to see that the print showed that same glacier extended close to the village of Grindelwald, near the railway line. It was such a remarkable piece of historical evidence about the retreat of glaciers that I bought it and it hangs on my dining room wall as a reminder of the impact of climate change on our planet. Even in the 20 years since I first saw the awesome sight of the Swiss glaciers in Grindelwald and also on the way to Zermatt, their retreat is very noticeable, a painful reminder of the tragedy of climate change and its dramatic consequences.

In 1850, 1745 square kilometres of Switzerland were covered by glaciers, but this area has shrunk dramatically to just 890 square kilometres now, having virtually halved. Each year, the retreat of the glaciers continues. The Swiss Academy of Natural Sciences has estimated that Swiss glaciers lost 3% of their total volume between October 2016 and September 2017, one of the biggest annual losses of glacial ice ever recorded (Swiss Academy of Sciences, 30th October 2017).

© The Author(s) 2018
R. Biswas, *Emerging Markets Megatrends*,
https://doi.org/10.1007/978-3-319-78123-5_12

In Africa, the fabled snows of Mount Kilimanjaro were celebrated by Hemingway in a short story with that title. Hemingway visited Tanganyika in 1933, providing the inspiration for his short story. However, the spectacular glacial ice fields that he must have seen at the top of the mountain have largely disappeared since that time.

> ...and there, ahead, all he could see, as wide as all the world, great, high, and unbelievably white in the sun, was the square top of Kilimanjaro.
> Ernest Hemingway, 'The Snows of Kilimanjaro', Esquire Magazine, August 1936.

The United Nations Environmental Programme (UNEP) has estimated that Africa's glaciers have lost 82% of their total land area since 1906, and are expected to disappear completely within the next decade. Other research on glacial retreat on Mt Kilimanjaro (Cullen et al. 2013) provides similar estimates, indicating that the glacial ice on top of Kilimanjaro has declined from 11.4 square kilometres in 1912 to 1.8 square kilometres in 2011, which is an 85% loss of ice cover over the past century.

Climate Change in Africa

According to the Intergovernmental Panel on Climate Change (IPCC) Fifth Assessment Report's assessment of Africa in 2014, evidence gathered indicates an increased warming over the previous 50–100 years. Mean temperatures for Africa are projected to rise by 2 degrees Centigrade by the end of this century compared with the late twentieth century mean. (Niang, I., et al., Africa. In: Climate Change 2014: Impacts, Adaptation, and Vulnerability. Part B: Regional Aspects. Contribution of Working Group II to the Fifth Assessment Report of the Intergovernmental Panel on Climate Change, 2014).

Due to the rapid growth of Africa's population projected over the next three decades, one of the most important potential threats from climate change relates to the impact on agricultural production and food security.

The implications of climate change for Africa will be complex, including reduced rainfall in North Africa and southwestern Africa, with increasing stress on water availability in some parts of Africa. These changes are also expected to reduce crop yields in affected areas, particularly because almost all agricultural production in Sub-Saharan Africa is still reliant on rainfall due to the lack of significant development of irrigation systems.

The total share of Africa's population that is still undernourished is estimated at around 22.7%, with 333 million people facing severe food insecurity in 2016, according to the International Fund for Agricultural Development (2017). The impact of climate change on crop yields combined with other factors such as rising population could therefore result in increasing food insecurity in Africa in future decades.

With climate change also expected to result in more severe weather events and natural disasters, some African coastal regions will also be vulnerable. In East Africa, the cities of Mombasa and Dar-es-Salaam are at risk from coastal flooding. Mombasa, which has a population of 1.2 million, is located on a low-lying island that is vulnerable to flooding and storm surges. Rising sea levels due to climate change will increase the land area vulnerable to inundation. Other African nations are also vulnerable to climate change and extreme weather events. For example, Nigeria is also vulnerable to flooding due to heavy rainfall, and major floods in 2012 caused significant economic damage to property, infrastructure and agricultural production.

Insufficient fiscal resources and inadequate planning for Africa's urbanization have contributed to the problems caused by climate change and more frequent extreme weather. Adaptation by many urban areas to cope with climate change will require considerable infrastructure investment in order to protect many urban populations from the impact of severe weather events.

However, unlike developed nations which have the substantial fiscal capacity to invest in flood prevention infrastructure, many African nations have large government debt to GDP ratios and high fiscal deficits, and will face mounting competing demands for public finances as their populations grow rapidly in coming decades. Consequently, the capacity of many African governments to invest in infrastructure to adapt to climate change is very constrained.

As part of the negotiations for the UN Framework Convention on Climate Change, developed countries agreed in 2010 to mobilize public and private sector funding of USD 100 billion to assist developing countries to adapt to climate change. The amount mobilized was estimated to have reached USD 62 billion by 2014. These funds being raised by developed countries will be particularly important for developing African countries given the fiscal resource constraints they face.

Asia's Vulnerability to Climate Change

The Fifth Assessment Report of the IPCC assessed that Asia has a significant vulnerability to the impact of climate change as a result of higher temperatures, more severe weather events and rising sea levels (IPCC Fifth Assessment Report 2014).

The impact of climate change through rising sea levels, changing weather patterns and more extreme weather events are expected to be particularly high in Asia. With many populous countries located in the Asian region, the impact of changing rainfall patterns due to climate change is an important risk factor for future agricultural production patterns.

Furthermore, much of Asia is vulnerable to extreme weather events such as tropical cyclones as well as flooding. The IPCC Fifth Assessment Report (2014) stated that Asia accounted for 27.5% of total global economic losses from weather-related disasters between 2000 and 2008.

A number of Asian countries have large river deltas with major cities located on the low-lying floodplains. These include Asian megacities such as Shanghai on the Yangtze River Delta and Dhaka on the confluence of the Ganges and Brahmaputra rivers. Bangkok, built on the floodplains of the Chao Phraya River, is also vulnerable to flooding, as is Ho Chi Minh City on the banks of the Saigon River.

The combination of rising sea levels and more extreme weather disasters could be particularly devastating for many Asian countries with large urban populations in such low-lying floodplains. Bangladesh is one of the most vulnerable nations to climate change, since an estimated 25% of the land area of Bangladesh is less than one metre above sea level. Bangladesh has already suffered considerable devastation from previous tropical cyclones that developed in the Bay of Bengal, creating high wind speeds that generated tidal storm surges that created tremendous destruction in low-lying coastal areas. The 1970 Bhola cyclone is estimated to have resulted in 300,000–500,000 deaths along the Bangladesh coastline. In April 1991, another devastating cyclone with wind speeds reaching up to 250 kilometres per hour hit the major city of Chittagong, causing storm surge waves of up to 6 metres, and resulting in an estimated 138,000 deaths with over 10 million made homeless by the destruction. Therefore improving resilience to extreme weather events is a key strategic priority for the Bangladesh government, including strengthening flood defence infrastructure and disaster management systems to prepare for the future impact of climate change.

In neighbouring, Myanmar, Cyclone Nargis resulted in over 130,000 deaths in 2008, with widespread flooding that resulted in the considerable destruction of agricultural crops. India is also vulnerable to severe weather events, with even the key commercial and financial hub of Mumbai, one of India's megacities, vulnerable to severe flooding on a regular basis. In 2005, heavy rains resulted in flooding in the state of Maharashtra that caused 5000 deaths, as well as causing severe floods in Mumbai that disrupted the city for days.

A key threat from climate change is also to food security, particularly, since a large share of the population of South Asia as well as Southeast Asia still are living in poverty and already suffer from malnourishment. The share of the Asian population suffering from malnourishment was estimated at 11.7% in 2016, according to IFAD (2017). While this is significantly lower than Africa's rate of malnourishment, which was 20% in 2016, nevertheless it still reflects that a substantial share of Asia's population still has inadequate food for their daily requirements. Moreover, due to the large size of Asia's total population, in absolute numbers the total Asian population suffering from malnourishment was estimated at 520 million people in 2016, more than double the number of people in Africa suffering from malnourishment.

If climate change has an adverse impact on crop yields, this could result in deteriorating food availability for a significant share of the population, particularly in populous nations with youthful demographics and growing population size such as Bangladesh, India, Indonesia and the Philippines. Moreover, the rate of malnourishment is significantly higher for South Asia, at 14.4% of the total population, than for the Asian regional average.

Rising temperatures associated with climate change can significantly alter rainfall patterns, impacting on crop yields. Global warming is expected to lower wheat crop yields in northern India due to the impact of higher temperatures, with more severe droughts also expected to lower crop yields in eastern China and some parts of Southeast Asia. However, in some regions of Asia, rising temperatures may improve crop output by allowing a second crop to be planted each year, such as in some parts of Pakistan. India is facing a growing water crisis due to the impact of rising demand for water from India's growing population, significant declines in groundwater levels due to heavy agricultural use of groundwater for irrigation, and lack of adequate investment by the Indian government in water storage infrastructure for decades. The impact of climate change is projected to worsen the situation in northern India, requiring accelerated government initiatives for management of water resources and investment in water storage infrastructure.

The World Resources Institute has estimated that 54% of India is already facing high or very high water stress, with the northeastern grain-producing states of Punjab, Haryana, Rajasthan and Gujarat facing particularly severe water stress with recurrent droughts having hit the region in recent years ("Three Maps Explain India's Growing Water Risks", World Resources Institute, 26th February 2015). During a severe drought which hit India in 2016, around 330 million people were impacted by the water shortages, with trains having to be used to supply water to the worst affected areas. Trains carrying water were sent to some districts in Rajasthan and Maharashtra when water reservoirs dried up for India, investing in water storage infrastructure will be a critical part of a long-term strategy to address the water crisis, improving the capture and storage of rainwater and managing groundwater resources in a more sustainable way to allow replenishment of underground water.

The IPCC Fifth Assessment Report (2014) also highlights the risk that due to climate change, rising sea levels could impact on rice production in low-lying coastal areas and river deltas, with Bangladesh, the Mekong river delta and the Irrawaddy delta vulnerable to significant loss of agricultural land due to rising sea levels.

In Bangladesh, which is a densely populated country, this creates major concerns about the risk that millions of "climate refugees" will be created as they lose their livelihoods as subsistence farmers and are forced to migrate to other parts of the country or try to emigrate abroad.

> People living in low-lying coastal zones and flood plains are probably most at risk from climate change impacts in Asia. Half of Asia's urban population lives in these areas. Compounding the risk for coastal communities, Asia has more than 90% of the global population exposed to tropical cyclones. The impact of such storms, even if their frequency or severity remains the same, is magnified for low-lying and coastal zone communities because of rising sea level.
>
> IPCC Fifth Assessment Report, Chapter 24. Asia. In: Climate Change 2014: Impacts, Adaptation, and Vulnerability. Part B: Regional Aspects. Contribution of Working Group II to the Fifth Assessment Report of the Intergovernmental Panel on Climate Change.

In the Pacific Island states, rising sea levels will also have devastating consequences in some nations that will suffer a substantial loss of habitable land. Amongst the most vulnerable according to the IPCC Fifth Assessment Report (2014) are the Marshall Islands and Kiribati, which could lose most of their habitable land if sea levels rise by half a metre. The Cook Islands, Tuvalu and Tonga are also among the most vulnerable to rising sea levels. The Maldives are also very vulnerable, with the capital city, Male, at risk of being completed submerged if sea levels rise by one metre.

The Maldives government is taking pre-emptive measures to avoid the risk that its inhabitants will become climate refugees by developing an artificial island called Hulhumale on reefs with a 3 m seawall to protect the artificial island. The Hulhumale project originally commenced in the 1990s to relieve congestion in Male, but has since become the government's strategic solution for rehousing inhabitants of other islands in the Maldives that become submerged due to rising sea levels.

For the Asia-Pacific region, the responses to climate change can significantly mitigate the impact, but will require considerable investment in infrastructure. Infrastructure to improve flood resilience in urban areas vulnerable to flooding is a key response, with many Asian governments having already commenced long-term infrastructure investment programmes to improve flood resilience. Ho Chi Minh City is investing USD 4.4 billion in new infrastructure to improve flood defence systems. Jakarta is also investing in improving flood defences and improving drainage of its canal systems.

In Thailand, the protracted 2011 floods resulted in economic damage estimated at USD 45.7 billion, according to World Bank estimates (December 2011), with USD 32 billion of economic losses in the manufacturing sector. The Thai government responded to the extensive floods by announcing a USD 11 billion infrastructure programme to improve infrastructure for flood defences.

In contrast to the determined response of the Thai government to the 2011 floods, India has not made substantial progress in mitigating flood risks in Mumbai. Despite severe floods in Mumbai in 2005 and recurrent episodes of flooding subsequently, the drainage infrastructure of Mumbai remains antiquated. The IPCC (2014) have called for substantial upgrading of Mumbai's drainage system, which would significantly reduce the economic losses due to flooding. As India's leading financial hub, major disruptions to Mumbai's commercial activity have severe economic costs for not only the city of Mumbai but for the entire nation.

Improving the resilience of agricultural production to climate change is also a key strategic response that Asia-Pacific nations can implement to mitigate the impact on crop yields. Use of new seeds developed to tolerate some of the more difficult growing conditions such as drought-resistant seeds can help to reduce the vulnerability of agricultural output climate change.

With many parts of Asia expected to experience more severe drought conditions due to global warming, improving irrigation systems and reducing reliance on direct rainfall will also help to improve crop yields. Countries, such as the United States, Australia and Israel are global leaders in agricultural irrigation technology for regions with very low rainfall, so accelerating such irrigation technology adoption could significantly contribute to managing the risks from climate change.

Implications for Latin America

As in the European and African glaciers, one of the strongest indications of the impact of global warming in Latin America is the retreat of the glaciers in the Andes, which has accelerated since the 1970s (IPCC 2014).

While climate change and the resultant rise in temperatures will impact upon Latin American food production, the implications are more ambiguous than for other developing country regions, notably Africa and Asia. Rising temperatures and increasing global demand for food may result in increased Latin American production of key agricultural products such as soybean and palm oil. As a major food exporting region with relatively low levels of malnourishment, Latin American may be able to gain an increased competitive advantage as a food exporting region as other regions face declining crop yields due to global warming.

However as with the Pacific Island states, the island states of the Caribbean will face vulnerabilities due to rising sea levels and increasing intensity of extreme weather events, notably the hurricanes that already devastate Caribbean nations all too frequently. As an indication of the scale of the devastation that can be wrought by hurricanes, the 2017 hurricane season was particularly damaging for the Caribbean, when Hurricanes Irma and Maria hit many islands. The island of Barbuda, part of the nation of Antigua and Barbuda, was so badly impacted that it became uninhabitable. The Dutch island of Sint Maarten, a self-governing country that is part of the Netherlands, was also badly devastated, but due to the support of the Dutch government received a Euro 550 million fund for reconstruction.

The impact of climate change on the small island states of the region is also manifested through coral bleaching due to rising temperatures, as well as soil erosion from beaches. Due to the importance of the tourism economy for many of the Caribbean nations, the combination of more frequent and severe hurricane damage, as well as coral bleaching and erosion of beaches in some areas could reduce the attractiveness of these destinations for tourism. Certainly, the devastation caused by Hurricanes Irma and Maria in 2017 caused protracted disruption to the tourism industry of a number of islands, including Barbuda, Dominica, Sint Maarten and the US territory of Puerto Rico. Since many Caribbean islands are also dependent on agricultural production for subsistence farming as well as for exports, the impact of severe hurricanes can destroy an island economy's economic output within days, by ruining a nation's agricultural crop as well as damaging tourism infrastructure.

Adapting to Climate Change

Developing countries are gradually implementing a broad range of strategies to adapt to climate change as scientific evidence increasingly indicates that the global response to control carbon emissions will not be sufficient to prevent significant climate change impact effects on many countries.

The vulnerability of least developed countries and small island developing states to climate change impact effects is particularly high. This reflects the dependence of many of these nations on agricultural output or tourism, both of which can be significantly impacted by extreme weather events such as cyclones.

The G-20, IMF and World Bank have also been at the forefront of efforts to use insurance solutions to try to mitigate the financial costs of natural disasters, working in co-operation with the international insurance industry to create innovative solutions. The Caribbean Catastrophe Risk Insurance Facility and the Pacific Catastrophe Risk Insurance Pilot are examples of progress towards such insurance schemes for small island states that are particularly vulnerable to the economic impact of such natural disasters. The new InsuResilience Global Partnership for Climate and Disaster Risk Finance and Insurance Solutions launched in November 2017 has created a new initiative for G-20 nations to assist a grouping of 49 vulnerable developing countries to mitigate the impact of climate change through innovative insurance mechanisms. The insurance industry is also developing new insurance products for cities to help mitigate the impact of natural disasters.

While some developing countries have the fiscal capacity to invest in infrastructure to improve resilience to natural disasters such as floods, the least developed countries often have high government debt levels and are dependent on international donor aid for a significant proportion of their infrastructure funding. As part of the COP21 Agreement on Climate Change, developed countries agreed to mobilize capital of USD 100 billion in order to finance adaptation to climate change by developing countries.

The private sector is also playing an increasingly significant role in financing solutions to address climate change. In February 2018, BBVA, Spain's second largest bank, pledged to mobilise USD 100 billion for green finance, sustainable infrastructure, social entrepreneurship and financial inclusion. In 2017, JPMorgan Chase committed to providing USD 200 billion in clean energy financing by 2025. In November 2017, HSBC pledged to raise USD 100 billion by 2025 for sustainable financing and investment.

An important area where banks are playing a key role is in the development of green bond financing. Green bonds are raised on international capital markets in the same way as normal bonds, but are used to fund green projects such as renewable energy infrastructure, sustainable land use development or that generate other environmental benefits. The international standards for designating a bond as a "green bond" are based on the International Capital Market Association's Green Bond Principles and the Climate Bonds Initiative's Climate Bond Standards. The total amount raised through green bonds annually has risen rapidly over the past decade, from around USD 4 billion in 2010 to an estimated USD 155 billion by 2017 (Climate Bonds Initiative, 10 January 2018). The World Bank has already raised more than USD 10 billion through the issuance of green bonds since 2008.

For developing countries, one of the most important priorities over the next decade and beyond will be to invest in infrastructure to adapt to climate change. Reducing vulnerability to extreme weather events and strengthening the resilience of food production to changing weather patterns will be among the key priorities for developing countries. This is particularly critical for least developed countries and small island states, which are among the most vulnerable to climate change.

13

Combating Terrorism and Organized Crime: Cryptocurrencies and Cybercrime

There has been substantial progress in the economic development of many developing countries over the past 50 years, with significant improvements in living standards and per capita GDP levels in the more successful emerging markets.

However, a large number of developing countries still remain mired in poverty, with weak institutional capacity and high levels of corruption. Many nations continue to be torn apart by civil wars and insurgencies, with some regions dominated by rebel forces or local warlords. Terrorist groups and organized crime gangs are able to exploit such failures of governance in some developing countries, which become swamps that provide fertile breeding grounds for terrorism and transnational crime.

The proliferation of terrorism and organized crime has resulted in a wide spectrum of international networks of criminal activity riding on the international wave of globalization and rapidly growing international trade and investment flows that has occurred in the past 50 years. These activities include the narcotics trade, human trafficking, slavery and counterfeiting. As organized crime gangs have accumulated vast financial resources and assets, their ability to embed themselves into legitimate commercial business activities and build strong networks with public officials in developing countries with weak governance has escalated.

The linkages between terrorist networks and organized crime groups are a rising threat, as terrorist networks utilize the well-established cross-border routes of organized criminal gangs to move terrorists and financing for terrorism across international borders.

© The Author(s) 2018
R. Biswas, *Emerging Markets Megatrends*,
https://doi.org/10.1007/978-3-319-78123-5_13

The Scale of Transnational Crime

The total global retail proceeds generated by transnational crime is estimated by Global Financial Integrity (GFI) at USD 1.6 trillion to USD 2.2 trillion per year according to their 2017 estimate (Transnational Crime and the Developing World, Channing May, Global Financial Integrity, March 2017). Of this total, around 30% is estimated by the GFI report as being attributable to drug trafficking, with around 50% being from a vast spectrum of counterfeiting. Other significant levels of criminal proceeds are derived from activities such as human trafficking, illegal mining and logging and crude oil theft.

With global GDP measured in nominal USD terms estimated at around USD 79 trillion in 2014, this GFI estimate of the total scale of transnational crime would be equivalent to around 2.8% of world GDP. This is a vast amount of revenue that is financing transnational crime each year, equivalent to the annual GDP of India in that year.

This is even higher than the United Nations Office on Drugs and Crime (UNODC) estimate for transnational organized crime in the year 2009 when it was estimated to be equivalent to 1.5% of world GDP (UNODC, Transnational Organised Crime the Globalised Illegal Economy).

While a large share of this annual revenue is likely to be expended on running costs such as wages for the criminal gangs and purchasing of their inputs, the profits remaining are financing the growing accrual of vast amounts of wealth for the criminal gangs.

The proceeds of these criminal activities are laundered through a variety of techniques, including the establishment of front companies that create an apparently "legitimate" business which can convert cash into bank deposits and other assets such as holdings of real estate.

A senior customs officer from a developed country once explained to me that criminal gangs often acquire restaurants, bars, nightclubs and other retail businesses that have large cash earnings, so that they can blend their illegal cash earnings into the legal cash flows, turning the illegal cash into bank deposits. Once their legal business has bank deposits, this money can be used to buy other assets, such as real estate. The funds can also be used to buy other businesses and establish new business operations in other countries, creating an international network of legal businesses as a front for their illegal operations.

Such international business operations by criminal networks can establish their presence in jurisdictions with weak governance, camouflaging their true operations under the veneer of legitimate business operations, gaining the support of public officials who may choose not to investigate too deeply into the true activities of their benefactors.

> Transnational Organized Crime is an abiding threat to US economic and national security. Criminals can play a significant role in weakening stability and undermining the rule of law in some emerging democracies and areas of strategic importance to the United States.
>
> James Clapper, Director of National Intelligence, "Worldwide Threat Assessment of the US Intelligence Community", US Senate Armed Services Committee, 11 February 2014.

With plenty of documented cases when even some of the world's best known multinationals have made corrupt payments to public officials in developing countries, the scale of payments to public officials by organizations controlled by criminal groups whose main purpose is crime is likely to be vast. The large flows of criminal funds are also used to fund insurgencies in some countries and finances local warlords operating in some countries in Latin America, Asia and the Middle East who maintain personal armies to protect the illegal trade of transnational organized crime gangs.

> Some states use Transnational Organised Crime (TOC) networks as proxies to engage in activities from which the states wish to distance themselves. TOC networks also have the ability to capture territory in states or portions of states and control it with violence and corruption of public officials. They often receive sanctuary as a result of providing social services, incorporating corruptive methods, and creating dependencies. TOC networks facilitate terrorism by providing money and services, such as selling weapons. They also engage in cyber-based theft and extortion and offer their capabilities to other cyber actors.
>
> Daniel R. Coats, Director of National Intelligence, "Worldwide Threat Assessment of the US Intelligence Community", US Senate Select Committee on Intelligence, 11 May 2017.

Transnational Organized Crime in the Digital Age

For decades, governments have progressively strengthened financial system regulation to try to prevent organized criminal groups and terrorists from exploiting the banking system for their criminal activities and for accumulating their assets. The Financial Action Task Force, an intergovernmental task force established to develop global standards for anti-money laundering, has established increasingly strict standards which most countries have progressively adopted. This has resulted in the strengthening of anti-money laundering rules for financial institutions worldwide. Nevertheless, despite these safeguards, criminal groups are becoming increasingly sophisticated in using alternative innovative solutions to access the financial system.

The latest estimates by the European Union Agency for Law Enforcement Co-operation (Europol), are that only a fraction of criminal proceeds in the European Union are intercepted by EU governments.

"Europol estimates that barely 1% of criminal proceeds in the European Union are ultimately confiscated by relevant authorities".
Europol Financial Intelligence Group, "From Suspicion to Action", Luxembourg, 2017.

As the scale of assets held by large organized criminal groups is very large in size, sometimes comparable to major multinational companies, these criminal organizations establish legal business entities in various jurisdictions worldwide and disguise their criminal operations with an overlay of legitimate business activities. This allows criminal groups to establish corporate bank accounts in financial institutions all over the world, using these accounts for large-scale international transfers.

Financial innovation and technology have also created new opportunities for criminal gangs and terrorists to conceal their financial transactions, as well as opening up new avenues for their criminal operations.

One of the most controversial and hotly debated areas of financial technology is the creation of cryptocurrencies such as Bitcoin, which are virtual currencies that so far have not been significantly regulated by central banks. As such cryptocurrencies can be used as a form of settlement of transactions but are not recorded by most regulatory authorities, use of cryptocurrencies can avoid many of the financial system controls that have been set up by government authorities to try to prevent money-laundering. There have been concerns among law enforcement agencies that cryptocurrencies are being used by criminal groups to transfer money internationally without any regulatory oversight. Some governments may have also tried to use cryptocurrencies to avoid sanctions. In March 2018, President Trump signed an execuective order banning all transactions by US persons or in the US related to digital currencies or digital coins issued by the Venezuelan government. The Venezuelan government had launched a form of cryptocurrency called the "petro" in February 2018, that may have been able to be used in attempts to circumvent US sanctions on Venezuela.

The Australian Criminal Intelligence Commission has highlighted the risks related to cryptocurrencies in its 2017 report on organized criminal activity in Australia.

The two key enabling technologies currently used to facilitate serious and organised crime are virtual currencies and encryption. Virtual currencies, such as bitcoin, are increasingly being used by serious and organised crime groups as they are a form of currency that can be sold anonymously online, without reliance on a central bank or financial institution to facilitate transactions.

Australian Criminal Intelligence Commission "Organised Crime in Australia 2017".

Global regulators have been in considerable disarray about what measures to take in regard to governance and regulation of cryptocurrencies as the price of leading cryptocurrency, Bitcoin, skyrocketed during 2017. So far, cryptocurrencies have been largely free to operate in a regulatory "white space" as regulators play catch-up with the rapid pace of development of cryptocurrencies. However, Asia-Pacific central banks have displayed increasing concerns about cryptocurrencies since 2017.

The People's Bank of China (PBoC) has been at the forefront of global regulatory efforts to clamp down on cryptocurrencies, with a ban on Initial Coin Offerings (ICOs) announced on 4 September 2017. A number of major cryptocurrency exchanges in China shut down during September 2017 in response to regulatory guidance by the PBoC.

The Governor of the Reserve Bank of Australia, Phillip Lowe, stated in a speech in Sydney on 13 December 2017 that the attributes of cryptocurrencies make them more attractive to criminals or those operating in the black economy rather than for normal financial transactions purposes, and that the current surge in investor interest in cryptocurrencies was comparable to a speculative bubble. The Reserve Bank of New Zealand Acting Governor Grant Spencer stated on 10 December 2017 that the surge in prices of cryptocurrencies "looks remarkably like a bubble".

The Indian government formed an Inter-Disciplinary Committee in April 2017 comprising representatives of government departments to prepare a report on the regulation of cryptocurrencies. The committee's report was submitted to the Indian government in August 2017, and Indian Finance Minister Arun Jaitley stated in his 2018 Budget speech that cryptocurrencies would not be legal tender in India.

The government does not consider cryptocurrencies legal tender or coin and will take all measures to eliminate the use of these crypto assets in financing illegitimate activities or as part of the payment system.

Finance Minister Arun Jaitley, 2018 Budget Speech, 1 February 2018

Although some governments are taking steps to try to prevent cryptocurrencies being used for criminal financing, many regulators worldwide have not taken any significant action to regulate the use of cryptocurrencies or to create a system of identifying bitcoin transactions. Consequently, the use of cryptocurrencies remains a major loophole in the international financial system that continues to enable financial crimes. Nevertheless, gradually there are increasing regulatory measures being implemented as governments realise that cryptocurrencies are being used as an unregulated currency for international payments and financial transfers by criminal organisations and terrorist groups.

In April 2018, the European Parliament voted in favor of increasing regulatory measures to regulate cryptocurrencies. The new EU legislation will require cryptocurrency exchanges and other platforms for cryptocurrencies to undertake know-your-customer verifications and other forms of anti-money laundering regulations in relation to cryptocurrencies. A number of governments, including the US Internal Revenue Service and some tax agencies of other governments have also begun to crack down on taxpayers who have not declared their capital gains from sale of cryptocurrencies. Although the process of regulation of cryptocurrencies has been slow, the regulatory net is increasingly being tightened to try to crack down on criminal activity related to cryptocurrencies. Banks in many countries are also banning the use of their accounts or credit cards to finance cryptocurrency purchases, both for anti-money laundering compliance reasons as well as due to concerns that slumping cryptocurrency prices could result in rising customer bad debts.

Digital payments technology has also created many other opportunities for criminals. Organized crime groups are also diversifying their operations into the new revenue opportunities related to cybercrime, including identity theft, credit card fraud and hacking of accounts. The most audacious example of how organized crime groups are able to rob banks was the Bangladesh Bank heist. Hackers managed to send instructions through the SWIFT interbank system instructing the US Federal Reserve Bank of New York to remit an amount of around USD 1 billion dollars from the accounts of the Bangladesh's central bank to various counterparties. Five transactions with a value of USD 101 million were completed, remitting funds to accounts in the Philippines and Sri Lanka. Although an alert bank executive in Sri Lanka queried the Sri Lankan transaction and halted the processing, the funds sent to the Philippines were successfully withdrawn, although a small proportion was later recovered. A number of other banks have subsequently had similar attempted hacker attacks, although so far none has been reported to have been successful. There are indications that some of these sophisticated cyber-crime attacks on central banks and commercial banks may have been orchestrated by state-sponsored groups operating from rogue states.

Asia's War on Terrorism and Organized Crime

Afghanistan is one example of a nation which has been ravaged by civil wars and conflict for decades, creating a fertile breeding ground for terrorism and organized crime. Afghanistan, which is one of the world's least developed countries, is the largest source of opium poppy and its derivate, heroin, in the world. UNODC has assessed that Afghanistan had 328,000 hectares of opium poppy under cultivation in 2017, up 63% since 2016 (UNODC, Afghanistan Opium Survey 2017).

The total value of Afghan opium production in 2017 was estimated at USD 1.4 billion, equivalent to around 7% of Afghanistan's total official GDP. This is estimated to be an increase of around 55% on the Afghan revenue from opium production in 2016, reflecting the large increase in area under cultivation.

Pakistan, Iran and various African countries have become important parts of the transhipment routes for Afghan opium to their major end markets for heroin in Europe and the United States. Opium remains a key source of financing for terrorist groups in Afghanistan and Pakistan, and therefore opium trafficking is a prime contributor to destabilizing terrorism and insurgent movements in Afghanistan and Pakistan.

> Afghanistan, in particular, continued to experience aggressive and coordinated attacks by the Afghan Taliban, including the affiliated Haqqani Network (HQN) and other insurgent and terrorist groups. A number of these attacks were planned and launched from safe havens in Pakistan.
> US Department of State, Country Reports on Terrorism 2016, Chapter 2, South and Central Asia.

In Southeast Asia, it is estimated that hundreds of nationals from Malaysia, Indonesia and the Philippines travelled to Syria and Iraq to join ISIS since

2014. These Southeast Asian nationals have been trained in extremist terrorist techniques and ideology, and as ISIS disintegrates as an effective force in the Middle East, it is likely that these hardened Southeast Asian extremists will return to their own countries to try to raise their own terrorist cells and seek to establish an Islamic caliphate in Southeast Asia. While their fantasies will certainly not be realized, it does mean that Southeast Asian governments will need to wage a protracted counterterrorism campaign to suppress these extremists.

Due to the highly capable police and military forces in Singapore, it is likely that Singapore will be successful in interdicting and suppressing extremist terror groups seeking to establish a presence in Singapore. A number of successful operations have already been conducted to prevent planned terrorist attacks and suppress extremist ideology being propagated by temporary workers from other Asian countries, such as Bangladesh.

In Malaysia, the police and intelligence services have had a strong track record in suppressing terrorist attacks, having prevented at least 19 attacks during the 2012–2017 period. Nevertheless, ISIS remains the most important security threat to the nation, with 105 suspected terrorists arrested in 2017, after 119 arrests in 2016.

Indonesia has suffered from a number of major terrorist attacks by extremist Islamist terror groups, including the Bali bombings in 2002, which resulted in 202 people being killed, and the coordinated suicide bombings of the Ritz-Carlton Hotel and the JW Marriott Hotel in Jakarta in 2009. Other major terrorist attacks included the bombing of the Australian Embassy in Jakarta in 2004 and another Bali bomb attack in 2005. These attacks triggered a strong response by the Indonesian government, with Indonesian police and counterterrorism forces mounting a protracted campaign to suppress terrorist networks. Major steps taken by the Indonesian government included the establishment of a National Counter Terrorism Agency in 2010 and the creation of a highly effective elite Special Forces unit, Densus 88, to spearhead antiterrorism operations following the Bali bombings. However despite years of intensive anti-terrorism efforts and considerable success, a new spate of terrorist attacks occurred in May 2018, with suicide bombings of three Christian churches in Surabaya and another suicide attack on a police station in the same city. According to the Indonesian National Intelligence Agency, around 1,000 Indonesians are estimated to have travelled to Syria and Iraq to join ISIS since 2014, with considerable concerns that returning extremists are creating terrorist cells after returning to Indonesia.

The war of extremist terrorist groups has also intensified in the Philippines. The Philippines is mainly a Christian nation, with over 90% of the population being Christians, but there has been a protracted government campaign to tackle the rise of extremist Islamist groups in the Muslim communities of the southern Philippines. The Abu Sayyaf extremist group has established the objective of creating an Islamic state in Western Mindanao and the Sulu archipelago, and has established links with Al Qaeda to further its aims.

Although the Aquino government did sign a peace treaty in 2014 with an Islamic insurgent group, the Moro Islamic Liberation Front, the peace process disintegrated after 44 police commandos were killed in a clash with MILF insurgents in January 2015.

The situation further deteriorated when President Duterte took office, after Islamic militants fought against government troops trying to arrest an Abu Sayyaf leader in Marawi City. The situation escalated into a protracted battle for control over the city which lasted for months. The battle started in May 2017 and ended in October 2017, indicating the tough fighting that the government forces experienced in order to liberate the city. Consequently Asia faces an ongoing war against terrorism for the foreseeable future, requiring increasing intergovernmental co-operation among Asian nations in implementing anti-terrorism strategies and joint operations to combat terrorist groups operating in the region.

The Threat to Africa

Much of Africa is vulnerable to the threat of penetration by terrorist networks and organized crime groups due to weak governance, the destabilization caused by regional conflicts, combined with the economic and social consequences of rapid population growth, low per capita GDP levels and high unemployment.

In Libya, which has been destabilized by years of civil war, various militia and extremist groups have controlled different parts of the country, creating a safe haven for terrorist networks and organized crime. This is comparable to the situation in some parts of the Middle East, notably Syria and regions of Iraq, where ISIS militants occupied vast tracts of territory since 2014 before being gradually pushed back by forces from an array of global and regional military powers.

The situation in Nigeria, Sub-Saharan Africa's largest economy, is also very unstable due to ongoing conflict between the Boko Haram extremist insurgents and government forces in some regions of the nation. The Boko Haram insurgency began in 2009, and has resulted in an estimated 20,000 deaths as well as 2 million displaced persons since that time. Other countries in the region have also been impacted by this insurgency, including Cameroon, Chad and Niger. With the population of West Africa projected to grow from 353 million in 2015 to 809 million by 2050, an increase of 457 million over this timeframe, the region is vulnerable to high levels of poverty and unemployment, creating rising vulnerability to terrorism and organized crime.

East Africa faces similar challenges, with extremist insurgent groups such as Al-Shabaab and ISIS having already established their terrorist networks in the region following a protracted state of anarchy in Somalia which allowed extremist terrorist groups to flourish. Kenya has mounted strong counter-terrorist operations with the support of allies such as the United States, but has nevertheless been the victim of numerous terrorist attacks, including the cowardly 2015 Garissa University College attack when terrorists massacred 148 innocent students and the 2013 Westgate Shopping Mall attack when 67 shoppers were murdered in an equally cowardly attack.

Both of these attacks were claimed by Al-Shabaab. These terrorist outrages have galvanized public support among the majority of Kenyans for tough counterterrorism actions by the Kenyan government, with its well-trained police and military forces making considerable progress in suppressing the militants. Global support by other governments through police and defence force co-operation with the Kenyan counterterrorism forces will continue to play a crucial role in suppressing terrorist networks in East Africa.

Implications for Developing Countries

The increasing global proliferation of international terrorist networks and transnational organized crime has benefitted from globalization, as the world economy has become more closely integrated through trade and investment flows. Criminal organisations and terrorist groups have been able to take advantage of rapidly growing flows of international travellers, air and sea cargoes, as well as financial flows in order to camouflage their activities. This has required an ever-growing need for governments to invest in border security to monitor international flows of people, goods and funds in order to interdict flows related to terrorism and organised crime.

With some developing countries being particularly vulnerable to such criminal organizations due to their relatively weak governance and lack of police and intelligence resources, a key global security challenge for the coming decades will be for the development of stronger partnerships between developed and developing nations to combat criminal groups. This will help to improve the resilience of many developing countries to international terrorism networks and transnational crime. In addition, developing countries will need to strengthen regional co-operation to combat terrorism and organised crime, as well as building government and private sector capabilities to fight cybercrime.

14

Conclusion: The Future Emerging Markets Landscape

The rising economic importance of developing countries in the global economy is one of the key global megatrends that have transformed the international economic order. Over the past four decades, the share of developing countries output in world GDP has risen from 25% in 1980 to around 40% by 2018. The rapid growth of developing countries as a grouping is reshaping the global geopolitical and economic order in a relatively short period of time. Further significant increases are expected over the next two decades in the developing countries' share of world GDP, as their average annual growth rate continues to outpace the GDP growth of the advanced OECD nations.

For multinational companies worldwide, this is forcing a rapid pace of transformation in their long-term strategic plans, as they refocus on the fast-growing consumer markets of developing countries. The large, mature consumer markets in the advanced economies of the United States and EU are growing at a much slower pace than during the past three decades, while the declining population of Japan is resulting in a gradual long-term contraction in the size of the Japanese consumer market.

One of the key global economic megatrends that is already well underway is the rise of emerging consumer markets, led by the rapid growth of the Chinese consumer market since 2000. Other large consumer markets in developing countries such as India, Indonesia, Brazil and Turkey are also showing strong long-term growth.

For corporate boardrooms around the world, this has meant that strategic planning for future revenue growth requires an increasing focus on fast-growing emerging markets of the future in order to drive revenue

© The Author(s) 2018
R. Biswas, *Emerging Markets Megatrends*,
https://doi.org/10.1007/978-3-319-78123-5_14

growth. However, in addition to building up their presence in the large emerging markets, many multinationals, including medium-sized companies, are increasingly looking towards the rapidly growing frontier market economies in Asia and Africa. While the size of these markets is relatively small compared to the BRICS economies, they offer high growth opportunities for a wide range of products and services. Developing Asian nations such as Vietnam, Bangladesh, Myanmar as well as Sub-Saharan African economies such as Ethiopia, Kenya and Ghana have consumer markets of significant size, with fast-growing household incomes and large populations.

However, for multinational companies that are used to operating in developed countries and upper middle income developing countries, entering these fast-growing consumer markets requires much more detailed and ongoing assessment of country risk involved in these emerging markets. The level of country risk in such markets can be considerably higher than in developed countries, with factors such as political risk, macroeconomic risk and payments risk being among the important considerations. Therefore, multinationals will increasingly need to establish more systematic risk management processes that consider these types of emerging markets risks when expanding their operations in these nations. When firms open production facilities or service centres in developing countries, they also need to have developed more detailed planning for supply chain disruptions or loss of service from such locations due to a wide range of risks, including conflicts, natural disasters and loss of critical infrastructure.

Recent examples of such episodes include the Thai floods in 2011 which caused widespread disruption and loss of production for many multinationals producing electronics and auto components in Thailand for their global supply chain. In Myanmar, Cyclone Nargis caused tremendous loss of life and catastrophic damage to the economy in 2008.

Perhaps the most ridiculous example of operational risks in emerging markets in recent times was when Cyprus suffered the loss of half its electricity generating capacity in 2011 when a power station was destroyed by an explosion, causing loss of power for much of the nation and then protracted rolling power blackouts. The circumstances of the explosion were incredibly idiotic, as 98 containers of munitions had been stored in the open sun for several years at a naval base adjacent to the power station and eventually self-detonated, destroying the power station and many other properties in the vicinity.

Another aspect of the risks involved in operating in developing countries relates to bribery and corruption. While these types of crimes are not limited to developing countries, the levels of corrupt practices can often be higher than in advanced economies. The Kroll Global Fraud and Risk Report for 2017/2018 highlighted that corruption and bribery is the fastest rising type of fraud, with the share of executives surveyed who reported episodes of bribery and corruption having risen to 21% in 2017, with reports of such incidents almost doubling compared with 11% in 2015 (Kroll Global Fraud and Risk Report 2017/2018, 10th Annual Edition, January 2018).

Despite the more complex risk environment in developing countries, the rapid growth of many consumer markets in developing countries will create significant new growth opportunities across a wide range of manufactures and services. Fast-growing household incomes create strong growth in demand for manufactures such as consumer electronics, autos and motorbikes, fast-moving consumer goods and consumer durables such as white goods. Rising household income levels will also drive demand for residential housing, underpinning growth in housing construction and a wide range of building products and home furnishings.

In the services sector, increasing household income levels will underpin demand growth for a wide range of services, such as banking and insurance, health care, communications services and business services. As countries progress to middle-income status, the capacity of their consumers to spend on retail goods, restaurants, tourism and travel will also grow rapidly. The boom in Asian commercial passenger air travel over the past decade highlights that these trends are already well underway.

However, despite these broad positive trends for developing countries as a grouping, the demographic changes occurring in different developing regions of the world have widely contrasting implications. Northeast Asia is facing the impact of severe demographic ageing, with Japan at the forefront of this silver tsunami. With the population of Japan projected to contract significantly over the next 30 years, the Japanese consumer market is expected to steadily decline in size, which could also result in a gradual decline in many of Japan's rural communities and small towns. A number of other Asian nations, including South Korea, China, Singapore and Thailand will also be impacted significantly by population ageing.

However, the youthful demographic profile of populous countries in Southeast Asia such as Indonesia and the Philippines, as well as in South Asia in India and Bangladesh will also create very large public policy challenges for governments as they try to deliver jobs growth for the large cohorts of youth joining the labour force each year.

In the African continent, the implications of rapid population growth and large increases in the population of working age are creating a demographic time bomb over the next three decades and beyond. If African jobs growth does not match the tremendous increases in working age population over coming decades, it could result in escalating poverty and unemployment, particularly in low-income Sub-Saharan African countries.

Addressing the implications of Africa's demographic outlook will require coordinated global economic policy action on a large scale, with an urgent global policy response needed within the next decade to prevent the scale of the issues from escalating. The G-20 has already recognized the need for international action to assist Africa with its industrial development. However, so far, large-scale funding to achieve an industrial transformation of Africa has not yet been mobilized by the G-20.

One of the key areas of policy focus will need to be on accelerating industrial development, to create new hubs of manufacturing jobs growth in Sub-Saharan Africa.

If the global community fails in the task of boosting African employment growth, the consequences will be felt in migration outflows, as the pressure to emigrate from Africa continues to mount due to rising unemployment, poverty and weak progress in improving living standards. A co-ordinated international development initiative for Sub-Saharan Africa is therefore required, similar in vision and scale to the Marshall Plan for the reconstruction of the devastated nations of Europe after the Second World War.

The changing technological landscape for manufacturing is also creating new challenges for developing countries, as industrial automation, robotics and The Internet of Things are altering the competitive landscape for many sectors of the manufacturing industry. Developing countries may be facing a growing technological and digital divide, as emerging markets with high technology industries, good infrastructure and abundant skilled graduates in technology and science are better positioned to become global hubs for high growth manufacturing industries. In contrast, nations which are reliant on agricultural and mineral commodities exports and have a relatively unskilled workforce may find it increasingly difficult to attract manufacturing investment and change the structure of their economies towards higher value-adding sectors.

Disruptive change is also transforming the global industrial landscape, as modern technologies such as artificial intelligence and big data are changing many professions and could result in dramatic changes in the future employment levels in some industries. Banking, insurance and accountancy industries are already being significantly impacted by these disruptive new technologies. New financial technology is also creating new competition for traditional retail banking from competitors in other sectors that can deliver digital banking solutions, such as telecoms firms. E-commerce is also having a significant impact on traditional bricks and mortar retailing, with large job losses in retailing already evident in some nations as e-commerce grows rapidly.

In this brave new world of rapid technological change, the future for the grouping of 47 LDCs is a particular concern, as many have a strong focus on primary industries, weak infrastructure and limited competitiveness in technology industries. Therefore, the developing countries grouping risks becoming increasingly fragmented into industrializing technology-focused economies that are strongly integrated into the global new economy, and another grouping of primary commodities dependent developing countries that lack significant technology industries and have weak human capital in IT and scientific disciplines.

A key determinant of competitive advantage among developing nations will be infrastructure quality, as nations compete to attract foreign direct investment as well as domestic investment flows. The quality of infrastructure for power and water, as well as transport infrastructure such as roads, ports and airports will be increasingly important factors for companies seeking efficient hubs for establishing manufacturing plants, R&D centres or IT-BPO campuses.

Therefore, mobilizing greater infrastructure flows for developing countries will be a key strategic challenge, with large infrastructure financing gaps in many developing countries requiring a greater role for private capital flows into infrastructure. With severe fiscal constraints limiting the scope for additional public sector resources to be invested in infrastructure development in many developing countries, one of the key public policy priorities for the coming decades will be to mobilize additional private sector financing for infrastructure development in emerging markets.

The use of private sector financial products and innovations to improve investment flows into developing countries is another key priority, with various insurance risk mitigation products that can be utilized to manage the higher risks involved in investing in developing countries compared with advanced economies. Insurance products can also be used to manage other vulnerabilities that can create significant economic disruption to developing countries, such as insurance protection for nations against damage from typhoons, earthquakes and other natural disasters.

Urbanisation is another major trend impacting on developing countries, as rapid growth in urban population results in growing environmental and social pressures in cities. Increasing traffic congestion, rising air pollution, inadequate housing stock and poor urban transport infrastructure are among the challenges facing many of the megacities in developing countries.

National, state and municipal governments in developing countries are therefore putting greater policy priority on improving urban infrastructure, as cities compete globally to attract new investment inflows. Increasing focus is being put on building greenfield smart cities or smart precinct projects that will become dynamic hubs for new investment by technology companies and other firms seeking high-quality infrastructure for their new plants or offices. Smart city technology is at the forefront of such urban developments, including intelligent traffic management systems, efficient energy infrastructure with continuous power and e-governance to ensure efficient delivery of government services.

Many large cities in developing countries also face significant environmental risks, with the impact of climate change expected to increase the vulnerability of low-lying cities built on coastlines or river deltas. This includes very large cities such as Jakarta, Dhaka, Ho Chi Minh City and Bangkok. Improving infrastructure to mitigate the risks of flooding or storm surges is increasingly important as the impact of climate change results in higher risks of extreme weather events occurring.

Overall, developing countries therefore face a complex mixture of opportunities and threats over the next three decades. The significant progress in economic development in East Asia has been a major positive factor in the overall progress of developing countries in reducing poverty. China's rapid economic development has made a very substantial contribution to overall poverty reduction among developing nations by lifting an estimated 800 million out of poverty since its economic reforms began in 1978. Globally, an estimated 1.1 billion people have been lifted from poverty since 1978. Therefore, China's progress in substantially reducing poverty has played a key role in driving global poverty reduction.

The transformation of China's economy from a low-income nation in 1980 to an upper middle income country by 2018 is a remarkable transition, with China on a path that will lift it into high-income status within the next decade unless some external shock or downturn due to domestic economic imbalances results in growth rates slowing down sharply. With the size of China's GDP having reached USD 12 trillion in 2017, the Chinese government has become a major source of development assistance to other developing countries.

The Belt and Road Initiative championed by President Xi Jinping is a vast initiative for infrastructure financing for developing countries that is expected to provide around USD 1 trillion for infrastructure projects in developing countries over the next decade. Therefore, China's economic ascent has created a major new powerhouse for development assistance, with large-scale financing already being provided to Asian and African countries.

Japan is also providing large-scale economic development assistance to developing countries, particularly in the Asia-Pacific region, while South Korea is also ramping up its development co-operation assistance.

The United States and Australia have also signed a Memorandum of Understanding in February 2018 to provide support for high-quality infrastructure development in the Indo-Pacific region. This will include a US-Australian Strategic Partnership for Energy in the Indo-Pacific region which will help to develop energy infrastructure with a focus on developing markets for gas, with both the United States and Australia being gas exporting nations.

Asian developing countries are the largest beneficiaries of the substantial flows of development financing already being provided by China, Japan and South Korea. Asian nations in the Indo-Pacific region will also benefit from the new initiatives for infrastructure development being launched by the United States and Australia.

For low-income Asian nations, this improves their prospects of rapid economic development, with many of Asia's thirteen LDCs set to graduate from LDC status over the next decade. However, the outlook for the LDCs in Sub-Saharan Africa is more challenging, with rapid population growth, low per capita GDP levels and continued dependence on primary commodities production being among the factors constraining their long-term prospects for graduating out of the ranks of the world's LDCs.

Geopolitical risks remain a key risk to economic development for many developing countries, notably in the Middle East, which has continued to be ravaged by wars in recent decades. Syria, Yemen, Iraq and Lebanon are among the Middle East countries that have been devastated by recent conflicts. In Africa, an increasing number of nations have suffered the impact of insurgencies, including the Boko Haram insurgency in Nigeria and the Al-Shabaab extremist grouping in Somalia which has also conducted major terrorist attacks in Kenya.

Despite geopolitical tensions between some of Asia's largest economic powers, notably disputed territorial claims between China and India over some desolate sections of the Himalayas and territorial disputes between Japan and China over the disputed sovereignty of the Senkaku/Diayou islets, the Asia-Pacific region has made substantial efforts at improved regional economic co-operation.

The ten member nations of ASEAN have created a nucleus for Asia-Pacific economic co-operation with their own success at creating a regional political and economic grouping that has improved regional political dialogue as well as creating the ASEAN Free Trade Area.

When ASEAN was created in 1967, one of its core objectives was to improve regional peace and stability in Southeast Asia, following the military tensions between Indonesia and Malaysia as well as Singapore during the period of *Konfrontasi* when Indonesian President Sukarno had triggered escalating military clashes by using Indonesian paramilitary forces to destabilize plans for the creation of Malaysia following British colonial rule.

Consequently, there were years of border conflict as the British military together with Malaysian forces fought against the Indonesian forces. This confrontation only ended when President Sukarno stepped down after the attempted PKI coup in Indonesia and Major General Suharto took power, giving his support to the creation of ASEAN to build a regional mechanism to build peace and security.

Since the 1960s, ASEAN has evolved as a powerful regional mechanism for strengthening political and economic ties among the ASEAN nations. Its role as a forum for regional dialogue has also grown considerably in recent years, both for economic and political co-operation. ASEAN leaders have regularly played an important role in defusing bilateral tensions among its member countries.

The role of ASEAN as a forum for regional security dialogue was also enhanced in October 2010, when ASEAN established a forum for ASEAN defence ministers to meet with regional partners. This forum is the ASEAN Defence Ministers Plus with Eight Dialogue Partners Forum (ADMM+). The eight dialogue partners are Australia, China, India, Japan, New Zealand, South Korea, Russia and the United States.

In the area of economic co-operation, the creation of the Chiang Mai Initiative also reflects the significant progress of East Asian regional coordination for the financial system.

This process of greater economic and political co-operation in the Asia-Pacific region over the past 50 years has made a significant contribution to the sustained economic development of the region, with relatively few major conflicts occurring during this time period to disrupt the region's path towards economic development.

However, regional flashpoints that have the potential to disrupt the region's economic development do still exist. The Korean peninsula remains an area of high military tensions ever since the end of the Korean War, with the potential for military clashes that could escalate into war. Due to the involvement of military superpowers in the Korean confrontation, the risk of conflict escalating into regional war has remained a risk ever since the Korean War.

Another major regional flashpoint is in the Indian subcontinent, with India and Pakistan having fought several wars since they became independent nations in 1947, with the first war between India and Pakistan taking place in October 1947, only weeks after both nations had become independent.

A major conflict also occurred in 1965, resulting in thousands of military casualties. Following the independence struggle in Bangladesh against the Pakistani military, another major war between India and Pakistan took place, with Indian forces liberating Bangladesh from Pakistan's military rule.

Meanwhile, there have been ongoing conflicts in some nations in the region, notably the insurgencies in Afghanistan and Pakistan which have resulted in large-scale civilian casualties as well as being a major obstacle to economic development.

Therefore, regional initiatives in the Asian region to strengthen political and economic co-operation will be critical to underpinning Asia's future economic development and prosperity.

The achievements of Europe in building regional peace and security after World War Two provide some lessons for the future of Asian co-operation. For hundreds of years, the European continent had been ravaged by repeated wars between European nations. Following two devastating world wars and millions of deaths in the twentieth century, European political leaders such as Konrad Adenauer, Robert Schuman, Winston Churchill, Charles De Gaulle, Willy Brandt and Jean Monnet were finally able to build lasting regional peace and political co-operation.

> Our constant aim must be to build and fortify the United Nations Organisation. Under and within that world concept we must recreate the European family in a regional structure called, it may be, the United States of Europe, and the first practical step will be to form a Council of Europe.
> Winston S. Churchill, Speech at University of Zurich, 19 September 1946.

Western Europe serves as a powerful example of how a region deeply divided for centuries succeeded in healing the bitter scars of conflict through political leadership by European statesmen who were committed to building unity and preventing future European conflicts.

If the major Asian powers can provide similar leadership for the Asian region, this could also provide a stable foundation for future sustained economic development and co-operation in Asia. Further strengthening of regional political and economic co-operation in Latin America will also help to create a platform for closer economic and investment ties between Asia and Latin America.

Despite the tremendous economic challenges facing many developing countries worldwide, one of the most powerful positive forces for future economic progress and development among the world's developing countries will be South-South co-operation. As the major emerging markets such as

China, India, South Korea, Brazil, Mexico, Indonesia and Turkey continue to ascend in the global economic rankings, their ability to become powerful drivers of economic development in other developing countries continues to grow. This has the potential to transform the global economy and lift hundreds of millions out of poverty over the decades ahead.

Bibliography

African Development Bank, *African Economic Outlook 2018* [African Development Bank Group] (2018).

Asian Development Bank, *Meeting Asia's Infrastructure Needs* (February 2017).

Balteanu, I., and Erce, A., *Banking Crises and Sovereign Defaults in Emerging Markets: Exploring the Links.* Working Paper 114 [Banco de Espana] (2014).

Bayly, C.A., and Harper, T.N., *Forgotten Wars: The End of Britain's Asian Empire* [Penguin] (2008).

Biswas, R., *Asian Megatrends* [Palgrave Macmillan] (London, 2015).

Biswas, R., *Future Asia: The New Gold Rush in the East* [Palgrave Macmillan] (London, 2013).

Biswas, R., Combating Organised Crime. In *Commonwealth Public Administration Reform 2004, Part Two: Democracy and Security.* Commonwealth Secretariat [The Stationery Office] (London, 2004).

Biswas, R., *Mobilizing Private Capital Flows for Infrastructure Development in the Asia-Pacific.* Discussion Paper 10 [United Nations Economic and Social Commission for Asia and the Pacific] (Bangkok, 2016).

Biswas, R., *Reshaping the Financial Architecture for Development Finance: The New Development Banks* [London School of Economics and Political Science, Global South Unit] (London, 2015).

Biswas, R., and Mendez, A., *The Long Crisis Facing Emerging Markets: A Roadmap for Policy Reforms* [London School of Economics and Political Science, Global South Unit] (London, 2016).

Blake, R., *Jardine Matheson: Traders of the Far East* [Weidenfeld & Nicolson] (1999).

Blood, Peter ed., *Pakistan: A Country Study* [GPO for the Library of Congress] (Washington, 1994).

© The Editor(s) (if applicable) and The Author(s) 2018
R. Biswas, *Emerging Markets Megatrends*,
https://doi.org/10.1007/978-3-319-78123-5

Cabezon, E., Hunter, L.,Tumbarello, P., Washimi, K., and Wu, Y., *Enhancing Macroeconomic Resilience to Natural Disasters and Climate Change in the Small States of the Pacific*. IMF Working Paper WP/15/125 [IMF] (June 2015).

Carreras, O., Philip Davis, E., and Piggott, R., *Macroprudential Tools, Transmission and Modelling* [National Institute of Economic and Social Research] (London, October 2016)

Chamon, M., and Garcia, M., *Capital Controls in Brazil: Effective?* IMF Paper, 15th Jacques Polak Annual Research Conference [IMF] (November 2014).

Cisco Visual Networking Index, *Global Mobile Traffic Data Forecast Update 2016–2021*. White Paper [Cisco] (February 2017).

Claessens, S., Ghosh, S.R., and Mihet, R., *Macroprudential Policies to Mitigate Financial System Vulnerabilities*. IMF Working Paper 14/155 [IMF] (Washington, DC, August 2014).

Clapper, J.R., *Worldwide Threat Assessment of the US Intelligence Community*. Statement for the Record, Senate Armed Services Committee (February 11, 2014).

Clement, P., and Maes, I., *The BIS and the Latin American Debt Crisis of the 1980s*. Working Paper Research No. 247 [National Bank of Belgium] (December 2013).

Clinton, B., *My Life* [Hutchinson] (New York, 2004).

Clutterbuck, R., *The Long, Long War: The Emergency in Malaya 1948–60* [Cassel & Co] (1966).

Coats, D.J., *Worldwide Threat Assessment of the US Intelligence Community*. Statement for the Record, Senate Select Committee on Intelligence (May 11, 2017).

Cohan, W.D., *The Last Tycoons* [Penguin Books] (London, 2008).

Cullen, N.J., Sirguey, P., Molg, T., Kaser, G., Winkler, M., and Fitzsimons, S.J., *A Century of Ice Retreat on Kilimanjaro: The Mapping Reloaded*. The Cryosphere, 7, 419–431 (March 2013).

Dikotter, F., *Mao's Great Famine* [Bloomsbury] (London, 2010).

Enright, M.J., and Hoffmann W.J., *China into the Future: Making Sense of the World's Dynamic Economy* [Wiley] (Singapore, 2008).

Executive Office of the President of the United States, *Artificial Intelligence, Automation and the Economy* [The White House, US Government] (Washington, DC, December 2016).

Farrell, B.P., *The Defense and Fall of Singapore 1940–42* [Tempus] (Stroud, 2005).

Ferguson, N., *Civilization: The West and the Rest* [Allen Lane] (London, 2011).

Galbraith, J.K., *A Short History of Financial Euphoria* [Penguin Books] (New York, NY, 1993).

Geithner, T.F., *Stress Test: Reflections on Financial Crises* [Random House Business Books] (London, 2014).

Ghosh, A., Ostry, J.D., and Qureshi, M., *Managing the Tide: How Do Emerging Markets Respond to Capital Flows*. Working Paper 17/69 [IMF] (March 2017).

Giegerich, B., *Europe and Global Security* [Routledge] (Oxon, 2010).

Greenspan, A., *The Age of Turbulence: Adventures in a New World* [Penguin] (New York, NY, 2007).

Griffith-Jones, S., *A BRICS Development Bank: A Dream Come True?* UNCTAD Discussion Paper No. 215 [UNCTAD] (March 2014).

Haldane, A., *Labour's Share. Speech Given at the Trades Union Congress in London* [Bank of England] (London, November 12, 2015).

Hall, J.W., *Japan: From Prehistory to Modern Times* [Tuttle] (Germany, 1968).

Hart, A.F., and Jones, B.D., *How Do Rising Powers Rise?* Survival Vol. 52 no.6, IISS (Dec. 2010–Jan. 2011).

Hijioka, Y., Lin, E., Pereira, J.J., Corlett, R.T., Cui, X., Insarov, G.E., Lasco, R.D., Lindgren, E., and Surjan, A., *2014: Asia. in Climate Change 2014: Impacts, Adaptation, and Vulnerability. Part B: Regional Aspects. Contribution of Working Group II to the Fifth Assessment Report of the Intergovernmental Panel on Climate Change* [Barros, V.R., C.B. Field, D.J. Dokken, M.D. Mastrandrea, K.J. Mach, T.E. Bilir, M. Chatterjee, K.L. Ebi, Y.O. Estrada, R.C. Genova, B. Girma, E.S. Kissel, A.N. Levy, S. MacCracken, P.R. Mastrandrea, and L.L. White (eds.)], pp. 1327–1370 [Cambridge University Press] (Cambridge, UK and New York, NY).

Hill, D., *The Gold Rush* [William Heinemann] (Sydney, NSW, 2011).

Hill, P., *Heisei Yakuza: Burst Bubble and Botaiho.* Social Science Japan Journal, 6, 1 (2003).

Howard, J., *Lazarus Rising* [HarperCollins] (Australia, 2010).

Hobsbawm, E.J., *Industry and Empire* [Pelican Books] (Great Britain, 1968).

Holslag, J., *Trapped Giant: China's Military Rise.* IISS [Routledge] (Oxon, 2010).

Hughes, J., *The End of Sukarno: A Coup That Misfired: A Purge That Ran Wild* [Archipelago Press] (New York, 1967).

IMF, *Asia and Pacific Small States Monitor.* Quarterly Bulletin, 5 (August 2015).

IMF, *The Liberalisation and Management of Capital Flows: An Institutional View* (Washington, DC, November 14, 2012).

Indonesia: The First 50 Years, 1945–1995 [Archipelago Press] (New York, 1995).

International Air Transport Association, *2036 Forecast Reveals Air Passengers Will Nearly Double to 7.8 Billion.* Press Release Number 55 (October 24, 2017).

International Finance Corporation, *Establishing Emerging Markets.* IFC History (Washington, DC).

International Fund for Agricultural Development, *The State of Food Security and Nutrition* [Food and Agricultural Organization] (Rome, 2017).

Jalan, B., *India's Politics: A View from the Back Bench* [Penguin & Viking] (New Delhi, 2007).

James, L., *Raj: The Making of British India* [Abacus] (London, 1998).

Japanese Ministry of Foreign Affairs, *Announcement of Partnership for Quality Infrastructure: Investment for Asia's Future* [Ministry of Foreign Affairs] (Tokyo, May 21, 2015).

Kaplan, E., and Rodrick, D., *Did the Malaysian Capital Controls Work?* National Bureau of Economic Research Working Paper 8142 [NBER] (Cambridge, MA, February 2001).

Kharas, H., *The Emerging Middle Class in Developing Countries.* OECD Development Centre Working Paper 285 (January 2010).

Kissinger, H., *On China* [Penguin Press] (New York, 2011).

Kroll, *Global Fraud and Risk Report 2017/18, 10th Annual Edition* [Kroll] (January 2018).

Krugman, P., *The Return of Depression Economics and The Crisis of 2008* [W.W. Norton] (New York, 2009).

Lee, J.K., *Korean War 1129* [Woojung Books] (Seoul, 2015).

Lee, K.Y., *From Third World to First: The Singapore Story: 1965–2000* [Times Media Private] (Singapore, 2000).

Lyman R., *Slim, Master of War: Burma and the Birth of Modern Warfare* [Robinson] (London, 2004).

Maddison, A., *Monitoring the World Economy 1820–1992* [OECD] (Paris, 1995).

Magnus, G., *Uprising: Will Emerging Markets Shape or Shake the World Economy?* [Wiley] (Chichester, 2011).

Mahbubani K., *The New Asian Hemisphere* [Public Affairs] (New York, 2008).

Mahbubani, K., *The Great Convergence: Asia, The West, and the Logic of One World, Public Affairs* (New York, 2013).

Mandela, N., *The Autobiography of Nelson Mandela Long Walk to Freedom* [Back Bay Books/Little, Brown and Company] (New York, 1994).

May, C., *Transnational Crime and the Developing World* [Global Financial Integrity] (March 2017).

Moller, J.O., *How Asia Can Shape the World: From the Era of Plenty to the Era of Scarcities* [ISEAS] (Singapore, 2011).

Moody's Investors Service, Credit Analysis, *IBRD (World Bank)* (January 31, 2014).

Moscow Times, *Russian Central Bank Increases Capital Flight Estimate by USD 38 Billion* (November 10, 2014).

Munich Re, *Pacific Catastrophe Risk Assessment & Finance Initiative: Rebuilding After Cyclone Pam* (March 20, 2015).

Myint, H., *Economic Theory and the Underdeveloped Countries* [Oxford University] (London, 1971).

Niang, I., Ruppel, O.C., Abdrabo, M.A., Essel, A., Lennard, C., Padgham, J., and Urquhart, P., *2014: Africa. In: Climate Change 2014: Impacts, Adaptation, and Vulnerability. Part B: Regional Aspects. Contribution of Working Group II to the Fifth Assessment Report of the Intergovernmental Panel on Climate Change* [Barros, V.R., C.B. Field, D.J. Dokken, M.D. Mastrandrea, K.J. Mach, T.E. Bilir, M. Chatterjee, K.L. Ebi, Y.O. Estrada, R.C. Genova, B. Girma, E.S. Kissel, A.N. Levy, S. MacCracken, P.R. Mastrandrea, and L.L. White (eds.)], pp. 1199–1265 [Cambridge University Press] (Cambridge, UK and New York, NY].

Nurse, L.A., McLean, R.F., Agard, J., Briguglio, L.P., Duvat-Magnan, V., Pelesikoti, N., Tompkins, E., and Webb, A., 2014: Small Islands. In *Climate Change 2014: Impacts, Adaptation, and Vulnerability. Part B: Regional Aspects. Contribution of Working Group II to the Fifth Assessment Report of the Intergovernmental Panel on Climate Change* [Barros, V.R., C.B. Field, D.J. Dokken, M.D. Mastrandrea, K.J. Mach, T.E. Bilir, M. Chatterjee, K.L. Ebi, Y.O. Estrada, R.C. Genova, B. Girma, E.S. Kissel, A.N. Levy, S. MacCracken, P.R. Mastrandrea, and White, L.L. (eds.)] [Cambridge University Press] (Cambridge, UK and New York, NY).

NEXI, *Annual Report FY 2014* (Tokyo, Japan, July 2015).

New Zealand Super Fund, *Annual Report 2015.*

OECD, *Annual Survey of Investment Regulations of Pension Funds* (2015).

OECD, *Small Island Developing States and the Post-2015 Development Finance Agenda* (July 2015).

Office of the Director of National Intelligence, *Global Water Security, Intelligence Community Assessment, ICA 2012–08* (Washington, DC, February 2012).

Office of the Director of National Intelligence, *National Intelligence Strategy of the United States of America* (2014).

Overtveldt, J.V., *Bernanke's Test, Ben Bernanke, Alan Greenspan and the Drama of the Central Banker* [Agate] (Chicago, 2009).

Pacific Regional Infrastructure Facility, *Infrastructure Maintenance in the Pacific— Challenging the Build-Neglect-Rebuild Paradigm.* Summary Paper (Sydney, 2013).

Poston, D.L., Alnuaimi, W.S.K., and Li, Z., *The Muslim Minorities of China: Towards Separatism or Assimilation?* Population Association of America [Princeton University] (Princeton, NJ, 2010).

Prestowitz, C., *Three Billion New Capitalists, The Great Shift of Wealth and Power to the East* [Basic Books] (New York, 2005).

Reinhart, C.M., and Rogoff, K.S., *This Time Is Different: Eight Centuries of Financial Folly* [Princeton University Press] (Princeton, 2009).

Reuters News, *Suspected Uighurs Rescued from Thai Trafficking Camp* (March 14, 2014).

Reuters News, *Global Forex Reserves Poised to Record First Quarterly Drop Since 2008/09* (December 17, 2014).

Rostow, W.W., *The Stages of Economic Growth: A Non-communist Manifesto* [Cambridge University Press] (London, 1960).

Roach, S.S., *The Next Asia: Opportunities and Challenges for a New Globalization* [Wiley] (Hoboken, NJ, 2009).

Rogers, J., *Investment Biker: Around the World with Jim Rogers* [Wiley] (Chichester, 2000).

Sachs, J., Bono, *The End of Poverty: How We Can Make It Happen in Our Lifetime* [Penguin] (Londona and New York, 2005).

Sanyal, S., *The Indian Renaissance: India's Rise After a Thousand Years of Decline* [Penguin & Viking] (New Delhi, 2008).

Schwab, K., *The Fourth Industrial Revolution* [Crown Business] (New York, 2017).

Scott-Clark, C., and Levy, A., *The Siege* [Penguin] (London, 2014).

Seymour, W., *British Special Forces* [Grafton Books] (London, 1986).

Smith, C., *Singapore Burning: Heroism and Surrender in World War II* [Penguin] (London, 2005).

Soros, G., *The New Paradigm for Financial Markets* (New York, 2008).

Soros, G., *The Crash of 2008 and What It Means* [Perseus Books Group] (New York, 2008).

Swiss Academy of Natural Sciences, *Fonte des glaciers suisses: presque un nouvel été record en 2017*. Communiqué de presse (October 30, 2017).

Standard and Poor's Rating Services, Ratings Direct, *International Bank for Reconstruction and Development* (April 2014).

Taleb, N.N., *Fooled by Randomness: The Hidden Role of Chance in Life and in the Markets* [Penguin Books] (London, 2004).

Tariq A., *The Nehrus and the Gandhis* [Picador] (London, 1985).

Thant, Myint-U, *Where China Meets India: Burma and the New Crossroads of Asia* [Faber and Faber] (London, 2011).

Thompson, J., *Ready for Anything: The Parachute Regiment at War* [Fontana] (London, 1990).

Transparency International, *Corruption Perceptions Index 2016* (January 25, 2017).

UK Prime Minister's Office, Press Release, *PM Announces Support for Small Island Developing States to Tackle Climate Change* (November 28, 2015).

United Nations Office on Drugs and Crime, *Transnational Organised Crime in East Asia and the Pacific: A Threat Assessment* (April 2013).

United Nations Office of the High Representative for Least Developed Countries, Landlocked Developing Countries and Small Island Developing Countries, *State of the Least Developed Countries 2017* [United Nations] (July 2017).

United Nations Department of Economic and Social Affairs, Population Division, *World Population Prospects, The 2015 Revision* [United Nations] (New York, 2015).

United Nations Department of Economic and Social Affairs, Population Division, *World Population Prospects, The 2017 Revision* [United Nations] (New York, 2017).

United Nations Development Programme, Commodity Dependence and International Commodity Prices. In *Towards Human Resilience: Sustaining MDG Progress in an Age of Economic Uncertainty* [United Nations] (New York, 2011).

United Nations Economic and Social Commission for Asia and the Pacific (ESCAP), *Economic and Social Survey for Asia and the Pacific* (2010).

United Nations Economic and Social Commission for Asia and the Pacific (ESCAP), *Estimating Infrastructure Financing Needs in Asia-Pacific Least Developed Countries, Landlocked Developing Countries and Small Island Developing Countries*. MPFD Working Paper 17/02 (May 24, 2017).

United Nations Economic and Social Commission for Asia and the Pacific (ESCAP), *Asia-Pacific Countries with Special Needs Development Report 2017: Investing in Infrastructure for an Inclusive and Sustainable Future* [United Nations] (2017).

United Nations Economic and Social Commission for Asia and the Pacific (ESCAP) Pacific Office, *Financing for Development: Infrastructure Development in the Pacific Islands*. MPDD Working Paper WP/15/02 (2015).

United Nations Conference on Trade and Development (UNCTAD), *The Least Developed Countries Report 2016, The Path to Graduation and Beyond: Making the Most of the Process* [United Nations] (2016).

United Nations Environment Program (UNEP), *Africa Without Ice and Snow.* Environmental Development 5, 146–155 (2013).

United Nations Industrial Development Organization (UNIDO), *Industrial Development Report 2016* [United Nations] (2017).

United Nations Inter-agency Task Force on Financing for Development, *Financing for Development: Progress and Prospects Report of the Inter-agency Task Force on Financing for Development 2017* [United Nations] (New York, 2017).

United Nations World Tourism Organization, *Chinese Tourists Spend 12 Per Cent More in Travelling Abroad in 2016.* Press Release 17046 (April 12, 2017).

US Department of Defense, *Annual Report to Congress: Military and Security Developments Involving the People's Republic of China 2012* [Office of the Secretary of Defense] (May 2012).

US Department of Defense, *Annual Report to Congress: Military and Security Developments Involving the People's Republic of China 2014* [Office of the Secretary of Defense] (April 2014).

US Department of Defense, *Annual Report to Congress: Military and Security Developments Involving the People's Republic of China 2016* [Office of the Secretary of Defense] (April 2016).

US Department of State, *Country Reports on Terrorism 2016, Chapter 2, South and Central Asia.*

Vayenas, C., *Democracy in the Digital Age* [Arena Books] (Bury St Edmunds, UK, 2017).

Von Tunzelmann, A., *Indian Summer: The Secret History of the End of an Empire* [Pocket Books] (London, 2007).

Vogel, Ezra, *Japan as Number One* [Harvard University Press] (Cambridge, MA, 1979)

Warren, A., *Singapore 1942: Britain's Greatest Defeat* [Talisman] (London, 2002).

Webster, D., *The Burma Road* [Pan Books] (New York, 2003).

Welsh, F., *A History of Hong Kong* [HarperCollins] (London, 1994).

Willis Towers Watson, *The World's 300 Largest Pension Funds* (September 2015).

Wolf, M., *The Shifts and the Shocks* [Penguin Books] (New York, NY, 2015).

World Bank, *Reducing Poverty by Closing South Asia's Infrastructure Gap* (2014).

World Bank, *The World Bank Supports Thailand's Post-floods Recovery Effort* (December 13, 2011).

Xi, Jinping, *The Governance of China* [Foreign Languages Press] (Beijing, 2014).

Yoong, L.Y., *ASEAN Matters* [World Scientific] (Singapore, 2011).

Index

© The Editor(s) (if applicable) and The Author(s) 2018
R. Biswas, *Emerging Markets Megatrends*,
https://doi.org/10.1007/978-3-319-78123-5